Praise for *Nine* ⸻

"It is the journey through heady, whiplash times that helps us understand where the nation is going . . . Perhaps [her elegy] for vanished homes in China required distance to write . . . A laojia [old home] exists not so much on a map but in the heart."
—*New York Times*

"[An] account of fiery, artistic defiance and a testament to the act of storytelling as a way to break the silence . . . Guo writes in the audacious, restless and fragmented prose that has become her imprint: a feverish style that can be as merciless as the world she portrays."
—*New Statesman* (UK)

"Rebellious, flamboyant and fundamentally optimistic . . . She writes frankly and furiously . . . Fascinating."
—*Scotland on Sunday* (UK)

"Gripping. . . In evocative, captivating prose that reads like fiction, Guo brings to life her lifelong struggles against the chains of poverty, gender, and censorship . . . A rich and insightful coming-of-age story of not only a woman, but of an artist and the country in which she was born."
—*Kirkus Reviews*

"The most compelling Chinese memoir since Jung Chang's *Wild Swans* . . . She's refreshingly fierce and funny."
—*Telegraph* (UK) (5 stars)

"[A] fierce portrait of coming of age in 1980s-1990s China."
—*Library Journal*

NINE
CONTINENTS

NINE
CONTINENTS

A Memoir In and Out of China

XIAOLU GUO

Grove Press
New York

First published in Great Britain in 2017 by Chatto & Windus, an imprint of Penguin Random House UK.

Published simultaneously in Canada
Printed in the United States of America

First Grove Atlantic hardcover edition: October 2017
First Grove Atlantic paperback edition: November 2018

Library of Congress Cataloging-in-Publication data available for this title.

ISBN 978-0-8021-2867-6
eISBN 978-0-8021-8932-5

Grove Press
an imprint of Grove Atlantic
154 West 14th Street
New York, NY 10011

Distributed by Publishers Group West

groveatlantic.com

18 19 20 21   10 9 8 7 6 5 4 3 2 1

For Marguerite Duras,
who gave me the faith to become an artist
during my low and hard years of struggle in South China

The soul can shrivel from an excess of critical distance, and if I don't want to remain in arid internal exile for the rest of my life, I have to find a way to lose my alienation without losing myself.

EVA HOFFMAN

CONTENTS

NINE
CONTINENTS

So many times I've seen England from the sky

The Past Is a Foreign Country

A wanderer, uprooted and displaced. A nomad in both body and mind. This was what I had become since leaving China for the West. It had been fifteen years of transit, change, forgetting and adapting. Then all of a sudden, at the age of forty, my belly was expanding. The earth had begun to exert a pull on me, a pull towards motherhood. On the second day of 2013, I found myself lying on an operating table in a hospital in London, my body hooked up by wires and tubes to a bank of humming machines. I was about to burst, literally. The moment the baby girl was pulled from my womb by Caesarean section I heard a cry – a sound that was at once familiar, but utterly surprising. There she was. Wrapped in a new towel with her wet, bruised little face against my breast. I embraced her with wonder and fear. This is good, I thought. This child will be rooted here. She will be a grounded person, unlike me, a peripatetic peasant, a cultural orphan.

Twenty minutes after delivery, we were wheeled into the maternity ward, filled with newborns and new mothers. Still in a haze of morphine, I heard all sorts of languages being spoken around me: Hindi, Arabic, German, Spanish, Polish. I remained in the hospital for the next three days, dressed in only a thin gown, trying to breastfeed and struggling to use the bathroom, shocked to see so much blood flowing out of me.

On the fourth day, when we arrived back home, I was surprised by a sudden urge to call my mother. I hadn't mentioned to her that I was pregnant once in those long nine months. As was typical of our relationship, we hadn't spoken in a while.

I dialled the dreaded number, embedded so deeply in my mind I could recite it in my dreams.

'Mother, it's me.'

'Oh, Xiaolu. I wasn't expecting your call.' Then immediately, 'Where are you?'

'London.'

'What's wrong? Why are you calling?' She was direct, almost rude. She had served as a Red Guard at the age of sixteen, a coarse and uneducated girl straight out of the rice fields. I always assumed that was one of the reasons we never got along.

'I'm fine,' I said. 'I wanted to let you know . . .' I found myself tongue-tied and unable to bring myself to say it. 'I just gave birth to a healthy baby girl.'

'What?' my poor mother cried. 'You just gave birth?'

'Yes. She is half-Chinese and half-Western.'

'My heavens! You were pregnant?'

After a few seconds of silence from her end, I thought she might at least ask the name of the baby, but instead she said, 'Are you coming back for Qingming Festival?'

Qingming is a day in April when we pay our respects to the dead. We sweep their tombs, burn incense and pray. I said nothing, only listened to her angry sobs through the telephone.

'You should come back! You don't even know where your father is buried! I want to move your grandmother's ashes from the village and put them next to your father. You should come back for this.'

This time, I thought, I have no excuse not to go. None. I might as well go and pay a debt of filial duty, once and for all. It's only a twelve-hour flight. I can do it. My whole adult life I had avoided going back to my childhood home as much as possible. Shitang, the fishing village where I witnessed my grandparents' depression and poverty, was a place I came to loathe. Wenling, where I spent my adolescent years, the cradle for my troubled relationship with authority, repelled me. When I left to study in Beijing in 1993, I promised myself: that's it, I will never return to this stifling backwater again. Ten years later, when I left China for Britain, I said to myself: from now on, no more ideological brainwashing. I'm not going to let myself be tripped up by my rotten peasant roots. But the time had come to face the past. To try to explain to my family how I had lived all these years. After all, I would have to explain it to my little daughter one day too. Just like James Baldwin said: tell it, go tell it to the mountain, tell it to your native kin, to the dead souls and the living souls. I would have to face them, one by one. No escape.

So, five days before Qingming Festival, I wrapped my new-born as warmly as I could and took a flight back to where my life began.

PART I | SHITANG: TALES OF
THE EAST CHINA SEA

Once upon a time, there was neither East nor West. There were neither animals nor human beings. Aeons passed. Water appeared. Algae and fish grew. Plants began to root themselves on sandy shores. Birds flew from one hill to another. More aeons passed – tigers, lions, phoenix, serpents, salamanders and tiny slithering creatures all found their quarters in the jungle to hunt and rest. But still, the world was quiet, as if waiting for some momentous event, the birth of some wicked and powerful creature. One day, Heaven's Eyes saw a piece of five-coloured stone shining on a mountain in the east. The stone kept shining until suddenly it burst into pieces and a monkey jumped out from the dust. The monkey had a handsome face, four long limbs and a slim body. He moved about in the fresh mountain air as he looked around with enormous curiosity. He then bowed to each of the four quarters of the sky, expressing gratitude for his birth.

The little monkey explored his world with gaiety. He fed on bananas and peanuts and drank from brooks and springs. He made friends with tigers and leopards, sloths and baboons. But one autumn day when the sun was going down, he suddenly felt sad and burst into tears. He raised his eyes to the risen moon in the east. He felt lonely. A great urge inside him told him to do something deserving with his life. But he didn't know what this great task could be. He stared at the moon slipping towards the west and fell asleep. During the night, he felt a drop of dew falling on his face. Then he heard someone speaking in his ear. The voice said:

'Little creature, you are not an ordinary monkey. You were nourished by the five elements of this planet, and have received the energy of heaven and earth from the beginning of time. You are the force of human life. You need to find the human world and to help a monk called Xuanzang to obtain the purest Buddhist scripture on earth. Once the sutra is secured, humans will achieve real knowledge of life and death.'

The monkey woke up under the moonlight, his ears still echoing with these words. Through the fragrant banana leaves, he felt a polar star shooting light right into his forehead.

Village of Shitang, Zhejiang Province,
where I spent my first seven years, 1970s

After I Was Born

I was born an orphan. Not because my parents had died, no, they were both still very much alive. Rather, they gave me away.

Of course, I don't remember anything specific about my first two years. No one in my family does. As a newborn, I had been given to a peasant couple who lived in a mountain village somewhere in our province by the East China Sea. Many years later, I was told a story that my mother couldn't raise me as my father had been imprisoned in a labour camp at the time. So that's where I lived, on that mountainside, for the first two years of my life. The only memory I have is a false one, told to me by my grandparents, who recounted the day when the barren couple from the highlands brought me, the unwanted child, back down the mountain to them.

Only a baby, and already given away twice.

The couple had found out where my grandparents lived and taken the long-distance bus all the way to our humble home. The first thing they did was place me in my grandmother's arms and say:

'This little child will die if she continues living with us. She is dying. You can see that. We have nothing to eat. We only manage to grow fifty kilos of yam every autumn. But we need to save them to sell at the market. So we have been feeding her the mashed leaves. But every time she sees the green mush on the spoon she turns her head away, or spits it out. She refuses to eat anything green any more! You know we don't have much rice, so the leaves are all we have. Look at her, her face is yellow and her limbs are weak. She never stops crying. She won't eat. She won't survive if she stays with us. So, take her back, we beg you! Take her back right now! We know we couldn't conceive, but we don't need a dying baby. We beg you to take her back!'

My grandparents were perplexed upon receiving me. They had nothing to say since they were not the ones who had sent me to this family in the first place. They took me without a word. From that day on, I lived with my grandparents by the sea, and my adopted parents returned to their yams, never to be heard of again. I was told later that the family bore the name Wong, that they lived on a mountain, with their yams, and apparently a few goats. Since the woman was infertile (or perhaps the man was infertile, but with peasants the woman is always to blame) she had no milk for me. I often wonder if she fed me with goat's milk, or whether their goats produced any milk at all. In China at that time no one drank animal milk. We were all lactose-intolerant. They must have fed me with soya milk before I had teeth. What else could they have done with a starving baby whose mother had decided to give her away to a family with no milk? I will never know.

Years later, when I pored over the map of the province and tried to find the mountain village where my adopted parents might have lived, I was struck by how many there were, scattered across the country, and how many nameless places were marked only by obscure yellow and green dots. Thousands of named hamlets, and many more anonymous ones. Was it Diaotou? Pingshan? Yongjia? Hengshantou? Changshi? Shifou? I gave up. After closing the map, I was told that most of these villages had become construction sites for the expanding cities. Even the mountains had been decapitated, their peaks shaved off in order to make way for roads or quarries to provide for the country's great development.

When I think of the first two years of my life, the image that spontaneously comes to mind is that of a small skinny goat trotting over bare mountains. Where is all the succulent grass that will satisfy her hunger? Where is the water to quench her thirst? The mountain is naked. There are only rocks and fertiliser-poisoned soil. But somehow the little goat managed to survive the impoverishment of her early life.

Grandfather

My grandfather was a bitter, failed fisherman. He was born in 1905, just one year before China's Last Emperor Puyi was born. I don't know if that was an ominous sign, an explanation for his fate – the last generation born under the imperial system was bound to be wiped out by new fashions. The day when he was born, his own father was apparently out at sea. In a fishing village, people say a child born while his father is at sea and the tide is rising will grow up to be a good fisherman. But the tide was receding when my grandfather emerged from his mother's womb. He never told me this himself. Other villagers gossiped about it on benches in front of their houses. But after hearing this story, I never liked watching the tide go out.

My grandfather used to own a fishing boat, and was able to make a living from selling fish on the dock every few days. The

boat was the only thing he ever cared for in his life. Nothing else
mattered to him. His boat, like others in the village, was painted
with two large eyes. The fishermen called them dragon eyes – a
boat is a dragon that conquers the waves. The vivid colours scare
away other sea creatures. Every few months, as was local practice,
he would repaint the eyes a dark red, and retouch the black and
blue lines along the body of the boat. From a distance, it looked
like a gigantic tropical fish, with jewel-like power. Every now
and then he reapplied a layer of tar, hoping that with a shiny
new skin it would ride the waves like a whale. After a big catch,
he let his boat bathe in the sun, fixing any broken bits, while
my grandmother helped mend the fishing nets. Then he would
launch the boat into the sea again, on one of those very early blue
mornings. He would sail far offshore, even with limited petrol
supplies. Sometimes he reached Gong Hai – the strait between
mainland China and Taiwan – beyond which further navigation
was forbidden. On the open water there were fewer vessels and
he felt the sea belonged to him. The fish were more abundant and
the eels fat and long. He would return two or three days later,
sometimes quite exhausted, carrying a good catch.

In those days, no one in a Chinese fishing village would
buy dead or even only half-dead fish – it was considered a bad
deal. In our kitchen we cooked everything alive – preserving
as much of the energy, the chi, from the sea as we could. So
as the fishing boats were returning, my grandmother and the
other fishermen's wives would gather on the beach with buckets
around their feet and wait. Once their husbands had hauled the
boats in, the women would rush to separate the catch immediately. Shrimps went into one bucket, eels into another. Snapper
were thrown into a basin of water, clams and crabs together

in a large barrel, and so on. Within minutes, the fishmongers from the village markets would arrive to pick the freshest items, peeling greasy notes from their pockets. There was no need for negotiation – the prices of shrimp, crab and snapper were always the same. With eels, a delicacy in the south, prices fluctuated with the season and the difficulty of catching them.

But those were the good old days, when the villagers were free-for-all sea scavengers. Then, in the 1970s, the Communist government decided to construct the Fish Farming Collective. Individual boats like my grandfather's were snatched away, to be 'managed' by the state. Fishermen were teamed together according to regional population, and then assigned a certain sector of the sea to fish in a big, industrial fishing boat. All catches belonged to the state, who would then distribute the harvest to every family according to a quota system. My grandfather was unhappy that his old way of life had been taken away, that time alone on his boat, away from the day-to-day grind and people he didn't like. Besides, he would have had to learn industrial fishing techniques with people he had never met before, under state supervision and with everyone reporting on everyone else behind their backs. He didn't have the character for that sort of life. He was a man born in the Qing Dynasty, the same age as our Last Emperor. For him, his days belonged to the Qing, not some quick-thinking Communist Party. So in the early 1970s, after his own boat was destroyed in a typhoon – one of those deadly storms that sweep up every summer from the South Pacific into the East China Sea – he gave up fishing. He became grumpy, spent his days drinking, and started hitting my grandmother regularly. From the age of three or four, I only really remember seeing him brooding in his room, a bottle glued to his palm.

Unfortunately, he had no other skills with which to make a living. He was starving and had virtually nothing to feed my grandmother and me. Then, one day, he found a big wooden board on a street corner. He took two benches from the kitchen and constructed a makeshift store outside our house. He would sell anything he could find – vegetables, pickled fish, shrimp paste, soap, nails and cigarettes. His cigarettes were a bit funny-looking, sold as singles, 'treasures' he found by the seashore. The cigarettes were originally packed tight in boxes like fancy Western biscuits. But storms and war with the Communists sunk many Taiwanese Nationalist boats and released their goods into the sea. Those 'treasure chests' floated ashore along with other flotsam and jetsam. And my grandfather, a proper sea scavenger, spent his days walking along the beach, picking from the goods. Somehow, he always found boxes of cigarettes, soaked through with seawater. Sometimes he would find stylish American cookies in brightly coloured tin boxes. Occasionally he would turn up with tinned food, typically beans. The cigarettes he would unpack and dry under the hot sun. He would then beautify them and sell them at a cheap price. This business worked for a while, but it depended on continued conflict in the Taiwan Strait – there wasn't exactly a daily supply of shipwrecks in the East China Sea, and currents were also liable to take what had been wrecked further south.

Still, my grandfather managed to sustain us with these meagre pickings, if only temporarily. Every day we drank watery porridge and ate boiled kelp. Our neighbours – families of the men who had joined the collective fishing boats – would give us some extra rice and noodles every now and then. My grandfather's scavenging days were numbered, we all knew that.

Village of Shitang

Some people said Shitang was an island, others a peninsula. It lay soaking in the salty water between mainland China and Taiwan, three hundred kilometres from the Taiwanese coast, the first place on the mainland to receive the dawn's rays every morning. In 2000, Shitang was in the news because a ceremonial sun statue had been built on a cliff facing east. The statue didn't look anything like the sun, but more like a tall, thin monolith out of *2001: A Space Odyssey*. It turned the village into a tourist attraction. But for the people of Shitang, it was odd. They had always known their village lay furthest to the east. Why, suddenly, was it such a big deal?

Shitang literally means stone pond. The word pond in old Chinese was associated with fish. Perhaps thousands of years ago, the area had been a salt-water lagoon next to the sea, before inhabitants built up the land along the seafront, just as Hong Kong or Macau had grown up on reclaimed marsh and swamp. Our family house was a small, green-coloured stone dwelling right on the horn of the peninsula. My grandfather lived upstairs, where he could look straight out to sea through a small window by his bed. In my memory, the sea was always yellow-brown, whether seen from my grandfather's window or from the beach. This yellow-brownness was to do with the large kelp beds growing in the shallow water by the shore. The kelp – we called it *haifa*, the hair of the sea – had tough stalks with broad leaf-like palms and long green-brown stripes. A swarm of shapeless sea snakes, they entangled themselves in the space between land and water. Despite its monstrous shape, we loved the taste. We either stewed it in eel soup or fried it with pork. We never tired of it, along with the tiny kelpfish we harvested from among the algae.

The soil was very salty in Shitang. It was not land suited to agriculture. There were barely any trees growing in the village. But gardenia trees are a determined species. They grew between rocks, their white flowers swirling in the salt-laden wind. It was the only type that could face the sea's yellow foam. I loved their strongly scented flowers. Women picked the buds to tie in their plaits. One day, thirty-odd years later, I stumbled across a gardenia in northern Europe. I breathed in the familiar scent under a clear European sky and cried. This tree didn't belong in my Western life. It was a sorrowful smell, if tinged with a warm feel of nostalgia. It took me straight back to my childhood on the typhoon-ridden coast of the East China Sea.

In that house, only my grandfather had a view over the kelp beds and the foamy sea. My grandmother and I lived downstairs, where the windows on two sides were blocked by our neighbour's washing lines, dried squid and salted ribbonfish hanging from poles. I couldn't say then whether I loved or hated that house. I lived there until I was seven. It was simply our house, our village. There was no comparison, no alternative. But years later, after I had left the village, I felt that Shitang had killed all tenderness in my heart. It had become a rock in my chest. Those hard corners, those jagged stone houses had turned me to stone too. The landscape made me merciless and aggressive.

Our street was originally called Anti-Pirates Passage. In the 1980s, the name was changed to Front Barrier Slope by the local authorities. The original name came from the Ming Dynasty. During that time, the area was under constant attack by pirates from the East Pacific, such that the local militia armed themselves with home-made guns and bombs for protection. Eventually, the village was returned into local hands. But that was four hundred years ago. It felt to me that nothing significant had happened since then, apart from when the local government replaced the Buddha posters in their offices with images of Mao. It had been a backwater, from the days of China's dynasties until now. The only dramatic stories came from the sea, from being close to Taiwan.

In the sixties and seventies, some local fishermen and villagers tried to cross the Taiwan Strait in secret, hoping they would be rewarded by the Nationalist government with gold and farmland as promised. Some succeeded, but very often they were recaptured and punished: someone's uncle and his brother were caught on the edge of international waters and sentenced to death. In the 1970s, no one had private radios or televisions. All news was announced at high volume in the street. Our house directly faced an electricity pole adorned with two loudspeakers. Every so often, in the early morning, we were woken by Communist songs followed by an announcement of 'shot at dawn' or 'life sentence'. Even though capital punishment was normal at that time, hearing these statements still horrified me. I had never witnessed anyone be shot, but the village gossip alone was enough to make me shiver.

Our street doubled as a market, with one end starting in the mountains where a Buddhist temple had been built, and the other end finishing at the beach and the open sea. From our little house we could always hear chatting, crying, arguing, haggling, cockerels crowing, children screaming, pigs oinking from day to night. There was never a moment of peace and quiet. It was simply the sound of China. There were always people every-where, life everywhere, noise everywhere, for better or for worse. My grandparents knew everyone in the village. They could spot an outsider instantly. My grandfather was always grumpy, so even though he knew everyone he never greeted anyone in the street. People would greet him and ask: 'How is your boat, Old Guo?' or 'Have you eaten today?' Local longhand for hello. But he never bothered to answer. He would just grunt, or pass them without even raising his eyebrows. My grandmother was the opposite, and greeted everyone she passed. But she also knew that her friendliness could not stop the village gossip about her relationship with her husband. No wonder, as gossip was the only form of entertainment available.

Grandmother

My grandmother was a kind, sometimes fearful woman. She had almost nothing, but she would still manage to scrape together small presents for the children who played out in the street: sweets, leftover rice, or some colourful seashells. So kind and voiceless, she was the most humble person I have ever known. I always thought that it was her decency that made her hunch-backed. It slowed her down, stopped her from walking even at a normal speed. Obviously, her tiny bound feet were a factor, but she never complained about them. Her back had been bent ever since I could remember, long before she had become an old woman. The nasty kids often laughed at me, taunting me with things like: 'Your grandmother is a big shrimp, she can only see her toes!' or 'Here comes the turtle on her hind legs!' Her thin, grey-white hair was always bound into a chignon behind her head, as her diseased and twisted spine made it difficult to wash her hair. She also slept poorly. Her long sighs and the creaking of her bamboo bed as she moved her twisted body would wake me up at night.

No one in remote Chinese villages had photos taken in those days. I have no way of knowing what she looked like when she was young. Perhaps she was a decent-looking girl, but surely always small and very skinny. Her parents arranged her marriage when she was still a child and at the age of twelve she was sent (or more correctly, she was sold) to my grandfather as a child bride for a bag of rice and eight kilos of yams. Her new home was not close; it took two days for her and her father to walk from their village to Shitang. But really, she came to fill her hungry stomach, without knowing that her old husband didn't have much rice in his rice jar either. This was the 1930s, when China was ravaged by civil war, when the Chinese Communists were fighting the Nationalist government. The Japanese invasion followed soon after, and their armies committed atrocities all over the country until 1945. My grandmother had a vague memory of the Japanese soldiers looting their house while they were hiding in a temple in the mountains. When they returned some weeks later, there was almost nothing valuable left, apart from a covered wok still sitting on the stove. She lifted the lid and found a big brown shit inside. She told me this story when I was about six and knew almost nothing about the world outside Shitang, which made me think that the whole Sino-Japanese War was to do with shitting in woks. She never said anything more about that time, despite having been witness to every war that had raged in China since the early twentieth century.

In the 1970s, people like us who lived in small villages were still chained to a feudal system, and women continued to be treated like cheap goods. My grandmother was still an outsider in this fishing community, even after living here for her entire adult life. Having grown up in an inland farming village, she didn't understand the sea and the lives of the fishermen. Just like all the other women in the area, she never set foot on her husband's boat, or on any other boat. To have a woman in your boat brought bad luck.

I often saw her crying alone. She would weep silently in the back of the kitchen or in front of a white porcelain statue of Guanyin she had hung on the kitchen wall. Her eyes were almost always clouded. Every day she prayed to Guanyin – the Goddess of Mercy – the most popular goddess in our region. When I was about five or six, and beginning to know a little of the world, she would tell me: 'Xiaolu, I have the life of a dog, it's hardly worth living. But I pray for you, and for your mother and father.' At that age, I had no idea what my parents were like and my grandmother was so reticent about our family background.

Nor did my grandmother ever talk about my grandfather, at least not in front of me. She was frightened of him. I saw how her limbs became stiff and she sometimes trembled when he came near. I never saw them lie on the same bed together, or even stay in the same room for more than half an hour. My grandfather barely ever ate in the kitchen with us. If he did, my grandmother would retreat, sitting in the corner, usually by the stove – a place that belonged to the woman in Chinese tradition. And she would eat only the leftovers. Grandfather preferred to take his rice bowl upstairs to his own room, where he could drink liquor by himself and chew on his own unhappiness. I think he despised her

deeply, partly because of tradition, partly because she came from
an inland family and didn't know how to be a fisherman's wife.
I was told that he had already decided on this hate the first year
they were married, her crime not knowing things like how to eat a
fish properly in a fisherman's house. In Shitang, we would always
start from the tail, never from the head. Eating the head of the fish
straight away was considered bad luck for a fisherman. But my
grandmother, who didn't know this and was concerned only to
show her modesty, would pick at the part my grandfather was not
eating. Furious, he left the table. My grandmother tried to learn
the local customs, but it was too late. She never gained his heart.

It was an awful partnership – he beat her almost every day,
for small things like not fetching a matchbox quickly enough
when he wanted to smoke, or for not cooking to his taste, or for
not being there in the kitchen when he was hungry. Or he beat
her for no reason at all. He kicked at her short, skinny legs, and
pushed and punched her to the floor. That was a normal sight in
our house. She wept only after he had left. And then she wouldn't
even get up from the cold stone floor. Despite my young age, I was
already numb from having witnessed this sort of scene too often.
Usually I would just hide. Who, in 1970s rural China, had not
encountered such scenes on a daily basis? I didn't feel close to my
grandfather as he never showed any affection or warmth to me,
but I didn't think he was in any way a monster, because where I
grew up, every man beat his wife and children. In the morning,
in the evening, at night, I heard our neighbours' sobs. First a
male voice shouting, the sounds of furniture being thrown, and
then the weeping of a mother or a daughter. That was village life.
It was normal. As long as I remain unmarried, I will be more or
less all right, I said to my young self then.

I remember how my old hunchbacked grandmother used her meagre savings to buy me an ice treat – the cheapest sort, made from only water and sugar. She would wrap it in a used handkerchief onto which she had coughed up her lungs and then come looking for me in the scorching summer afternoon, to give me that little morsel of sweet ice. But by the time she found me, rolling around in the dirt or play-fighting with a bunch of kids in an alleyway, she would unpack her snot-ridden handkerchief to recover what was left of the treat. The ice would have already melted, of course, and I would be left with only a thin little stick with an ice clot attached. 'Suck it quickly!' she would cry, out of breath from her search. I would suck it out of thirst, like a street dog. That was how my grandmother loved me, although I didn't know what 'love' meant then. No one had ever taught me that concept in the village, at least not verbally. Later, once I had grown up, I came to realise how much she loved me. She really cared for me. An ice treat cost five cents, the same price as a vegetable bun. A luxurious love by our standards and for that I should have stood by her, especially when my grandfather lost his temper and threw his fists at her. But I was too small and too scared. I would hide wherever I could. Tears fell down my cheeks too, but not for my grandmother. I cried out of anger, a rage, that I had been born into such a shithole and out of an overwhelming sense of desolation.

The Goddess of Mercy

The small white statue of Guanyin above our kitchen table had been there as long as I could remember, and she was there until the day I left Shitang. She was always covered in dust, but my grandmother's cataracts prevented her from seeing how dirty the statue was. Guanyin stared out into the dimly lit kitchen, her expression devoid of meaning or feeling, alongside the old bench and its flaky paint, the broken umbrellas, and my grandmother's comb that lay silently on the windowsill, missing its teeth.

Guanyin has often been compared to the Virgin Mary, maybe because some representations show her carrying a willow branch in one hand and a baby in the other. But the story of our Goddess of Mercy is not about raising a future god. My grandmother, who preferred to pray to Guanyin rather than Buddha, identified with her, woman to woman. Guanyin bestowed her compassion on all those grief-stricken wives and unlucky daughters.

Guanyin: 观音 – her name literally means one who listens to the cries of the world. Legend has it that some thousand years ago she was the daughter of a cruel king. One day the king asked her to marry a wealthy but unloving man. She told the king that she would agree to marry, as long as the union would ease the three great misfortunes of mankind; ageing, illness and death. If her marriage could not help with any of these sufferings, she would rather retreat into a life of religion. When the father-king asked who could possibly ease these sufferings, his daughter mentioned a doctor she knew who could cure all of these ills. Her father was furious, as he wanted her to marry a man of power and wealth, not a healer. He punished her, forcing her into a life of hard labour, giving her little to eat and drink. But still she was unyielding. Every day the king's daughter begged to be allowed to enter the temple and become a nun. Finally her father agreed, but ordered the monks to give her the toughest chores in order to break her spirit. But Guanyin was such a kind-hearted person that even the animals around the temple wanted to help her. Her father, seeing this, became so frustrated that he tried to burn down the temple hoping that she might perish in the fire. Guanyin was trapped, but as she was dying, a white tiger saved her and took her into an underground world. When she woke up she found herself in the land of the dead. Guanyin gazed upon the suffering souls around her and heard their cries. But her gaze soothed the crying children and soon they began to smile and play; the men stopped punishing themselves and started to find peace within; the dried willow trees flushed green again; the dead lotus began to blossom in the stagnant water. While in Hell, Guanyin witnessed the horrors that human beings had to endure and was overwhelmed with grief. Filled with compassion, she released the good karma she had accumulated during her life, and freed all the suffering souls back on Earth. From then on, the world worshipped her, calling Guanyin the Goddess of Mercy.

This was one of the few stories my grandmother told me, and I remember my first reaction was: 'Grandmother, why can't all women stay unmarried like Guanyin?'

My grandmother looked at me and shook her head. Then she sighed. 'Women have to get married. Otherwise we are punished.'

This seemed like a bad rule for women, I thought. They were punished either way. Just look at my grandmother. I could understand why she prayed to Guanyin every day. Women like my grandmother were not valued for themselves. She was a dutiful daughter, then the dutiful wife, and dutiful mother, until eventually she was abandoned and forgotten.

During the Cultural Revolution, however, the Goddess of Mercy was to be punished yet again. In the early 1960s, Western symbols like the Virgin Mary or Jesus Christ were banned and destroyed. But some of the underground Chinese Christian groups venerated the Virgin Mary by disguising her as a statue of Guanyin holding a child; a cross would be hidden in an inconspicuous location on her body. So this half-Chinese Goddess half-Western Madonna survived for a while, until one day Mao announced his 'anti-feudal' and 'anti-superstition' movement. The government in Beijing declared that anything linked to China's feudal past (such as images of kings and queens, grassroots religious practices, temples, etc.) should be destroyed. Overnight, anti-feudal public meetings in the village market square were set up and statues of the Goddess of Mercy were smashed, the hidden crosses in Guanyin's robe cast into oblivion along with the little baby in her arms. My grandmother hid her precious porcelain figure in her wardrobe until the middle of the 1970s, when images of Guanyin were finally allowed again, and my grandmother could regain her faith in an afterlife through prayer – surely the next life would be better than the one she had endured so far.

Swordfish

Everyone in Shitang was crazy for swordfish. The good fishermen often boasted about how many they could catch in a season (sometimes they did the same for eels). As for eating them – whether steamed, grilled or fried – the fishermen's wives paid extra care in their preparation. The fishmongers in the market would always try to keep them alive as long as possible after extracting them from the salty water, in order to maximise their succulent texture. For me, swordfish were strange creatures. I especially found their long, sharp bills threatening – like swords cutting through water, piercing anything that obstructed their path.

Our next-door neighbour, Da Bo, was about forty-something (I imagined my father to have been the same age because Da Bo had four daughters who were close to me in age). Da Bo was a skilled fisherman with a good reputation; unlike my grandfather who had wrecked his boat and then lost everything, Da Bo always kept his boat in a good condition and sailed it frequently. He fished with his own boat even after the Fish Farming Collective formed in our region. I would go with his daughters to the dock and wait for him to return. His four daughters all bore the same name, *Feng*, which means Phoenix, but were distinguished by number. So from the oldest to the youngest they were called Yifeng (Phoenix One), Erfeng (Phoenix Two), Sanfeng (Phoenix Three) and Sifeng (Phoenix Four). You would think they had been treated badly by Da Bo and his wife, as they were only useless girls, not longed-for sons, but in my eyes they were not mistreated at all. Da Bo loved them just as he would have loved sons. It made me wonder about my parents. If they had loved me, would I have been living with them?

Once, while we were playing in Da Bo's backyard, he taught us how to catch swordfish. 'The swordfish is the fastest of all the fish in the sea. They can swim down to two thousand feet below the surface of the water and then swim back up again in one go. Can you imagine that?' Da Bo stared at me, his bloodshot eyes glistening. Just like the swordfish. I shook my head weakly.

'It's very difficult to catch them, that's why they are so prized.' He spoke as his hands untangled the fishing net. His wife was holding the other end, trying to spot any bits that needed mending.

'So how do you catch them?' I asked eagerly.

'How? Because I never sleep! I catch them by moonlight, when the sea is calm. I don't like having any other scavengers around me, you see? Swordfish are powerful predators because they have large fins. They have very few enemies, only whales are strong enough to attack and eat them. I take my boat out in the dark and then I circle quietly, choosing spots where the shrimps live because swordfish love shrimps. My old heavens! Those bastards are so quick! They can dive so quickly at the brush of a hook or harpoon. And when hurt, they can run their swords through the bottom of our hulls. Once, I saw them form a gang and attack the sides of my boat! And one of the swordfish was about four metres long. It was half the size of my boat! I thought, those bastards will destroy it!'

'Then what happened?' I asked, terrified by his story.

'They made holes everywhere and water came in. But in the end, I was fully prepared, and with strong gloves I snatched the four-metre-long monster and smashed his head with my oar!'

Da Bo stood up, took out a small knife from his pocket and cut a piece of dried swordfish hanging from a branch of his bay tree. He handed it to me. I took it and put it straight into my mouth. After chewing on it for a long time, I decided my teeth were not strong enough. It tasted like salty steak, but felt like a piece of wooden cardboard. I couldn't swallow it. I would have preferred to eat my grandfather's shoes. So I spat it out. Da Bo didn't take offence. He just laughed.

Since I rarely ate swordfish, I had assumed it must be delicious, when not dried and salted. Of course my grandmother could hardly afford such a delicacy. She would only buy the cheapest creatures from the sea – small crabs and fiddly shrimps for making a kind of pickled-fish mash. Otherwise she would buy jellyfish. Jellyfish were cheap. You could get a big bowl for just five fen. And I loved the sour spicy pickled white globules in ginger sauce. That was my idea of luxury, my swordfish without the proud sword.

The Hui

When I was six one of our neighbours told me that I was Hui, not Han Chinese. I didn't know what he meant. He said Hui don't usually eat pork, but we ate pork ravenously when we had the chance. Pork was the best. We would eat any meat available in the village, including dog and cat. So I went back home and asked my grandparents about the Hui. But my grandfather refused to explain. He had taken to only ever speaking in monosyllables. And my grandmother couldn't help me since her family's ancestors were Han. All she said was: 'Don't ask me! You know your grandmother is illiterate. I can't even write my own name.'

So I went to see the stationmaster, the man in charge of our village's long-distance bus service. I had heard people say he had made it to the outside world many times and knew lots of things. Besides, he was a member of the Communist Party. Not that I knew what that meant then, but I gathered that it was no easy achievement. So I walked up the hill, all the way to the bus station with its wide view of the coast.

'What are Hui, stationmaster?' I asked. He was standing by the ticketing window, holding a book of bus tickets and a pen. A whistle hung around his neck which he used when it was boarding time. But it was noon, and all the buses had already left. He was having some time to himself, chewing roasted sunflower seeds while monitoring the station.

'Hui? They are descended from the Mongols or the Turks. Your ancestors were Tartars.'

'Tartars?' I didn't understand a word he was saying.

'Yes. They were from the west of China, that is, Central Asia. They were very powerful and brutal people. Haven't you ever heard of the Mongols?'

I shook my head. How could I, in such a village?

'They ride horses and sleep in yurts on the grass. They don't like growing rice, nor do they know how to fish.'

'They sleep in yurts on the grass?' I was caught by that image, thinking it could be fun living under a giant umbrella beneath the sky.

'You might be a descendant of the Mongols. You know, one out of every three hundred Chinese is related to Genghis Khan, the great emperor of the Yuan Dynasty. I bet you are one of them!'

A descendant of Genghis Khan?

'But, stationmaster, you mean I don't come from around here? I come from the place where people ride horses and sleep on the grass?'

'Yes. And when you grow up, you'll be just like your Tartar ancestors. You'll carry a long knife and conquer the world.'

I was never a girly girl. For some reason I was always drawn to epic stories of heroes. So I was impressed by what the stationmaster had told me. Carrying long knives and conquering the world. It was unimaginable for a skinny girl like me. It sounded strange but wonderful!

'Your grandfather should know where your family comes from. Ask him.'

'But Grandpa doesn't like to talk. You know that. He doesn't even speak at home.'

As we talked, a bus full of passengers arrived. Chicken cages, wedding quilts and piles of luggage had been tied to the roof. The exhaust was so thick it made me want to throw up. The stationmaster jumped back on duty. He blew his whistle loudly and made signs to the bus driver.

As he was directing the driver he turned to me and said: 'One day, when you see your parents, they will tell you where you come from.'

I watched the passengers climb down from the bus, covered in dust, carrying their chickens and shopping from the nearby town. I tried to form an image of my parents. I was told they had to work elsewhere in a newly built town, a whole day's bus journey from here. Surely I had already met them, given the fact that my mother had given birth to me. But my poor head was otherwise empty of details about them. Neither did I feel I missed them. How could a child who had never lived with her parents miss them? How could someone who doesn't know what love is, miss love?

In 1970s China, we lived an uneducated, rural life with no television, no books or magazines, and no access to information that wasn't state-controlled. With Communist ideology running from top to bottom, there was barely any room for personal discussion about love or intimacy. I don't ever remember having heard the word 'love' before I had turned twelve or thirteen. No one ever mentioned it. Or if I did hear it, it would have been used in propaganda about Mao and the Communist Party. But they would use the word *re ai*, 热爱 – literally 'hot love', or passionate devotion. You were supposed to devote yourself entirely to the Communist Party and Chairman Mao. Personal love was the last thing one should be concerned with. I wondered, years later, whether that was why my grandmother took to crying alone in her kitchen corner so often. There was so little love in her life. And she didn't 'love' or understand Communism and the ideology of Chairman Mao either. She probably loved her son, my father. But he barely ever came home. We were abandoned by him and by my mother, or by the idea that you should 'devote your life passionately to Chairman Mao and the Communist Party'.

Pirates of the East China Sea

During the Ming Dynasty, some four hundred years ago, local militia used to march through our street, Anti-Pirates Passage, before going off to fight the Japanese pirates. The stationmaster was descended from one of those fighters and would tell stories about this brave forefather.

'Do you know why we called those pirates *wokou*?' the stationmaster asked me once while I was listening to him recount the heroic deeds of his family.

'*Wokou*?' I shook my head. It was a very old word, a word only very old people used.

'*Wo* means short people, dwarves, like the Japanese. *Kou* means bandit – in this case they were sea bandits.' The stationmaster squatted down and, using his index finger, wrote the two characters in the sand: 倭寇. The characters had so many strokes and composed by all sorts of radicals. They looked incredibly complicated. As I watched him writing in the sand with his finger,

I wondered if I would ever learn to write, especially characters like these ones. I couldn't understand how any adult knew how, it looked an impossible task in my eyes. No wonder my grandparents were illiterate.

'The *wokou* – the Japanese pirates – lived on small islands out there in the ocean, between us and Japan. They were poor, and lived like savages compared to us – we were in the midst of the wealthy and civilised Ming Dynasty. The *wokou* didn't fish or grow vegetables like we did. They lived on boats and went along the Chinese coast, robbing the locals of food and clothes. They killed lots of people too . . .'

Killed people! How terrifying, I murmured in my heart. I would never want to meet those dwarf pirates.

'Some of them were also Chinese. They lived on tiny islands in the East China Sea. They helped the Japanese to loot our towns. We didn't understand their dialects. No one understood anyone from outside their part of China really. But my great-great-great-great-grandfather could tell if they were pirates or not, even when they were still miles out to sea.'

'How? Because they looked different?' I asked.

'Yes, they wore very shabby clothes – ragged robes and torn hats. And as I told you, they were much shorter. They were midgets, vile, nasty midgets! Their boats were not well built, and they were not well mannered. Also, if you looked closely, there were no fishing nets hanging from the side of their boats, because they were lazy people! They only robbed, never worked.'

'So how did your great-great-great-great-grandfather fight them?' I was eager for the real story, as the stationmaster was always getting sidetracked.

'Ha! He volunteered to fight after the dwarf bandits attacked the village! They always attacked in the night. They looted and murdered people in their beds, taking pigs and rice with them and running back to their boats before dawn. Then the Ming emperor sent a general called Qi Jiguang. General Qi was a legendary military man. He trained my great-great-great-great-grandfather and all the other local farmers and fishermen. He taught them how to use guns and swords, and how to swim. Can you imagine! No one in Shitang could swim at that time but we had been fishermen for centuries.' The stationmaster paused to see if this important point was clear to me.

I shook my head, then nodded with great seriousness. Yes, I could imagine that. Because my grandfather was a fisherman and he had never learned to swim. He, like us, believed sea demons would snatch him if he went into the water. So he never liked the idea of learning to swim.

'But it must have been difficult for the general to train the fishermen to swim, because they would be scared of being eaten by sea monsters,' I said, picturing the fishermen spluttering around in the water.

'You are right, Xiaolu. You are a clever girl.' The stationmaster patted me gently on the head. 'But General Qi was from inland and he had been sent by the emperor. So he didn't care what our fishermen thought about sea monsters and he was very forceful with his rules. In the end, he trained all our men, and even got everyone in the province to build forty big warships!'

Wow. I was impressed by this story. This general sounded like the real hero, not the stationmaster's x3 great-grandfather, who was actually just some low-level soldier.

'So in the end, we beat the dwarf pirates. They didn't dare get so close to the coast again! And our villagers learned how to build very big ships. So big that you could bring everything you needed to live on them for days on end!'

'And what happened to your great-great-great-great-grandfather, stationmaster?'

'He died in battle. Many of our fishermen perished. Nasty sea bandits!' the stationmaster cursed.

People said you only became a hero if you died in battle. Otherwise stationmaster's family would not have been descended from a hero. It had earned the stationmaster respect in the village. I wandered off, my mind full of images of those big ships. I would like to have lived on one of them with all the food and water and supplies I might need, and free to go wherever I wanted.

An Unusual Visit

I never knew my grandparents' names until the day the local government sent someone to our street for the census. It was the end of 1970s. The One Child Policy had just been announced, and the government had started to pay attention to identity registration. My grandparents couldn't even recognise their own names printed on the form, of course, let alone write them. Everyone in the village called my grandfather 'Old Guo', which gave only his family name. And my grandmother was simply 'grandmother' to everyone, or sometimes *shi* – 氏 – which means 'wife'. It never occurred to me that my grandparents had personal names, nor did I ever bother to ask what they were. Being nameless in this respect was common for an old woman like my grandmother at that time. So when household registration started in Shitang at the end of 1978, it was a very confusing moment for everyone. The government not only needed the exact details of people's identities (including name, age, place of birth, political status, children, etc.), but they also had to name each street with a metal plate and add numbers to each door so the postmen could find every house, and the government could keep an up-to-date record of every family and their movements.

In those few weeks, we kids followed the census officials from door to door, giggling and laughing at their curious activities in the village. When the two officials approached our house, I was so excited that I sat straight down beside my grandmother. My grandfather was not at home and I thought I could help my grandmother answer some of the big questions that they might ask her.

The two men wore grey Mao suits, glasses and chain-smoked. One of them was probably the leader, as he looked older. The younger one had thicker glasses and acted like a secretary or assistant. He had a row of ballpoint pens in his top pocket and carried a dozen registration sheets. They sat opposite us, on the bench where my grandfather usually sat. Then the older one asked my grandmother:

'How many people live in this house?'

'How many?' My grandmother stared at the man, thinking for a bit. Then she answered with a question: 'When?'

The man was a little confused and in turn questioned her: 'What do you mean *when*? It's a simple question, how many people live in this house?'

Then the assistant suggested: 'Two? Three?'

My grandmother looked a little offended by what they had asked. But she was a humble woman, so she explained with her simple words: 'But, officer, you should ask which year. I have lived in this house for the last fifty years and the number of people has always been changing. You know, there have been at least five or six people living in this house at any time: my husband and I, my son and his wife, then my grandchildren, sometimes my mother's family's cousins. Now, it's different. My son left us a long time ago. My mother's family barely visits. When my son got married, he and his wife left with their child. But I am still waiting for them to come back and live with us. Maybe they will come tomorrow. Maybe they will come back during Moon Festival. I don't know. So it's not that simple.'

The two officers gaped at my grandmother and then looked at each other in dismay. The assistant was going to write some numbers on his sheet, but he consulted his boss first. 'So should I write six or two?'

The other cursed the younger man. 'You are playing flute to a cow, little brother! Granny just doesn't understand our question.'

By this point, I was growing impatient, so I gave the answer: 'Three, officer. Three! My grandfather, my grandmother and me are the only ones living in this house.'

The officer praised me and his hand went into his pockets. He took out a piece of candy and gave it to me. I popped it into my mouth at once.

'So tell me everyone's name,' the assistant continued as he wrote on his form. 'What's your granddaughter's name and age?'

Before I could answer for myself, my grandmother began: 'Guo Xiaolu. She is five.'

'But we need to know her exact date of birth.' The assistant stopped writing and looked up. 'When's your birthday, little girl?'

I stared at him blankly. Birthday? I had never heard of such a concept. I was born already, why would I need that now?

'When's your granddaughter's birthday, granny?' the boss asked, stamping out his cigarette. He then lit a new one.

'I don't know exactly,' she answered. She looked as confused as me, then added: 'She was given to us when she was nearly two. There were no papers with her.'

'What is your name, granny?' the assistant chirped.

There was a silence. Then both of the men looked at my grandmother, taking long drags on their cigarettes, their bleary eyes like needles in the haze of their exhalations.

'I have no name,' she replied.

'What do other people call you?' The boss didn't seem at all surprised by her answer. They already knew that very few old women had names in our village.

My grandmother just shook her head.

'Is it fine with you if we just write your name as Guo Shi?' the secretary enquired.

It must have sounded reasonable to my grandmother, since *Guo Shi* literally meant 'wife of Guo'. And I saw my grandmother nod her head.

But the boss was not happy with this outcome. He turned to his assistant. 'Don't you remember what the chief said to us about this yesterday? It's feudalistic to call a woman merely someone's wife. We can't do this again or we'll be sacked.'

'Before my marriage,' my grandmother began hesitantly, 'my parents called me Second Sister, because I was the younger daughter in the house.'

'Second Sister? That's no good,' the boss officer said dogmatically.

'So what shall we do?' The younger man raised his head from the registration sheets and looked grave.

'We have to find out this woman's real name!' the boss cried firmly. Then he turned to my grandmother and leaned towards her as if she was now a very important person.

'Listen, granny, do you have any papers related to your family? Any original household registration papers?'

'Papers?' My grandmother shook her head. 'Maybe my husband has some.'

'Where is your husband?' the man said.

'Oh, he's out. He only comes home to eat.'

The two men looked at their watches. It was just after lunch, so my grandfather wouldn't be back until late.

'Show me where he keeps his papers.' The officer was now looking really annoyed.

My grandmother didn't move. And I knew why. So I explained: 'My grandfather would be very angry if anyone entered his room. He would beat us.'

The assistant gave me a glance, not impressed by what I had said.

'What's your husband's name? And age?' the officer said.

'Guo Liangcai. He will be seventy-two this year,' my grandmother said.

I was very surprised. Because this was the first time I had heard my grandfather's full name. I didn't expect him to have such an ordinary name, just like all the other men in the village. Suddenly, he seemed different to me. His name was like a new hat.

'Which *liang* and which *cai*?' The assistant raised his pen, but hesitated. In Chinese many different characters have the same pronunciation yet are made up of different characters, and you had to be educated to know which character to write.

'Oh, I don't know,' my grandmother answered. 'I only know that his name is Guo Liangcai. You know we can't write.'

Now the assistant was beginning to get very frustrated. He looked at his boss for instruction. But his boss seemed to have lost his patience too. He choked on his cigarette and then asked: 'And I suppose you don't know your husband's exact birthday either?'

My grandmother's eyeballs rolled upward, as if she was hoping an answer would fall from the heavens. I knew she was really thinking, since thinking always had that effect on her small, damp eyes. Then she said: 'I know that he was born around the ninth day of the ninth moon. But that is according to the lunar calendar, officer.'

'Well, we have to find out the date in the Western calendar,' the secretary said with a weary voice. 'We don't use the lunar calendar any more in our registration documents. It's our new policy.'

He started on his fifth cigarette. The whole kitchen was full of smoke. My eyes felt itchy and I had to rub them constantly. Then I heard one of the men say:

'Have you got some tea, granny? We could wait for another ten minutes, maybe your husband will appear.'

My grandmother stood up and poured some water from the bucket into the wok. Since she barely washed the wok (in order to save oil and any leftover nutrients from the previous dish), I could see that the water in the wok had turned a brownish tinge.

But my grandmother could not see this. She replaced the lid and set the water on to boil as the men smoked, oblivious of us.

'I really can't do this job, brother! You can see for yourself, most people here are illiterate and don't know how to write their names. And even if they showed us their family paperwork, they wouldn't even be able to point out their own name on the page. What's the point of the census? It's totally inaccurate!'

'There is a positive side to it, brother, even if our resources are limited,' his colleague tried to soothe him. 'At least the government can gather information about the number of children. After all, the government's main concern is population control.'

'So I suppose we don't need to give them any packages today?' The assistant looked at his boss, as he reached for his bag.

'No. No need,' the officer answered wearily.

At that age, I didn't understand what they meant by 'give them any packages'. Only many years later did I realize that they were talking about distributing condoms to married couples to stop women getting pregnant.

That afternoon, the men drank two cups of oily green tea, and ate my grandmother's red-bean cakes, which were as hard as rocks. But my grandfather didn't return home in time. As the dusk was falling outside in the street, the two men dried their cups and stood up.

'We might come back tomorrow, or another time, granny,' the assistant said. They had finally stopped smoking.

My grandmother and I watched them disappear into the twilight, both of us wondering what these government men really wanted from us. We could offer them nothing apart from my grandmother's oily, dirty tea and inedible cakes. Even now, decades later, I wonder occasionally what they wrote about us on those registration forms. It seemed that millions of people's lives were turned into arbitrary, accidently created fictions, made up by the state. The real lives of the people were unimportant to officialdom.

The Child Bride

After the visit by the two government officers, I became quite curious about my grandparents' stories. I now knew my grandfather's real name, but not where he was from, and I knew even less about my grandmother.

'If your name was Second Sister before you married my grandfather,' I asked her, 'you must have a family name? Like my family name, Guo?'

'We were the Liang family.'

'Liang?'

'Most people in Peach Knot Village were related to the Liang family. I had many cousins and uncles before I left Peach Knot to marry your grandfather. But I don't know how they are doing these days.' My grandmother paused, and then added slowly: '. . . or whether they are still alive.'

'Peach Knot? Were there peach trees in your village?'

'There used to be lots of peach trees. But they were all cut down, and we planted tea and rice instead.'

'Oh.' I was disappointed. Peaches were my favourite fruit. It was hard to grow peaches in Shitang because they rotted quickly in the humid hot air. I usually only got to eat two or three during the festival season when the villagers donated fruit to the Buddhist temple on the hill. I would go to the temple once the ceremonies were over and steal most of the offerings from a grand porcelain bowl in front of a statue of Buddha. My focus was on the peaches and dates especially – they were the sweetest.

'What about your older sister? Where is she now?' I asked. My grandmother had never spoken about her own family to me.

'She married into a family not far from Peach Knot.'

'And did she have children and grandchildren?'

My grandmother shook her head. From the doorway, I could see the afternoon sun casting long shadows across everything outside in our street. She got up and started preparing our dinner, bringing the conversation to a close.

But I persisted. 'Why didn't she have any children?' I was surprised. As far as I knew, every single woman in Shitang had many children, and once she became a grandmother, she had plenty of grandchildren too.

'She had a ghost marriage.' My grandmother fetched a small axe and began to chop some wood behind the stone stove.

'A ghost marriage? What's that?'

'When she was very little, maybe only three or four years old, she was engaged to a man who was fifteen years older than her. But by the time she had turned fourteen and they were supposed to get married, he had died from some illness. Our parents and his parents would not break the arrangement, since his parents promised to give us a donkey for the marriage. So on the day the wedding was supposed to take place, we went to their village to get the donkey. My sister was wearing a red dress and sat in the front room of their house. Once all the relatives were gathered, my sister knelt and bowed three times to her parents-in-law with a framed photo of her dead husband beside her.'

'Oh. So she got married to a picture . . . !' I imagined a young woman in her red gown lying on a bed, in the dark, beside a framed photo. At least the photo wouldn't beat her! 'Did your family get the donkey afterwards?'

'We took it home after eating a big meal at their house. But my sister had to stay and serve the family for the rest of her life. When we left with the donkey, my sister cried so hard it was as if she was going straight to hell that night. My mother and I cried too. Only my father left without saying anything, pulling at the donkey. That was the last time we saw my sister.'

I pondered upon this for a while. What was better, I wondered: to live with a ghost husband, or with a real live grumpy violent husband who barely came home? I thought long and hard, but couldn't decide. Then, suddenly, I remembered the donkey.

'How about the donkey? Is it still alive?'

'No, the donkey died a long time ago. It died before my father married me off to your grandfather. My mother died a year after the donkey.'

'Oh . . .'

My grandmother was wiping her eyes with her dusty and blackened hands. I didn't know if it was because dust from the stove had got into her eyes or if she was crying. She then put the chopped pieces of wood into the stove and lit the fire.

'Did you get a donkey when you married grandfather?' I asked eagerly.

'Don't be silly. Have you ever seen a single donkey in Shitang? What would you want animals for if you live right next to the sea? There's no land here. Too much water. If people here saw a donkey they would think they had met a dragon, or a donkey-dragon!'

My grandmother now stopped wiping her eyes and returned to the story. 'My father and I had never met your grandfather, but someone came to our village looking for unmarried daughters. He told us a fisherman needed a wife and he could give us some bags of yams and rice if my father agreed to marry me off. So my father said yes, even though I was still a young child. The man went back to Shitang first to inform your grandfather and also to prepare the yams and rice for us. And we waited. We waited for years for him to return, but no one showed up. My father was so angry he nearly went looking for another family to take me.'

The image of an angry father was forming before my eyes: he looked just like my grandfather, his eyes bulging as he brooded on his pipe in a dimly lit kitchen. 'Why was he angry? Because you were getting old?'

'No, I was still young. I was only twelve.' My grandmother rose from the stove, began to chop a long belt of kelp, and threw the pieces into a wok of water.

I wondered about being twelve years old. I had just turned five and I would be married off just seven years later if we were to follow this tradition. Perhaps I would get two donkeys, even though the animals would belong to my grandparents and not me.

'It seemed like we waited a lifetime,' my grandmother continued. 'But finally the man came back to Peach Knot and he brought a sack of rice and three bags of yams on a horse cart. He said to us: Guo Liangcai, your future husband, was pleased with the marriage proposal and urges you to come to Shitang as soon as possible.' My father was relieved. We packed all the clothes I had: two shirts and the mended trousers that had belonged to my dead mother. We steamed some buns and off we went. It was

early morning. My father and I carried all our stuff and followed
the man. I didn't realise your grandfather's home was so far away.
The horse cart didn't come with us — we couldn't afford it, so we
just walked. We walked across the mountains, along dirt paths.
I remember seeing a peacock in the bush. I tripped, because my
feet ached so much. I sat down in the dirt, holding my aching feet
and watching the peacock running away from us. My father said
it was a good sign. The peacock is your husband. He is waiting
for you. I almost burst into tears because my bound feet hurt
from so much walking. On the first night, we had to sleep by
the roadside and were bitten by a swarm of mosquitoes. By the
second day, we had already eaten all the buns and we were still
very hungry. My father was furious with the man, because he had
promised us it would take us only one day to walk to Shitang.
We walked and walked, and on the third day we arrived. As we
came down from the mountains, I caught a glimpse of the sea.
I was so frightened. It was the first time I had seen so much
water! There was water everywhere! And those waves! Then a
gust of salty wind blew against my face and I thought I couldn't
breathe! I was so scared! How would I survive here with such a
strong sea wind and bare rocks everywhere under my feet? But
my father assured me that there was much more food in a fishing
village. He made me believe that life would be better in Shitang
compared to Peach Knot.'

At this point, the kelp had begun to boil. It gave off a very
particular glue-like fishy aroma. My grandmother chopped some
ginger and added it to the soup.

But I was not satisfied with my grandmother's story. I had
seen a few big weddings in the village when families married off
their daughters. Sometimes they even hired a band with drums

and trumpets and marched through the streets with the bride sitting in a big bamboo chair carried by four men. Then a huge banquet would be held at their house. Sometimes the banquet spread out onto the street, if the family was rich and had many relatives.

'Did you have a wedding when you arrived? Or a banquet? Were you given a red dress to wear?'

My grandmother shook her head as she spooned a bowl of kelp soup from the steaming wok. Then she explained.

'On the first day your grandfather did arrange a small banquet for me and my father. But of course he didn't cook. He was a bachelor and barely knew how. Our next-door neighbour helped to prepare three or four dishes, none of which I had ever tasted before. We had sea-cucumber soup, a plate of steamed razor clams, and a local dish they have always cooked for weddings in Shitang: fried green-bean noodles with shrimp and chopped squid heads, served in a large basin.'

In those days, sea cucumbers were cheap and the local fishermen caught them wild from the deep sea. These days, they are all farmed near the docks and are tasteless and slimy, just like the rice porridge we ate every morning, which I hated.

'That was the best meal I ever had in your grandfather's house. Then I discovered he was as poor as my father. The next day, my father left. He was still drunk, but told me when he left that he could finally die knowing both his daughters had found good homes to go to . . . But what did he really know about such matters?'

My grandmother sighed. Her sigh was so long and so heavy that I worried the ceiling might fall on our heads. She said no more. By the time she had served up the third bowl of kelp soup, my grandfather had returned home. As usual, he had been out all day by the harbour, scavenging for abandoned items and dead fish. That day, he brought a small bag of clams. He looked weary. He dropped the clams in a bucket by the stove, and glanced towards his bowl – his was bigger and a different colour to ours. He took his soup bowl silently, mounted the wooden staircase and disappeared into his room. After his footsteps settled down, my grandmother and I sat at our table and chewed our kelp quietly. We both felt a little frightened whenever my grandfather was around. My grandmother became especially timid when he was upstairs. He might scream out at any second because the soup was too hot, or too salty, or contained no meat. He was often grumpy about the fact that there was no pork, forgetting that he was the one responsible for bringing it home.

The Drowning British

The next time I went to the bus station, I found a brand-new wooden placard hanging on the front gate of the station, with large, freshly written characters on it. They had been painted in red, and looked very important. The stationmaster was standing in front of two buses and supervising passengers as I walked through the gate. His wife was checking tickets and punching holes in them with a rusty pincer. From the shouting and talking, I could make out that one of the buses was supposed to be going towards Ningbo, the other to Zhoushan, big seaport towns and the furthest destinations you could get to from our village by bus. It would take, I was told, at least eight to ten hours non-stop along the bumpy mountain roads to get to either.

Once the buses had gone, I caught the stationmaster's attention.

'Stationmaster, what's written on the new placard on the gate?'

'The official name of the station,' he answered, slightly impatient at my curiosity. He walked into the ticket office and brought out a half-eaten sugar cane. He bit into it as he stood under the salty noon sun. I could see that he had recently lost some teeth; two or three were missing since I had seen him last.

'So what's the official name now?'

'Wenling County Shitang Village Model Long-Distance Bus Station,' he mumbled through a mouthful of sugar-cane pulp.

I repeated the name. It seemed very long to me. I didn't know our station was officially a 'model' station. But I was not surprised that it had been awarded a prize, considering how much effort and attention the stationmaster and his wife gave it.

'Wenling County? Where's that?' I asked. This was the first time I had heard of such a name.

'Wenling is a big inland town with straight, flat roads. Our village and the other surrounding ones belong to Wenling. They've got a mayor, who tells us every day what to do.' He spat out some of the pulp and added: 'You know what, Xiaolu? That's where your parents live and work.'

'Oh . . .' I didn't know they were so close. The idea of my parents was still so abstract and not as appealing as the sound of this inland town called Wenling. I was curious that this place should have power over us, that they could control our lives here in the village.

'Have you ever been there?' I asked.

'No. But I have been to the places near Wenling. Like the islands around Zhoushan, for example,' the stationmaster said proudly. 'The population is at least ten times more than here. The fishermen are professional and have lots of fishing festivals all year round.'

'Islands?'

'Yes, you can't miss them. Your grandfather used to live on one of them, before he settled here.'

Once again, I was taken aback by this information. Why was it that *no one* in my family had told me anything about their lives? I would have done better being the stationmaster's daughter. At least I would know where I came from and who my parents were.

'So my grandfather lived in Zhoushan on an island? Did he have a boat?'

'Yes, he was very brave and went everywhere, looking for sea eels and having adventures.'

'What kinds of adventures?'

'Lots. He even fought in the war against the Japanese, when he was young.'

'Really?'

'Once, during the war, he and other fishermen saved hundreds of foreign soldiers from drowning and being eaten by sharks!'

'What foreign soldiers?' I had no idea what the stationmaster meant.

'That was a long, long time ago. Thirty years before you were born, Xiaolu.' The stationmaster's eyes moved to his wife, who was sweeping with a broom. She was cleaning up the sugar-cane pulp he had spat out on the floor.

'You are too young to understand this, but Zhoushan was a very important place for foreigners. As important as Hong Kong back then. The foreigners were called *the British*. They came from a tiny place on the other side of the world. They had big noses, yellow hair and hairy bodies. They had been causing trouble for us Chinese for a long time. They forced us to buy bad things, like something called opium. They liked to live by the port because the seafood was the best and the beaches were very beautiful!'

'Wow.' I was a bit scared, but I would have loved to have met the yellow-haired foreigners. 'Were the Big-noses angry with the Japanese?'

'Yes, they were fighting them too. In 1942 the Japanese came and attacked the locals. The fishermen of Zhoushan preferred the Big-noses to the Japanese dwarves. The Japanese had captured many Big-noses in a big battle. And they were taking them in ships across the sea to Japan, passing Zhoushan en route. It was a massive boat, but it sank after being hit by some other Big-noses, called Americans, near your grandfather's island.'

'Why did they do that?'

'The Americans were fighting the dwarves too. The British Big-noses on the Japanese boat were drowning, so your grand-father and some of the other fishermen seeing this all unfolding from the beach felt pity for the Big-noses and wanted to help, because they hated the Japanese. No one in this world is as cruel as the Japanese! Your grandfather and his friends pushed out their fishing boats and rescued the Westerners with their nets and oars. Because of this brave act, the fishermen were honoured by the government. The Big-nose Chief of Hong Kong wanted to thank the fishermen, your grandfather included, who was among the bravest. They promised them a brand-new shiny boat with a motor, not just sails. But the boat never arrived. Some people must have stolen it on the way. Bastards!'

The stationmaster paused, and knitted his brow.

'Motherfuckers! The British Big-noses should have learned their lesson that we Chinese are kind people because we have forgiven them for what they did to us during the Opium Wars. I hope they will always remember that!'

I felt completely overwhelmed by this war story. I couldn't understand why all these foreign Big-noses were fighting on our Chinese coastline. Why a Japanese boat was carrying Big-nose prisoners from the other side of the world. And why the American Big-noses bombed them. My head was exploding. I certainly didn't want to live through war, but I was happy to hear that my mute and bad-tempered grandfather had once been a hero, and kind-hearted, a man of mercy, a man who helped others. Even foreigners.

'But why did my grandfather move here?' I asked. The islands of Zhoushan sounded a better place to be. In my eyes the beach in Shitang was always smelly, and the village festivals only ever celebrated dead people.

'I don't really know. But usually fishermen moved around with their boats, especially when they were still single. They would sail from coast to coast and settle only when they got married.'

My grandfather had the reputation of being a man of no words and no particular stories to tell. Perhaps he had lost his memory from all the drinking? Had he been numbed by a hard life? Did he feel proud of having saved those foreigners from drowning? Would he have been happier if he had stayed in Zhoushan rather than moving here, to this small, rotten peninsula? In Zhoushan he could have entertained his granddaughter with tales of the past, but here in Shitang he was mute, nothing but a failed fisherman who had lost his boat and hated his hunchbacked wife.

DDT (dichlorodiphenyltrichloroethane)

My grandfather, the professional sea scavenger, was now seventy-three years old. He staggered along the shore with a large, empty sack slung on his back, his steps heavy and his breath short. He was looking for anything valuable by the water: driftwood, containers, dead crabs, or even dead bodies. If he could find a dead body he could at least harvest the man's clothes and shoes and sell them. It was 1978, and I was five years old. I remember one evening, going out with my grandmother to look for him when he didn't return. He had been coughing hard for days and she made for the shore, expecting to find his dead body lying in the sand. When we returned to the pitch-black house, he was already upstairs, sound asleep in his room.

Then, one day, my grandfather was too tired for his walks along the beach. He woke up and started coughing up blood as he ate his morning bowl of unsweetened rice porridge. He was sick, but we didn't know from what. There was only one traditional herbal medicine shop in the village, which had a simple clinic attached. He was not treated with modern scientific knowledge. He was too sick to continue his little business. His son, my father, wasn't very filial in the traditional Chinese sense. He didn't send much money home to his parents. Nor did my parents come to visit. For days, my grandfather limped around inside our house, coughing and wheezing heavily. Occasionally he went outside, but only got as far as leaning against his empty grocery table. His eyes were like two empty holes, his face grey and lifeless. Acquaintances who passed on the street gave him one or two cigarettes, but he smoked bitterly. Before long the seasonal typhoons arrived, and the violent storms and cold rain shut him back inside the house again.

One morning, my grandfather didn't come down for breakfast or lunch. Grandmother hobbled up the stairs to his room on her tiny, bound feet. I was in the kitchen carving a little boat out of a big cuttlefish bone, the sort of thing I always did with fish skeletons. Then I heard my grandmother scream. She clambered down the stairs.

'Go get Da Bo! Or find someone, anyone!'

I ran round to Da Bo's house and pushed open their door.

'Come quick!' I screamed. 'Grandmother is crying! Come!'

I ran back upstairs, and saw my grandfather lying on the floor. Beside him, empty cartons had been tossed on the ground, along with a half-drunk bottle of Bai Jiu – a very strong local liquor the fishermen drank in the cold weather. My grandfather's eyes were wide open, but not moving. They looked like the eyes of a dead fish. I fell on my knees and shook my grandfather's arms. But they were limp. Then my grandmother reappeared, sobbing and hysterical. Da Bo pushed past her, followed by his wife.

'I should have called you last night!' my grandmother was wailing. 'Why have you done this to me? What did I do to deserve this?'

'Terrible! He must have poisoned himself by mixing DDT with the alcohol.'

My grandmother knelt down, touched my grandfather's body and started up her crazed screaming again.

At that time every household was given bottles of DDT and other fertilisers for free by the government, even though Shitang was not best suited to cultivating crops.

Unable to understand what was happening, I squatted down on the floor, and watched in silence, utterly bewildered.

Half an hour later, crowds of people had gathered in front of our house. My grandfather's body was being carried down to the kitchen by a few men. One of them tried to close my grandfather's eyes, but they refused, they were stuck as if locked open. Suddenly, a cry:

'A warm towel, quick!'

My grandmother stood up and grabbed a towel hanging by the washbasin, then poured some hot water from a bottle onto it. The old man took it and covered my grandfather's eyes. A few seconds later, he removed it and everyone could see that my grandfather's eyes were shut. Satisfied, the man handed the towel back to my grandmother and began giving orders. I looked again at my grandfather's corpse in his black cotton clothes, stiff and motionless. His skinny feet were naked save for a pair of broken grass shoes. His mouth was grey and dry like the lips of a dead shark. Now I began to feel frightened. The villagers whispered to each other at first, but soon their chatter grew louder and almost excited. 'He drank DDT, did you hear?' or 'He didn't get on well with his wife and children, no wonder he took action!' or 'He must have felt desperate!'

I was only five and a half. I didn't understand death. But somehow the scene tormented me, and I felt a deep sense of shame in front of all those people. My grandmother had told me that dead people became ghosts. But I didn't see any ghosts dressed in black flying around the room. All I felt was a searing anger, and an icy-cold loneliness somehow emanating towards me from the shrivelled body. No one talked to me. No one explained the situation. I am sure, even today, that I was enraged by that scene. Our house had become a place for public gossip over a corpse and its poison. I hated the feeling of indignity and shame as it lingered that afternoon and for long afterwards.

I don't remember much of what happened during the days that followed my grandfather's death. All I can remember is that we barely went upstairs after that. I was too frightened to enter the room by myself. I thought his ghost might be living up there, and might visit us. I was terrified by noises at night. Since I had always slept in the same bed as my grandmother, I would wake her and ask her to listen. But she would merely open her rheumy eyes and sigh in the dark.

My grandmother wept for days, and wore black for the rest of her life. But I soon felt numb. Sometimes, as my grandmother and I ate our porridge in the kitchen, I felt his presence, as if he was upstairs in his room, slurping the same porridge and cursing under his breath. He was the same shadow in death as he had been in life, and I accepted his continued presence without much thought. The room upstairs was the driest in the house. Sometimes my grandmother climbed up there to drape ribbonfish from a pole under the ceiling. When the wind came and blew through the windows, the long and pale-coloured ribbonfish were like a row of hanging men, swinging weightlessly in the stale air.

The Medicine Master

One summer morning, after a week of unrelenting typhoons, the sun returned to the sky and began slowly heating up our rain-drenched village. Water was everywhere. People came out of their houses, either to fix broken windows or clean up ravaged front yards. Out on the beach, I was playing with Da Bo's children. Then we saw Da Bo swimming under a cliff where the rugged edge always trapped drifters. He was trying to secure a large box against the constant onslaught of the waves. Eventually he managed to grab hold of the big metal box, and climbed up to where we were playing.

'What's inside?'

'Don't touch it! Move back, it might explode!'

A local fisherman was once injured opening a box of bombs he found among drifting debris. Not that he had known there would be bombs inside. Damned Taiwan Nationalist pigs! he cursed miserably when one of his toes was blown clean off. After that, the people of Shitang were more careful with mysteriously packed foreign objects that came adrift on the shore.

We retreated a bit, but soon returned, impatient to see what it was. It was sealed perfectly.

'The foreigners sent it!' one of the kids screamed upon seeing the strange letters that adorned the surface of the package.

'They must be American cookies!' I said. I really hoped it contained some exotic foreign sweets, the kind once found by one of the fishermen.

Da Bo dragged us away again. He told us to watch it from a distance, but not to let anyone take it. He then went to borrow an axe from some guys on the docks. Minutes later, he returned along with two more men. Excitement rose when they caught sight of the metal box.

'It can't be a bomb,' one man exclaimed. 'They wouldn't put writing on it if it was.'

'It must be supplies sent by the Westerners to the Taiwan navy!' the other said.

'Unless the American imperialist pigs want to kill us all and that's why they used such a big box. It might still contain a bomb!' Da Bo reasoned fearfully.

Despite the differing opinions, the three men began to chop at it. We kids were a bit scared by this point and ran to hide behind some rocks. It took them a long time to get it open. We saw them looking confused as they stood staring at the contents. I ran back with the other kids, and was greeted by a sight I'd never seen before. Thousands of small pills packed in different glass bottles, each bottle labelled with foreign letters. The pills had various colours and shapes; some were big white tablets, others round like fish eyes, brown and transparent. For a long while, we all stood gathered around these neatly packed bottles of pills, not knowing what to do with them.

'Western medicine,' said one of the men, breaking the silence. 'We can take the box to Doctor Ruan, he'll be able to tell us what they are.'

'Don't be stupid!' Da Bo scoffed. 'Doctor Ruan knows no more English than us! How would he know what these pills are?'

The Chinese for doctor is *Dai Fu*, literally Medicine Master. Doctor Ruan ran a herbal medicine store and knew about every grass and root in the world. Patients came to see him, told him what was wrong, he would check the tongue and press his fingers to their wrist to check the pulse. Then compose a herb mix from the jars on his shelves and give his patient instructions on how to cook the herb soup and when to drink it. I used to hang out at Doctor Ruan's shop every now and then, so I had picked up some knowledge – orange skins for a cough, mint roots for a stomach ache, *lingzhi* mushrooms for the kidney, ginseng for women, and so on.

Doctor Ruan was checking a woman's pulse when we arrived. The woman, who looked sickly and pale, was somewhat irritated by our interruption. The three men laid the box on the counter and said loudly to the Medicine Master: 'Dai Fu, we found these in the water, maybe you can find some use for these Western pills!'

Doctor Ruan let go of the woman's wrist, and examined the bottles in the box. He sighed heavily. 'Western pills. I wish I could read the instructions!'

He then grabbed some brown-coloured herbs from a jar on the shelf, and a handful from another jar, weighed some seeds from a drawer and mixed them with some oyster-shell powder. He wrapped the medicine in a piece of thick brown paper and told the woman to cook it slowly, and drink the concoction twice a day for three days.

As the woman paid her bill and thanked him for what seemed like an eternity, the Medicine Master put on his glasses and began to study the small labels on the pill bottles more closely, as if he could understand them.

The villagers said it took the Medicine Master three years to identify every bottle in the box. Apparently, he physically tested each one, either on himself or on his patients, and kept a very detailed diary of what effect each type of pill had on the body. No one died from his experiments, at least not that I heard. All we knew was that, in the end, he sold the pills with properly labelled Chinese characters written in his own hand. They were very popular and sold quickly, despite their expiry dates.

The Heart Sutra

'*Form is not different from emptiness, and emptiness is not different from form. Form itself is emptiness, and emptiness itself is form. Sensation, conception, synthesis and discrimination are also such as this . . .*'

My grandmother sat beside our dining table 'reading' a Buddhist sutra, the pages crumbling like dried, old cuttlefish. Her index finger was moving along the lines as she chanted. She 'read' slowly, word by word, her finger carefully pointing at each character. But wasn't my grandmother illiterate?

Even now, I don't fully understand how my grandmother read a whole book of sutras. I knew then that she was regularly reading at least two scriptures – one was the Heart Sutra and the other was the Diamond Sutra. And she really did read each character, line by line, on those brown, smelly pages. One day I did an experiment. I grabbed the book and asked her to close her eyes. I flipped and messed around the pages and then randomly pointed to a character by covering the others on the page. I asked her to open her eyes again and tell me what it said. She fixed her eyes on the strokes, but shook her head blankly. Then she tried to remove my hands from the page so that she could locate the character in the text. Of course I refused. 'Ha, I won!' I yelled mercilessly, having proved my grandmother was indeed illiterate. She could 'read' because she first listened to others chanting, and then synced the sound to the position of the character in the text. Even I, just six, could manage that.

Years later I discovered that the Heart Sutra is the shortest of all the Buddhist scriptures, with only 260 Chinese characters in total; the English version comes to only sixteen sentences. So my grandmother could easily recite it by heart and 'read' each word aloud. My grandmother told me that the Heart Sutra had been found two thousand years ago in an ancient Indian temple, written on a palm leaf.

Even though I was a rebellious child and hated the rituals, I still remember most of the Heart Sutra, just from listening to it being chanted every day as a child. '. . . *All dharmas are empty – they are neither created nor destroyed, neither defiled nor pure, and they neither increase nor diminish . . .'*

'What is a dharma, Grandmother?' I asked.

'Dharma . . . I don't know exactly. But maybe it's about the *right* way of living.'

'The right way of living? What's the right way?'

My grandmother didn't give me an answer, but merely repeated the sutra: '*All dharmas are empty . . .'* Then she went on: '*This is because in emptiness there is no form, sensation, conception, synthesis, or discrimination. There are no eyes, ears, nose, tongue, body or thoughts. There are no forms, sounds, scents, tastes, sensations or dharmas . . .'*

I repeated in my heart: there are no eyes, ears, nose, tongue, body or thoughts. How bizarre! What did it mean? There is nothing? Where are they then? Where are we? Do we exist or not? Knowing my grandmother wouldn't answer me, I stopped questioning and carried on chanting with her: '*There is no field of vision and there is no realm of thoughts. There is no ignorance nor elimination of ignorance, even up to and including no old age and death, nor elimination of old age and death. There is no suffering, its accumulation, its elimination, or a path. There is no understanding and no attaining.'* And then, a short beat, and the conclusion: *'Because there is no attainment, bodhisattvas rely on Prajñāpāramitā, and their minds have no obstructions.'*

I don't know if my grandmother understood the meaning of those lines. I certainly wasn't affected by any of it. You don't have to understand them, people said. You will understand the meaning by chanting them every day year after year. But still I didn't get it. It was very strange to talk about emptiness when Shitang was full of cries and laughter and talk of births and deaths. With my grandmother's chanting echoing in my mind, my heart was bored and grew ever wilder. I wanted great excitement. I wanted whatever I saw – balloons, sweets, picture books, beautiful clothes, butterflies and hair clips. I wanted things, not strange ideas about empty forms and suffering. My grandmother's mournful whisperings and dead texts only made me even more restless and desperate.

Nine Continents

There were two temples in the village – a Buddhist one and a Taoist one. The Buddhist one my grandmother used to go to was located on West Hill. It had survived the Cultural Revolution of the early 1970s, though there hadn't been much revolutionary activity in our remote village. But the second temple, which my grandmother and I rarely visited, was a dark and spooky place behind East Hill dedicated to the Taoist pantheon. It was buried in a bamboo forest and looked sad in the shadowy light of the hill. The temple walls and roof were broken in parts. People said it had been destroyed during the Cultural Revolution, and life had never really returned. I once saw a green snake lurking nearby, and once or twice rats scampering around and making nasty noises where the villagers were supposed to kneel down and pray. I was terrified of the place.

The Taoist temples of my childhood were always more frightening than the Buddhist ones. At least the Buddhists put up friendly statues of the Goddess of Mercy, the Kitchen God, or a fat Happy Buddha. But the Taoists preferred grotesque half-human, half-monster figures. The one near the village was always pitch black, and completely lacking in chi. Nevertheless, a couple of Taoist monks had made it their home. We called them Daoshi. The Daoshi were desperately poor, because none of the villagers ever went out there to donate food or money. They barely had enough for a candle or an incense stick for the temple jars. And the place was permeated with a strange smell, the kind of stench you might associate with Hell – dead, menacing, mouldy and dank. It was rare to encounter the Daoshi, but if you did, you would notice they always wore those long robes and square-toed grass shoes you only otherwise saw in traditional opera, as they practised their strange and mysterious rituals.

On one occasion, my grandmother managed to get a Daoshi to talk to her. This monk was an old man, as old as my grandmother. His long white hair had been combed and tied in a chignon on the top of his head, just like my grandmother's. He was sitting in the yard, grinding a ball of herbs into medicine.

'Daoshi, will you be so kind as to take a look at my grand-daughter?' Grandmother begged. She laid a few oranges she had brought with her beside the herbs by way of an offering. But the old man didn't even look up. His pestle and mortar continued to make grinding noises, and I thought I saw some rusty powder resulting from this activity. His face was not as wrinkly as my grandmother's, nor was it anything like the walking corpses that populated our village.

'Daoshi, look at this child! Her face is yellow and her bones are almost poking through her skin! I worry about her.'

I was a bit scared by the monk's stoic manner, and I tried to hide behind my grandmother. A few moments later, the monk cleaned the dirt from his hands and glanced at me as my grandmother dragged me closer.

'She's got a broad forehead, don't worry.' His voice was deep and husky.

My grandmother nodded earnestly, and at the same time pushed me forward. I felt like a little chicken about to have its head chopped off. The monk took my left hand, opened my palm and studied the lines for a few seconds. He took my right hand and examined that too. Then he dropped my hands and went back to his work. He ground some more powder and collected it together in a bowl with a broken edge. The whole scene looked shabby and beggarish.

'The girl is a peasant warrior,' the old monk announced.

'A what?' My grandmother hesitated. 'Did I mishear you? A peasant warrior?'

But the monk didn't repeat himself. Just as I was about to ask him myself what a peasant warrior was, he spoke again.

'She will cross the sea and travel to the Nine Continents,' he announced slowly but clearly as he plucked some dried leaves from a nearby plant.

In the old days, people used the phrase 'Nine Continents' to describe China, or even the whole world. It was a metaphorical phrase because very few people had even been to the farthest reaches of the empire. It was quite an intellectual concept for my grandmother, and the monk's announcement stunned her. I, however, wasn't impressed. Somehow, I didn't believe him.

The Daoshi gave no more explanation. The monks didn't like to talk. Instead, he stood up and took the bowl of powder into his clay hut. My grandmother followed him. 'Do you mean she will conquer her fate and travel the world?'

'Travel the world. Yes, she will.' These were his last words, and with that he disappeared into his little hut at the back of the temple. We normal people were not permitted to enter a monk's house. So we stood outside, not knowing what to do. The temple was deathly quiet, only a cicada could be heard screaming with full force in the tree above our heads.

At that time, Chinese people barely travelled. A monk wouldn't either, unless he had particular standing like Xuan Zang in the Tang Dynasty, who was entrusted with the task of recovering a set of original sutras from a sacred place far, far away. Travel was simply not a part of our lives. Besides, every Chinese household was strictly registered and monitored through a powerful administrative tradition that originated in imperial times. If a subject left the place of his registered home, he would lose his beneficiary and social status. On top of that, no one had the means to take to the road. The country was vast, bisected by high mountains and long rivers, and even in the 1970s, it lacked any modern infrastructure to enable travel. People unfamiliar with an area could get lost and starve to death. But, for some reason, my grandmother took this palm reading as a good omen. She was happy with the monk's words, perhaps a bit inspired by the idea. As we walked home along the mountain path buried by long grass, she kept repeating the monk's message.

'We will wait for that day, Xiaolu. You will travel the Nine Continents and achieve great things when you grow up. Only the Daoshi can see this.' She paused, struggling for breath. Her bound feet and hunchback made it difficult for her to traverse the hills. She leaned against a tree and almost looked sad. 'But I don't think I will live long enough to see that day.'

Travel the world. I had nothing to say about this. I couldn't read palms. And I was too small to understand what the 'future' meant – it was an impossible concept for a peasant child. All I cared about was the here and now. I wanted everything as soon as I could get it. I didn't want to wait for the future.

I have never forgotten the encounter in the gloomy temple. Even today, the sight of a Taoist monk still makes me feel giddy, and slightly fearful. How did that mysterious man with the chignon know my future, when I knew absolutely nothing?

Tourists on the Beach

To my young eyes, the East China Sea was always brown, churning the refuse and rubbish the villagers dumped in it every day. Or else it was greasy and dirty, because of the oil plant they built nearby. When all was still, you could hear the oil-drilling machine working somewhere out at sea, and soon this sound replaced the usual patter of the village. The sea was never beautiful or majestic for me. But for others the sea appeared very different. This I discovered one day, when a group of students came to Shitang.

I was wandering alone as usual by the thick green-brown kelp bed, looking for shrimp and tiny crabs when I saw some college students around eighteen or nineteen in age arriving with their teacher. They didn't talk like us villagers. Even in my ignorance, I could tell they were civilised people from a civilised place. I quickly realised from their conversation that they must be studying art. They wore white sun hats and carried army-green shoulder bags. With their clean trousers and clean shirts, they looked beautiful and elegant. Their skin was much whiter than ours. Their teacher said something, and they began to take out their sketchbooks and draw the landscape.

I was fascinated by them and stood very close, watching them drawing. One of the college boys was drawing a boat on the horizon. He used coloured crayons, a sort of oily stick of wax I had never seen before. The way he sketched the waves was messy but quite dazzling. To my astonishment, the brown-coloured water transformed to blue on his paper.

For a moment, I was dumbfounded. So I asked him: 'But the water isn't blue, is it?'

He raised his eyes, looked at me with some amusement and answered: 'Maybe you're right. But in my eyes, it is.'

I was at loss for words and absolutely taken by what he had said. Then I ran to a girl nearby. She was tall, her black hair strong and thick like the strands of seaweed before her. Gardenias bloomed across her purple shirt. She was a beauty compared to a scruffy, yellow-skinned girl like me. I stood on my tiptoes and watched her. She was sketching some of the fishermen's wives repairing fishing nets by the kelp bed. These women, normally so ugly and rough with their straggly hair and muddy trousers, suddenly became stylish and even charming. I was mesmerised by her drawing, and stayed by her side as she began to apply colour to the sketch. She worked on the buoys tied to the nets:

yellow, blue, white, pink, purple. I had never noticed such colours in reality. She finished her sea landscape with a sunset. Or was it a sunrise? The sun was half orange, half red. I was astonished. I pointed urgently to the sea where no sun was visible on the horizon, and cried:

'But there's no sun there! Only grey clouds!'

The girl just smiled. Without responding, she began to paint the sea with a mix of red and blue.

It was one of the happiest days of my life. I chatted with the students and I loved being around them. I made brief friends with the beautiful girl with the long black hair that afternoon. She told me they were from an art school in the capital city of our province. Hangzhou, she called it. I imagined it must be very far away from here. They were on their Life Drawing summer trip, and were taking the last bus back at four o'clock. Ah, four o'clock! How I wished terribly that I could go with her, to the city of Hangzhou, and to study at that magical art school. I wished she were my big sister. In fact, I wished the whole group were my siblings. I missed them before they had even left. Time passed too quickly, the light in the sky changed. They began to gather their things, packing their colours, pens and paper. In a panic, I decided to follow them to the bus station. As I walked with them, the beautiful girl with the purple shirt said she would come back to visit, and hoped to meet me again. 'Really?' I was so happy to hear that, as if that promised future was all that mattered to me. I cared for, and dreamed of, nothing else, as long as those young artists returned to our village. By four o' clock, the stationmaster's long, loud whistle blew, and the group waved as the bus pulled away. Off they went, disappearing along the newly paved mountain road, leading to the outside world.

From that day, I waited for them to return. But of course, they never did and I never saw them again. But those young artists had snatched my heart. I knew I could no longer stay in the village, and all I needed was to wait for my chance to leave. That afternoon, an hour after they left, a sunset danced above the kelp-entangled beach. The colours had been taken out of the girl's picture, a scarlet red on a deep blue sea. I stood on the sand and watched as it trembled almost imperceptibly above the contours of the lapping waves. It was astonishing. Those art students had seen what I was unable to, even though I knew the village and the sea much better than they did. From that afternoon onwards, I knew I wanted to become an artist. I would devote my entire life to that end.

Madame White Snake

It was my last summer in Shitang. I was six and a half. Like a grasshopper, I was starving and restless. I was hungry for new things and quickly bored. It felt like there was nothing in the village that could nourish and calm me. The typhoon season came and it rained heavily. As storms swept overhead, drenching the village for days on end, the streets were emptied. I spent my afternoons in the village auditorium, which was the only regular space for entertainment in Shitang.

Most traditional Chinese operas are very long, based as they are on folklore and oral histories. It can take up to twenty hours to finish the fifty, sixty or even one hundred acts. When I was young, people typically brought food and drink and spent every afternoon over the course of five or six days watching the opera.

If they skipped some acts, they waited for the reprise. Entry was free, as all cultural entertainment in those days was state-funded. That summer, the auditorium was playing the opera *Madame White Snake*, based on an ancient tale that originated in our province, Zhejiang.

Everyone knows the story of the Legend of Madame White Snake in China. I think I must have heard it first when I was still in my mother's belly. The love story captures everyone's hearts, whether you are a little kid or an elderly man on your deathbed. Escaping the tireless typhoon rains, I entered the auditorium. I was so haunted by the garishly painted actors and the fancy stage decorations, that I went back again every day for five days. I hid backstage, among the sets and props. There I could touch the dazzling costumes and shiny wooden swords, plastic willow trees, paper pavilions and mini-sized pagodas. It was the best place in the entire village. My playground, my fantasy land.

A white snake spirit lives deep in the waters of West Lake in Hangzhou, one of China's ancient imperial capitals. She has been practising Taoist magical arts for centuries, when one day a young medicine man named Xuxian crosses over Broken Bridge. By accident, he drops a packet of herbs into the water. The white snake swallows the medicine, and gains another five hundred years' worth of magical powers, drawing together her and Xuxian's fates in the process. But another spirit, this time of the tortoise, is also desperate to be immortal and thus grows jealous of the white snake's powers.

To please the medicine man, the white snake transforms herself into a beautiful woman in a silky white dress and conspires to bump into the young man on the bridge in the rain. He lends her his umbrella, and the pair fall in love and get married. In the meantime, the tortoise spirit has accumulated enough powers to take human form, and he transforms himself into a Buddhist monk called Fahai. He approaches Xuxian and tells him to give his wife sorghum wine during the Dragon Boat Festival, which turns the unsuspecting wife back into a white snake. Her delicate husband dies of shock upon realising her true identity.

At this point in the story I had already been at the opera three afternoons in a row. The white snake then travels to Emei Mountain, where she steals a magical herb that can bring her husband back to life. But Fahai, the tortoise turned monk, is a spiteful man. He tries to separate the happy couple again by imprisoning Xuxian in Golden Mountain Temple. But Madame White Snake uses her powers to flood the holy site and rescue her husband. The couple give birth to a son and call him *Mengjiao*, meaning 'dreaming of a dragon'. It's a very ambitious name, and promises much later in the story. But the evil tortoise turned monk will not be defeated and so he fights Madame White Snake and traps her in a pagoda.

At the end of the fifth day, the drama reaches its climax. The story jumps ahead twenty years, as Mengjiao scores the top result in the imperial examination. Triumphant, he returns home to visit his parents, defeats the monk and frees his mother. The family is reunited. But the monk flees and returns to the bottom of the lake. Fearing punishment, he hides inside the stomach of a crab. Legend has it that the yellow part inside the shell is his evil body.

My heart still hung in the air and I was in a state of nervous excitement as the opera ended. I had watched the actors eating a banquet of steamed crabs. But wouldn't the tortoise-turned-crab spirit manifest himself in everyone's stomachs? Or was it all hinting at trouble yet to come? The happy family would never truly be happy, because one day their stomachs would cramp and perhaps they would all die from the pain.

Returning to my grandparents' house, I decided to never eat crab again. Or maybe just the claws. And I told everyone else not to risk it either. 'Don't eat the yellow bit, Grandmother! It's the body of the tortoise turned monk!' But she never listened to me. She gobbled every last bit, from the shell to the glands, from the gills to the legs. I really worried that one day I would find my grandmother walking sideways and every kid in the village would laugh at me. If she was a shrimp before, she risked adding crab to the mix. It was too terrible to bear.

I also spent days wondering about the umbrella they had used in the opera. It was made from white paper, dotted with pink cherry blossoms, and had a green fringe. The Chinese character for umbrella is pronounced *san*, which sounds the same as the character for separation. Couples and families are very careful about using umbrellas in China, believing them to bring bad luck – lovers will be separated, sons and mothers will lose touch, and so on. Since Madame White Snake had met her future husband under an umbrella, it was no wonder that things had turned out the way they did. I'll never use an umbrella, I said to myself, nor give one to the people I loved. Had my parents been using an umbrella the day I was born? Was it raining as I emerged from the womb?

I still hadn't met my parents. I had no idea what to expect. Did they look like my grandparents? Was my father also hunch-backed like his mother? Maybe he wasn't as bad-tempered as my grandfather. Maybe he was talkative, like Da Bo from next door. And my mother, what was she like? The village women all had long braids, or if they were married they tied their hair up in a bun. What kind of hair did she have, and what kind of clothes did she like to wear?

I tried to picture them as I left the auditorium. I wasn't angry with them; I didn't know what to feel. Outside, the familiar street market lay deserted under a fish-belly white sky. Everyone had gone home for dinner. I felt desolate as I walked back to my grandparents' house. My mood was grey, like the typhoon-drenched walls of every house in this old village.

Meeting My Parents

One afternoon, as I was sitting in the dark auditorium watching a new opera, some kids came and told me to go back home.

'Xiaolu, your grandmother is looking for you!'

I ran back home, thinking my grandmother had probably bought me an ice stick, or some sweets as a treat. But as I stood on the threshold, I saw two strangers sitting in the kitchen. A man and a woman. The man was slender and wore glasses. The woman was much shorter, and bore a stern expression. She came straight up to me and took hold of one of my skinny arms. She looked me up and down and in a very strange accent said: 'Ah, Xiaolu, you are so big now!'

I was nearly seven years old.

Then I heard my grandmother's voice from behind the woman: 'This is your mother, Xiaolu. Call her Mother!'

I stared at the woman, perplexed. I sort of understood what she was saying, but her accent and words were alien to me. She clearly didn't speak the local Shitang dialect. As most of the fishing families here had immigrated from Fujian Province many years ago, we spoke a dialect called Mingnanhua.

The man then moved closer, while staring at me like I was some curious animal. These strangers made me very uneasy.

'And this is your father. Call him Father!'

The man with the glasses patted my head lightly and smiled. He had big hands and long fingers and an almost gentle look, so different from the gruff faces of the fishermen in the village.

I was mute. I withdrew to the corner of the room, unable to say these strange words, mother, father. I couldn't do it, not that day.

So that was it. I had finally met my parents. Oddly enough, I don't really remember how I felt at that particular moment, perhaps a little anguished. I don't think I had a clear concept of what it meant to have parents. I was very aware that something had been missing in my life, that I didn't have parents like other village kids did. But still, it didn't feel like a significant moment at the time. The only change I noticed was the new tea bags and rice cakes on the table.

My departure from Shitang came very suddenly. I wasn't even aware it was really happening, that I was leaving my poor grandmother behind, all alone in the house. I was given no time to say goodbye to the friends I usually played with out on the street, nor did I realise that I might never see them again. In my confusion, I heard my parents say my things were packed. I didn't have much, just a few shirts, pairs of trousers and my slippers. And we would be going soon, before the last bus left for the night.

'Where are we going?' I asked in distress, looking up at the two adults.

'We are going home, to Wenling,' my mother answered in her strange accent. She had a rough peasant manner; she was not instantly likeable. Not that day, nor later.

'You're going to school,' my father added, in a friendly voice. He didn't have an accent, he spoke just like my grandparents.

I don't remember if I cried. I didn't really understand what was going on. My grandmother walked all the way to the bus station with us. We had to move very slowly along the cobbled alleyways, because of her bound feet. The other villagers greeted my grandmother, and each time we stopped she would introduce my parents to the other old men and women. 'This is my son, Xiuling,' she pointed to my father. 'He's here to take my granddaughter to school.' My grandmother was visibly proud. I noticed that she didn't introduce my mother to the villagers. I wondered if she felt the same as me, that this woman with the strange accent was a bit scary. Sometimes my father recognised someone in the street and went to pat the man on the shoulder and say a few words. He had lived in these streets until he was nineteen years old.

Eventually, however, we arrived at the bus station. The stationmaster was there, whistle around his neck, cleaning the car park with a broom. He instantly greeted my father and grandmother, offering them a handful of sunflower seeds from his pocket.

He fished out another handful and put them in my pocket.

'Xiaolu, didn't I tell you that your mother and father would come to take you to the big city? You have a great life ahead of you. And your father will give you the best education.'

I nodded as my parents smiled to the stationmaster. A great life ahead of me. It sounded promising and I was excited to hear this, although I still didn't understand what my future might hold. As we jumped onto the bus, I saw my grandmother's eyes welling with tears. She was crying. She took her handkerchief from her pocket, the same dirty handkerchief she used to wrap my ice lollies. She wiped her eyes with it, but the tears were pouring down her cheeks.

My heart felt so heavy, my throat became tight. But then came the weight of my father's hands; he was holding me in the bus seat.

As the bus began to pull out, my grandmother followed us. I heard her trembling voice: 'Xiaolu, send me letters. The neighbours will read them to me!'

I nodded. Then she yelled, her voice hoarse now: 'Do what your parents say, won't you?'

But my grandmother's last words were carried away by a gust of dusty wind. The sea blew the salty breeze into the bus, and I smelt the familiar fishy odour of Shitang.

Suddenly, I realised what was happening around me, and I was seized by such an indescribable fear and sadness that I burst into tears. My throat hurt from the effort of holding back. But I couldn't bear it any longer, and I started to howl. It felt like the end of the world. Even though I had been an unhappy child living with my grandparents in Shitang, I was still scared to be dragged from the only life I had ever known. The bus was moving like a coffin, and with an overwhelming sense of hopelessness, I turned back to watch my grandmother until she became a small dot in the distance.

The bus journey was tortuous. I had never left the village before, nor had I ever taken the bus. As the diesel started to burn and the disgusting smell entered my nose and lungs, I threw up on the seat. My father opened the window and lifted me up so that I could stand and vomit outside. My mother gave me a napkin to wipe my mouth. Today it takes under two hours to make the journey, along a smooth highway, but back then it took twelve bumpy hours along twisty mountain roads, before the plains of Wenling opened out before you. They had begun building tunnels and roads around the mountain, but most of the people in Shitang never left the village. The journey was dusty, noisy and exhausting, and you could feel the uneven rocks being crushed underneath the tyres. Passengers were constantly being thrown into the air and bounced back onto the seats. My head was spinning, my vision became blurry and my ears ached. Each time the bus made a turn, my throat seized and I threw up. This lasted for two or three hours until I had nothing left to bring up. Weak and miserable, I stood on my seat and looked out of the window and howled in agony.

My grandfather, a Hakka fisherman, 1970s

PART II | WENLING: LIFE IN A COMMUNIST COMPOUND

Another three thousand years have passed since that moonlit night when Monkey heard the whispering voice in his sleep. Monkey travelled from continent to continent in search of the human world, until he arrived in a land called Tang Dynasty China.

In this rich and curious land, the Tang emperor established a grand capital called Chang-an. Inside the city walls there were countless markets selling silk, porcelain and exquisite jewels. Beyond the city walls there were miles of rice and sorghum fields where farmers ploughed for generations. But the Tang emperor was an idealistic man. He wanted the country's future to be animated by a strong spiritual life. One day he assembled his officials and announced that he wanted to find the most enlightened Buddhist monk in the country to teach in the Imperial Court. So the officials went in search for the man. Finally, in a dilapidated temple hidden in a pine forest by the South China Sea they found a monk called Xuanzang.

Xuanzang knew every single scripture by heart. When he was told that he had been chosen by the emperor to teach in the Imperial Court, he said that he would only do so if he could travel to India to obtain the original Buddhist sutras. The emperor agreed, and sent him a white horse as his companion, as well as two diligent assistants – Pigsy and Sandy. On a golden-rayed autumn morning, the monk and his disciples left Chang-an for India.

As soon as Xuanzang and his companions left the city walls of Chang-an, they began to experience difficulties. They had to travel in harsh weather through Gansu, Qinghai and Xingjian in the Gobi Desert. On the thirty-seventh day of their journey they had only arrived at the edge of the desert.

Thirsty, hungry and exhausted, the pilgrims sat by a little stream on the edge of the desert. After they drank some water and ate their last remaining food, Xuanzang urged his companions to return to the road. But Pigsy was too hungry to go on and Sandy was too weak to walk. Just then, a yellow-pink sandstorm swept down from a distant dune. The sky turned dark and the storm howled and swallowed everything in its path. The two disciples lay down on the ground, trembling with fear that the end of the world had come. But the monk kept praying. In the howling wind they heard an unearthly voice: 'Master, I am coming to protect you!' Gradually the storm calmed. Xuanzang and his disciples opened their eyes and discovered they were surrounded by exotic fruits they had never seen before. Then suddenly, a handsome monkey appeared and told them to eat the fruits before they began their journey again. Xuanzang was a little confused. The creature bowed to the monk three times and said: 'Master, I was sent by Heaven to assist you in your journey. Please let me accompany you.'

Xuanzang gave the creature a Buddhist name, Wukong, meaning Emptiness Knower. He told the monkey that he must tame his cunning trickster nature and Wukong now promised he would obey his master. When the sky turned blue, the pilgrim team stood up and proceeded into the desert.

The first time I met my brother, aged almost seven

Wenling

In the autumn of 1980 I finally started primary school. Me, the seven-year-old street urchin, suddenly dressed in a school uniform and told to sit still and recite Tang Dynasty poems, no questions allowed.

Wenling literally means Warm Mountain. It was a modest, middle-sized town, home to thousands of newly trained peasant workers. If you were to visit Wenling today, you would find a totally different place from the hilly town of my childhood. When I arrived it was at the beginning of a period of massive transition. Ten years later, the mountains had been flattened, highways squashed the fields, and the population had tripled to a million and half. The green Wenling of 1980 is very different from the overpopulated, traffic-choked, polluted Wenling of today.

The name Warm Mountain summed up the landscape perfectly. Unlike Shitang, of which every corner was forged of rock stained by saltwater blown in from a yellow sea, Wenling was verdant and calm. It sat in the bottom of a basin, so the air was warm and sticky. Bamboo, orange and mulberry trees were our staples and they grew everywhere, in front of houses and along the streets. Rice paddies and residential buildings sat side by side, encircled by tea plantations and rapeseed fields, and beyond that, yams climbed up their wooden frames along the motorways.

This was the China of the early eighties: town and nature, with no real separation between the two.

Wenling was a big city in my eyes, with middle schools and high schools, and many new streets and gleaming residential blocks. So much to explore. Slogans and propaganda posters adorned the walls and, although the paint had faded, they were still legible. *'Up into the Mountains, Down to the Countryside!'* *'Learn from the Peasants, Learn from the Workers!'* *'One Child is Better!'* The most common slogans praised our great leader, *'Long Live Chairman Mao!'* or *'Chairman Mao is the Red Sun in Our Hearts!'* The Cultural Revolution had ended four years before I arrived in Wenling, but visually the town was still saturated in its propaganda. Everyone here looked quite different from the citizens of Shitang. Most people worked in factories. Wenling had a very big plastics industry, as well as shoe making and a gigantic silk factory where my mother worked. But there were also lots of peasants living on the edge of the town and on the hillsides, growing their rice and vegetables.

Everything about life here was different from the rugged Shitang. In my grandparents' village, everyone lived in their own house – even the poorest fisherman had a small shed to call his own. But in Wenling, families lived together in compounds newly built by the government. No one was afforded an autonomous life here. Every adult belonged to a work unit, run by the state. During the day our parents worked in factories and offices. In Shitang, women were housewives, gossiping about their men on their doorsteps after lunch. But here, the women were full-time workers. Apart from the elderly, you never saw anyone just sitting in front of their house, contemplating the clouds, as was normal in Shitang. Everyone in Wenling seemed to be very proud of their work and dedicated to building a strong industry. My new surroundings seemed much nicer and more modern than my grandparents' draughty stone house, yet I wasn't sure if I was going to be happier here.

The big news for me upon arriving in Wenling, however, was that I had a brother. He was two years older than me, and we hated each other immediately. The reasons for our enmity were many and complex. We had never lived together. He was nearly nine when I first met him. I noticed how his upper lip quivered and how he squinted at me through his glasses, as if I was an irritating pest. I was an invader, a threat to his material and emotional comfort. My brother had an instant prejudice against me and I was convinced that this attitude was encouraged by my mother, who had given me away to the goat-herding Wong family for adoption when I was born. The hierarchy in our family was obvious: my father was most important, then my brother, then my mother, and I was the insignificant flea unworthy of attention. At mealtimes my mother would save all the precious pork for my father and brother. If I reached for the meat, she would beat my chopsticks back and order me to wait until the men had finished eating. I was her last concern. Not only that, but I was also one of the youngest in the compound, and became an easy target for the boys. Warm Mountain turned out not to be so warm after all.

My Mother

The first conflict with my mother came about over language. Unlike my father, who spoke both the Shitang and Wenling dialects, my mother could only speak Wenling Hua. It must have been those roots, sharing a first language with my father, that turned me into my father's child. Both my father and I were raised by my paternal grandparents; we had inherited the same traditions from the fishing village. So in the beginning, I didn't want to talk to my mother and my brother, and my mother was disgusted by what came out of my mouth.

'She speaks like your barbarian fishermen! She even behaves like them too!' Then she grabbed my dirty shirt. 'Look at her sleeves! Look at the layers of snot and dirt! She is one hundred per cent peasant!'

My mother despised peasants. I couldn't understand why. In my eyes, in Wenling, you were either a peasant or a worker. No one was richer or better than the other. Years later, I was told that it was the legacy of the Cultural Revolution that made my mother behave like this. Chairman Mao's policy of sending city people to the countryside didn't build respect between them; instead it alienated one from the other. The youth from the cities desperately wanted to go back home and the peasants felt disrespected.

Later, I learned that my mother's family had in fact been from real peasant stock. In the Chinese Household Registration system, fishermen and farmers belonged to the same caste, it was stamped in their documents: Peasant Household. And this status would determine what kind of job you could get and where you were allowed to live. When I grew a bit older and had learned to read and write, I found my mother's ID card: *Li Heying. Date of birth: 3 May 1949. Peasant Household.* What a revelation! I was indignant. How could my mother despise me and treat me like a second-rate person?

For generations, my mother's family had worked with buffaloes in the rice paddies. But rarely were they blessed with a
fat year. Since Wenling was in a mountainous region, peasants
could only grow their crops on uneven patches of rocky hillside.
Irrigation was difficult. You had to physically carry water buckets
uphill in order to water the crops. Year in, year out, the weather
worked against them. It was either drought or floods, and either
way the crops were ruined. The family's bad luck continued right
up until the 1960s, when my mother's generation were trained
as factory workers to serve Mao's ambitions: they were building
China into an industrial nation that could compete with Western
imperialism.

That was how my mother, who only had three years of basic
education and could just about write her own name on a registration form, escaped the farming life. She didn't take up work in a
factory, but instead joined the propaganda dance troupe attached
to the association of local Red Guards, aged just fifteen. She was
no great beauty – I've seen a photograph of her as a young girl –
certainly not beautiful enough to be selected for the Red Guard's
propaganda team under normal circumstances. But she had the
red and right background which suited their vision. She came
from a straightforward peasant family and had a young innocent
heart ripe for persuasion. So she was given an army uniform and
an official armband, upon which was sewn the golden characters for 'Red Guard'. Her plaits were cut short and she wore a
green army hat with a red star on it, a brown leather belt tightly
wrapped about her waist and a Little Red Book placed next to her
heart, tucked into the left breast pocket of her uniform. She and
the other teenagers were trained to chant lines from it, followed

by cries of '*Long live Chairman Mao, long live Chairman Mao, may Chairman Mao live for a million years!*'

Throughout the 1960s my mother and the other Red Guards went around the local theatres and performed in the streets, 'educating the masses'. No one at that time was encouraged to get a higher education. '*Ignorance is pride*', as one of the slogans from that period went. Of course, such was the revolutionary, peasant spirit. Perhaps my own rebellious spirit came from my mother, as little as I wanted to admit it considering how much I hated her during those years.

It was impossible for me to get close to my mother – she was always nervous about something. She never asked me how I felt or what I wanted. She flew into a rage if I didn't obey her, if I didn't wash the vegetables properly, or if I broke a bowl by accident. It was as if she had been bitten by a rabid dog. I certainly didn't want to be bitten in turn. She had a heart of stone, that's how it felt to me. She was just like the uncompromising ideology of Maoist China – inhuman, unchallengeable and full of contradictions.

Iron Plum and Red Lantern

From the day I started school in Wenling just before I turned eight, I discovered how my mother spent her time. During the day my mother worked in the town's silk factory and at night she and a selected group of workers rehearsed and performed revolutionary opera. By the end of 1970s, the legacy of the Cultural Revolution still reigned supreme. One of its manifestations was the continuation of the local performance groups and operas for the revolution, invented in the 1960s by Madame Mao. They combined a particular style of modern ballet with stories of the glorious Red Army. This mix created its own form of visual language for depicting heroes and villains. Normally the heroes would be the proletariat or Communist soldiers, the villains the landowners or Nationalist traitors. My mother's silk factory was a major industrial base in Zhejiang Province. So it had its own opera and entertainment troupe. And on one occasion, fittingly, my mother was chosen for the leading role – Iron Plum from the famous opera *Legend of the Red Lantern*.

It was a very big deal in our compound that my mother had been chosen to act in a revolutionary opera, even if it was just an amateur production. So almost every evening, after we had finished dinner, my brother and I would take our homework to the silk factory theatre where my mother was rehearsing with other worker-actors. I had always felt baffled by my mother's former-Red-Guard attitude towards life and how it conflicted with her peasant background. This opera only fuelled my confusion. It was set in the 1930s: the Nationalists controlled the country and the Communists were conducting underground activities in Japanese-occupied territories. One day the father of our heroine, Iron Plum, is taken away and jailed by Nationalist soldiers. Iron Plum's family now lives under the threat of police retaliation. She is told by her grandmother that her parents were working underground for the Communist Party and had sacrificed their lives for the revolutionary struggle. After hearing this heroic story, Iron Plum decides to follow their example and joins the revolution.

My mother worked hard in rehearsals, so as not to disappoint the audience. The opera didn't require much singing, but lots of physical movement and some very stiff poses, like spinning around a tree with a gun on her shoulder, singing. Each night, I would hear my mother complaining to my father about her exhaustion and lack of sleep. She would eat some leftovers in the kitchen, still be practising lines from the opera: '*Now I finally understand my family's mission. I will raise the red lantern to light the path of the future.*' She would speak doubtfully: 'We still have to sing the praises of the revolution, despite no longer believing in such things.' My father never said anything to contradict his wife. Before long they would both be asleep, after a hard day's work, leaving me awake and confused on my small bed wondering about my mother's comments.

Since my mother was always occupied – either working in the factory or rehearsing for her opera – and my father was at his work unit all day long, I was expected to take care of most of the housework. My brother, the only son in the house, wouldn't even touch the kitchen sink. I was around eight or nine – only a couple of years after I'd left Shitang – when I began cooking for the family, washing the clothes, mopping the floors and feeding the chickens after school. Perhaps it was natural for a daughter to take over the household duties from her mother? Nevertheless, I hated it. Why should I be the one to do everything? And what was the use of doing housework at all? Chairman Mao had slept in dirty shirts for almost half a century but that hadn't hindered him from being the most powerful man in China. My grandmother had barely rinsed our bowls after each meal, because they would be just used again a few hours later for the same porridge. I resented being forced into such futile activities merely because I was the daughter.

Most of all, I wanted to go out to play. I wanted to know what city kids did and what they talked about. But I didn't seem to have the things the other kids had. My clothes were always roughly mended hand-me-downs from my brother. I didn't have any friends. I was lonely. I wanted to be cared for and loved and I missed my grandmother. Especially after my father went to visit and came back to report that she had become very frail and she could no longer see much. I imagined my grandmother sitting in our stone house where my grandfather had committed suicide, with hardly any food and even less companionship. How did she endure the solitude? Did she still pray to Guanyin every day? Did she still weep in the dark kitchen? I constantly wondered how she was and I felt miserable, for her and for myself.

My Father

My father was the only one in the family I could connect to. He had a sensitive heart – partly because he was a painter and partly because he grew up by the sea, which imbued him with a fisherman's spirit with which I was familiar. He was born in 1931, a significant year for China. Japan took advantage of the civil war between the Nationalists and the Communists to invade Manchuria. At the same time, Mao Zedong created his first Jiangxi Soviet Government in southern China with only two thousand men. In those days people desperately needed a great leader, and a revolution for the oppressed. He described to me the poverty of his childhood in Shitang: 'Your grandmother, my mother, was sold to my father for a few kilos of yams. And I never owned a pair of shoes until I was thirteen.' My father was supposed to become a sea scavenger like my grandfather. But he didn't continue that family tradition. Instead, he wanted to paint, which surprised everyone.

For some odd reason he didn't really explain to me, he began to become obsessed with drawing and painting as a teenager. I was intrigued by this, as I still recalled my encounter with the art students on the beach. Had he had a similar experience? My father shook his head. He realised that Shitang offered him no possibility to pursue his artistic dream. So he left my grand-parents at the age of sixteen and went to study at the province's teacher-training college, where he received free accommodation and an education. The school was for proletarians, promoted by the Communist Party in the 1950s. There he was trained to paint and write calligraphy. They only used traditional Chinese ink, though in his free time he painted with any and every material he could find: squid ink, dye, chalk, crayon, watercolours, oil paints. Everyone said he was a better painter than his teachers, and that his calligraphy was superb. He was an excellent student. At nine-teen he joined the Communist Party and began teaching. There was a big shortage of teachers at the time, so he was required to teach anything and everything, although he mostly concentrated on literature, painting, geography (even though he had never left our province) and physical education (he was good at basketball). In his spare time he wrote poems and published sketches. He was grateful to the party and to Mao for transforming him from an obscure fisherman's son into an educated citizen. That was, until 1956, when he was caught up in the first nationwide politi-cal purge following the so-called Hundred Flowers Campaign. This was when his troubles began.

The Hundred Flowers Campaign was a movement in which the Communist Party encouraged everyone to openly express their opinions about the regime. 'The policy of letting a hundred flowers bloom and a hundred schools of thought contend is to promote the flourishing of the arts and the progress of science,' Mao said at the time. Believing the party to be sincere, my father joined in wholeheartedly. He was keen to find solutions for the problems of the time, especially to improve the lot of the impoverished peasants who were forced to give away the entirety of their harvests to the army and the state. Since he was very good at drawing, he created a series of comics to show how the peasants were suffering and the negative consequences of the 'collective farming' policy, which he then published in local magazines. Lots of people saw them and agreed, and party members from the province paid attention to his opinions. But my father didn't know that the government was also weeding out the 'poisonous flowers'. Before a year had passed, Mao began a counter-campaign to rid the party of those who didn't share his ideology or his solutions. More than half a million intellectuals, including my father, were targeted and condemned to labour camps. Overnight, my father, a 'model teacher' in a country school, was thrust into the storm of an ideological purge and fired from his job.

'I was sent to Changshi, a mining region in our province, to do hard labour,' he mentioned to me once.

'What sort of labour?' I asked eagerly, not understanding what he was really saying. I thought about the men in Shitang: they were either fishermen or labourers. Everybody worked with their hands. In fact, so far every adult man I had known was a labourer or a manual worker.

'The sort of labour that one normally wouldn't want to do. The work was dangerous, and physically very hard,' he said, but he wouldn't go into details. Maybe he didn't want me to feel sorry for him, or he simply thought I wouldn't understand. Some years later, my mother filled in what my father had left out. He had worked in a quarry, blasting away rocks with dynamite, then carrying stones down the valley for construction work. No one wore helmets and injuries were a daily occurrence. In the evenings, the men had to write page after page of self-criticisms, to purge themselves of their 'capitalistic thoughts'. It had to be done with absolute sincerity – sarcasm, false notes or exaggerations would result in further denunciations and even more severe punishment.

Class Enemies Getting Married

My parents met in the 1960s, in one of the village recreation centres where my mother sang and danced with other Red Guards to 'educate' the peasants. This was the story my mother told me when I was a bit older.

'We were class enemies,' she said.

'What do you mean, class enemies?' I asked, finding the concept too abstract.

'It means I was a Red Guard, and he was a Stinking Number Nine. I was obliged to beat and spit on him.'

In contemporary Chinese culture, intellectuals were classified as number nine in a system of classes – lower than manual workers or doctors. During the Cultural Revolution, people resurrected the term, or else referred to them as 'capitalist dogs'.

'You mean you met Father while beating him up? And you spat on him?' I couldn't bring myself to believe this was true.

'Yes. Exactly! I couldn't see his face, as he was kneeling on a stage with a big placard with a black cross on it hanging around his neck.'

'And it said Stinking Number Nine on it?'

'Yes. We chanted slogans and sang revolutionary songs while they dragged class enemies onto the stage. They were forced to squat down as we read the charges out, things like "Anti-revolutionary Poisonous Weed" or "Bourgeois Poisonous Flower", whatever was written on their placards. Some of them trembled and wept while we shouted at them. Then the head of the Red Guard team told us to teach them a lesson. I went straight to your father, spat on his head and kicked him in the spine. He didn't fall over or make any noise. He remained on the floor, looking stubbornly up at me.'

My stomach churned when I heard this. After a few seconds of silence, I asked again: 'Was that *really* the first time you met Father?'

'Yes, how else do you think we could have met?' my mother answered dismissively. 'People like him didn't live with the rest of us. He was either out in the fields or locked up in the labour camp.'

'But, I mean, did he look right at you while you spat on him and kicked him?'

'I don't remember. We were a group of Red Guards, we got carried away in the moment. We didn't really mean it.' My mother's tone was dry, so shockingly matter-of-fact.

'But you ended up getting married?'

'We went to the re-education camps to monitor the capitalist dogs and stinking intellectuals. I saw how your father lived in a pig shed and worked day and night. He was so skinny and he could barely see. He struggled with the work. I took pity on him, and brought him clean water and some vegetable buns. He looked like he might faint at any second.'

'You took pity on him?'

'Yes. I also thought, why would such an honest-looking man be a capitalist dog? Maybe the party had misunderstood, not that I dared say that out loud. We ended up like comrades really, until the year he was set free and returned to Wenling.'

'Then what?'

'We decided to get married.'

'And Father was happy with that?' I asked.

'Are you being deliberately stupid? He felt grateful to me. Which other woman at that time would have dared marry such an outcast? He was a public enemy! Without me, he would probably still be living in a pig shed and eating from a trough.'

I heard different versions later from our neighbours. Apparently it had been a very dramatic decision for my mother. People shunned my father, to protect themselves from his bad reputation as a class enemy, in case there was a further political purge, my mother's family included. My grandmother was especially adamant that her daughter not marry him. My mother's brother beat her and threatened her, saying that she would never be allowed to return home if she went to see my father again. She was locked up in a room and all her clothes and shoes were taken away, so that she couldn't escape. My grandmother said she would rather her daughter die than marry an anti-revolutionary Stinking Number Nine. Despite all this, my mother was not to be dissuaded. One night, she managed to escape through the window. She ran half naked through the street, straight to my father. He dressed her in his clothes. With no shoes on her feet, they went the next morning and registered their marriage.

'Your mother was so brave and romantic. At that time no one even dared to talk to your father. They avoided him like the plague. But your mother didn't care about any of that,' one of our neighbours in the compound told me.

'Their story is just like *The Weaver Girl and the Cowherd*. The Weaver Girl's mother created the Milky Way to keep them apart, but just like the girl from the story, that wasn't a big enough obstacle for your mother!' another old woman in the compound told me, her eyes glistening. The Weaver Girl was the seventh daughter of Mother Heaven, and her job was to weave white clouds for the sky. Bored and lonely up in the sky, the Weaver Girl decides to visit Earth, where she meets a simple cowherd. Of course, they fall in love and she stays. Mother Heaven is so furious that she takes out her giant hairpin and scratches a river in the sky to separate the two lovers. This was how the Milky Way was formed. I thought to myself: *The Weaver Girl and the Cowherd* is a sad story, but my mother and father's had a happy ending. Well, so far, it seemed.

My mother's family lived on the outskirts of Wenling, but from what I'd heard, I imagined my maternal grandmother to be an awful and cruel old lady, who tried to stop my parents' love. I bet she also had a giant hairpin, like most old women.

So my mother saved my father's life? Even though she spat on him and kicked him on their first encounter? It was hard to believe. There must have been some love between them, but no one ever used that word. In fact, I don't think I ever heard it in our family; there were never fancy words like 'love' in a family's life in China then.

I always felt that my mother kept a lot of things from me, lied even. She never told me that she had rebelled against her family to marry my father. Perhaps she worried that I would be inspired by her example. She also never told me whether she had joined the Red Guard house raids, where they targeted the houses of the suspected 'anti-revolutionaries' and smashed everything up, sometimes even torturing people in the process. She had barely participated in any 'real' revolutionary acts – that work was reserved for young men, she told me. She only chanted and danced in the Taizhou Region Red Guard 8th Rebel Group Dance Troupe. I would never know exactly what she did in those years. It had already become a kind of myth to my generation.

After marrying my father, she quickly fell pregnant with my brother. She left the Red Guards and started working in the large silk factory. Zhejiang was the centre of the silk industry, and at least three thousand women worked every day in my mother's factory alone. I remember how I used to enter the factory and look for my mother. I walked past rows of noisy silk-binding machines which were extracting silk from the silkworms. Each machine whirled softly and was in perpetual motion; collectively it was overwhelming. The air was stiflingly hot, and an intense odour of mulberry leaves hung thick around me. It felt like some layer of Chinese Hell for worm corpses, manned by women in white robes. My mother appeared out of the gloom, standing among the lines of workers, her hands soaked in warm water and her fingers busily sorting the wet silkworms with a small brush. She skewered the silkworms and roasted them on top of the hot machines. She used to give them to me as an after-school snack, and I would sit eating them in a corner of the throbbing factory. They tasted of mulberry leaf and burnt meat. I probably ate at least a thousand of those hot little bugs over the years, a token amount of protein to make up for all the years I spent living with my grandparents and eating mainly rice porridge and kelp.

Shaolin Kung Fu

I had been living in Wenling for some years, but still my brother and I seemed to lead, largely, parallel lives. I had thought we might play together or that he would protect me. But none of that had happened. He was the centre of the Guo family. I was the afterthought. We kept our distance. My overwhelming memory of my brother as a young boy was his love of Shaolin kung fu.

In 1982 a truly astonishing film called *Shaolin Temple* came out starring a nineteen-year-old Jet Li, who had swapped a life of professional martial arts for that of an actor. He replaced Bruce Lee as the ultimate Chinese hero in the minds of all young boys, my brother included. We lived right next to Wenling People's Cinema and it was possible to slip through the back door from our compound without buying a ticket. So we children used to sneak into screenings all the time. We were blown away by *Shaolin Temple*. It was one of the very first Chinese martial arts films not to focus on fighting, but to emphasise love, the beauty of nature and the poetic spirit of the monastic life. None of us had ever been to the real Shaolin Temple, which was far away in Henan Province in central China. But we all knew about it, this mysterious temple with 1,500 years of history in teaching young monks how to fight. For us, it was a sort of children's version of the basic ideas of Buddhism and even Taoism, those deep philosophical things only old people understood. I was absolutely taken by the picturesque mountain landscapes and mesmerised by the pretty actress Ding Lan who sang while herding rams in the wild forests that surrounded the temple. But I soon realised the reason for my brother's adoration of the film was very different to mine. He was fascinated by the magical power of Shaolin kung fu, especially its techniques and philosophy. He murmured the names of the martial art forms and walked around kicking non-stop. The film was a massive commercial success in China and was shown in cinemas for months. My brother could never be found after school and neglected his homework, because he was watching the film again and again. He wanted to learn every combat move that Jet Li and the Shaolin monks made. He even practised silently in the dark of the cinema, while the other audience members were enjoying the forbidden love story between the apprentice Jet Li and the singing cowherd girl.

The monks in the film were performing a kind of qigong martial arts, and I could see that all of the boys were attempting moves like 'the 18 Hands of Luohan'. It was said that this particular form had been created by an Indian Buddhist monk called Bodhidharma. When Bodhidharma visited the Shaolin Temple, he taught the monks a series of exercises which imitated the gestures of arhat statues (in Chinese we call them *luohan*). The method focused mainly on palms, fists and hooked hands, as well as twists and flicks of the wrist.

I was never a fan of all this kicking and fist throwing. I kept at least a ten-metre distance from my brother when he was in kung fu mode, but still I was destined to be on the receiving end, by virtue of being the youngest girl in the compound. Every time they hit me, I recall the words of the master monk to his disciples: 'Martial arts are for defence, not for killing or hurting people.' It looked like none of the boys had remembered this line, even though they had seen the film so many times. When my eleven-year-old brother demanded to be allowed to join the temple, my father asked him if he was prepared to get up every morning at five and train for a whole day, without ever being allowed to eat meat for the rest of his life. 'No meat?' My brother thought about this for a few days and then never mentioned the idea again.

Even though Shaolin kung fu became a national obsession for Chinese boys throughout the 1980s, most of them grew out of it eventually and moved on to 'real life'. Strange when you think about it, that these teenagers, who once punched and kicked each other, settled so easily into their obedient roles. Perhaps it was also to do with the incredible number of martial arts films produced, leading to very poor production, and indeed, overproduction. Audiences lost any appetite for it and young people discovered other objects for their zeal. I don't remember when exactly my brother stopped watching kung fu films. But I remember he spent more and more time in my father's studio learning ink painting, which my father encouraged of course. He also became more and more introverted, as if those blots of ink absorbed his youthful energy. He began to smoke too, and by the age of fifteen, he would sit on my father's chair, enjoying a cigarette, while my father was out at meetings. His legs dangled beneath the ink-soaked table, his unfinished mountain and river painting laid out before him. I didn't say much about his work; whenever I tried, he only looked back at me with those weary kung fu eyes.

'You know nothing about art,' he hissed like a snake, 'so just shut up.'

My brother and I are just as distant today. The idea that he was the official child of the family and that I was nothing but an unwanted girl dominated everything about the way we behaved at home and outside. This distance gradually turned into a sort of mutual respect for each other's lives. At sixteen he left us to study fine arts in Hangzhou.

Life in a Communist Compound

Life was centred entirely around our compound. We lived in a typical Communist worker compound, built in the 1960s. Forty families lived together in a mix of dwellings that were fused at some point around a large, central courtyard. We had one public shower room and one toilet block with five holes to squat over. Each family was given two rooms: one for cooking the other for sleeping. We cooked downstairs and slept upstairs. No one had any secrets. Everyone left their front doors open. Mothers and children rushed in and out of all the homes as if they were their own. I remember two donkeys and a mule lived in the compound, too, belonging to one of the families who used to be farmers. Now that they were factory workers, the donkeys were retired and spent their days wandering around the yard or periodically roaming into the distant fields for fresh grass. The sight of them reminded me of the poor donkey my grandmother's family had received in exchange for their elder daughter's ghost marriage. Here in Wenling animals seemed redundant. No one worked on the farms, and everyone was busy learning how to operate machines. Every few days a crowd would gather in front of our kitchen, staring at a brand-new electricity generator or a mechanical rotisserie and trying to get it to work. Machines seemed to be taking over our lives.

Of the animal kingdom, only chickens had retained some purpose in this new world. We owned a multitude. They were everywhere: in the back and front yards, under the beds and chairs, sometimes flapping onto the dining table while you were eating. As a result their excrement covered our floor, but no one seemed to mind. The adults were too busy to care about hygiene. Every few days we would check if the hens had laid eggs. Eggs were our main source of protein. But frequently they would hatch before we could harvest them. My favourite thing was to watch the small chicks crack through the shells and pop out, all wet and soft. They were my pets, my little friends.

But the yard had been stripped of any grass. So to feed the chickens we kids were sent out to collect grass and grain from the fields outside the compound. Somehow, the number of chickens reduced steadily each year. I remember one morning walking to the public toilet where I found a whole bunch of dead chicks floating in the cesspit. Our toilet was actually nothing more than a huge hole in the ground. Someone had left the door open, and the chicks had stumbled into it. It was a very sad sight, seeing their little beaks popping up through the sludge, along with their dull blind eyes. The adults said the poor animals must have been thirsty or hungry and gone searching for water in the night. This started happening repeatedly, as we never fenced in the chickens. I found it horrifying and would often avoid going to the toilet, until one day there were no more chickens left in the yard.

One afternoon, I noticed that the adults were cleaning up the small hall of our communal building where furniture was usually stored. They were converting it into an auditorium. Then they brought in a box-shaped object with a smooth, shiny front, like an insect's shell. Someone said it was a 'television'. It would educate us. It was eight inches across and only showed black and white. Its long aerial was two antennae like a beetle. We kids were extremely curious to see what would come out from this compact and mysterious box. We waited impatiently for the adults to adjust the channels, although there were only two or three on offer in China at that time.

From that day on, everybody would bring their benches and eat their supper in front of the television's glowing light. It was a revolution in our evening lives. After the news at seven o'clock, where we could see our country's leaders shaking hands with important people, films and drama series would follow. Subject matter ranged from the Communist defeat of the Nationalists to stories about the anti-Japanese war of the 1930s. I loved these programmes. They had stirring, patriotic soundtracks, often sung by young women, whose soaring voices would pierce my ears and my heart. It was unashamedly propaganda, but beautiful all the same. The television allowed me to access a vastly larger world than the one I had known in Shitang. In Shitang there had been very few man-made images, apart from the fading prints that hung on old flaky walls. Colour came in the form of gaudy sweets packaging, or the old, eerie Buddhist statues. Television was an explosion of image, and my imagination swam in this new, artificial world.

The Trial of Madame Mao

After the arrival of the television, we compound families were bound even closer together. One day we received an official notice: all adults were told to gather for the seven o'clock national news to watch the trial of Madame Mao. Of course the children followed the command as well. It was November 1980, four years after Chairman Mao's death. The show trials of the Gang of Four had just begun. We children used to shudder in fear at just the name, the Gang of Four, as if they were a monstrous cannibal-istic horde that might appear at any moment in our courtyard. Despite our youth, we were told that the Gang of Four was a political faction composed of four Communist officials includ-ing Mao's last wife Jiang Qing, and that they were evil criminals who had plotted against Mao. I was eight and a half years old and fascinated. Mao's wife plotting against her own husband? Why would she want to do that? It would surely make her public enemy number one.

The trials were televised nationwide for several weeks. They made a very strong impression on me. Now, as I look back, the event seems like a symbolic moment in our recent history: before the Gang of Four no Communist high officials had ever been put on trial. I think by showing the Gang of Four in the dock, our then leader, Deng Xiaoping, wanted the people to realise that a new era had begun. This was his time and he was showing that he disapproved of the manic political purges of Mao's time.

My father was always the first in our compound to take up his position before the television to watch the trials. All the neigh-bours would sit beside or behind him. We guessed that he was especially concerned about the fate of these officials, having been punished during the Cultural Revolution himself. Even though his name had now been cleared and he had been promoted to work in Wenling's Cultural Bureau, he still felt insecure. One evening, just before the trial broadcast was about to begin, he tried to explain the background to me and my brother. During

Mao's violent class struggle in the 1960s against so-called 'revisionists' and the 'bourgeoisie', nearly a million Chinese had been sent to labour camps. And by the end of the Cultural Revolution in 1976, at least 35,000 intellectuals had died, either by committing suicide or being tortured to death. The Gang of Four was responsible for these purges. But still, when Madame Mao appeared in front of the court, I just couldn't connect the image I saw with what I had been told about her. I asked my father: 'Is she really the Chairman's wife?'

'Yes, she was,' my father confirmed.

'But how come? She looks just like a man!' I exclaimed loudly. 'She's very ugly, and kind of spooky!'

No one responded to my comments. They just stared at me, then turned their heads back to the TV screen.

It's true, Madame Mao looked terrible on-screen. Her hair was cropped short like a middle-aged man. She wore a pair of plain glasses with scratched black rims. Her grey Mao suit looked uncomfortable on her, as if she had stripped it off someone in the street. Her face barely registered any expression and there was an icy look in her eyes. She was most unattractive. I wondered how and why our Chairman had married her, and why would a woman in such a position want to undertake a 'counter-revolution'? As we followed the televised trial for weeks, I desperately wanted to understand this new thing called 'politics'. After all, I sensed the deep involvement of my parents in the events of this period. With so much about them still unknown, how could I not want to know a bit more about it?

As the trial approached its end, I began to understand, or, rather, began to take in what my father had explained to me:

Madame Mao Jiang Qing was initially accused of conspiring with Lin Biao – the then vice president of China – to assassinate Mao. Other members of the Gang of Four were charged with planning an armed coup to usurp power in 1976, when Mao was frail and close to death. Ultimately, the charges that stuck to Madame Mao focused on her systematic persecution of artists and intellectuals during the Cultural Revolution. Among other things, she was accused of hiring forty people in Shanghai to disguise themselves as Red Guards and ransack the homes of writers and performers. She had even been a famous actress before she married Mao! Why would a once famous actress want to persecute actors and artists?

'But why were there no posters or images showing what she was like when she was an actress?' I asked my father.

'That would make her look worse,' my father answered, somewhat impatient with my constant questions.

'Why? What's wrong with being an actress?'

'That would prove her bourgeois decadence. A Shanghai actress wearing all that make-up could never be a real Communist comrade.' My father turned back towards the screen.

Every evening Madame Mao appeared unrepentant. She would not confess her guilt. I remember that for every question the court asked, she would only answer 'I don't know'. The crowd watching was livid – it seemed no one liked Madame Mao. At some stage during the televisation, my mother began to be drawn in. Perhaps because she had been a Red Guard and under Madame Mao's command. But even she despised her.

'Without that manipulating wife, Chairman Mao would have remained sober. But she manipulated him with her pillow talk and got control over him!'

That was my mother's self-assured judgement of this supposed evil woman. In my young head, I wondered if it was simply that she was a woman. Had she been a man she probably wouldn't have been the object of such intense national hatred.

There had been reports that Madame Mao planned to defend herself by cloaking herself in Mao's mantle, saying that she had done only what Mao had approved. As the trial got under way, Jiang Qing dismissed her assigned lawyers, deciding instead to represent herself, answering with just a cold 'I don't know'. A few days later, she argued that she had been obeying the orders of her husband and that therefore she was innocent. She said, in front of the whole nation: 'I was Chairman Mao's dog. I bit whomever he asked me to bite.' I didn't have a clear opinion of her then, but my father was furious. He stood up from his bench and shouted in rage at my mother: 'No wonder things have been going so wrong over the last fifteen years – these people are totally mindless! Including Mao's own wife!'

No one in our hall dared to comment. Everybody was still tormented by their own political involvement in the Cultural Revolution, an episode in which wives denounced husbands, neighbours denounced each other, and students denounced professors. Years later, when I came to the West and first heard the Lou Reed song 'Growing Up in Public' with lines such as 'Some people are into the power of power/The absolute corrupting power, that makes great men insane', I thought, how could a Western musician manage to write such an accurate account of Chinese life? It was exactly how we grew up – under the absolute power of the collective. No one had any secrets – to have a secret was to betray the state. Everyone had to be absolutely loyal to the government, and the government was the party.

The trial finally drew to a close at the end of January 1981. Madame Mao was sentenced to death with a two-year reprieve. Then in 1983 her death sentence was commuted to life imprisonment. But she didn't want to live, and several years later she committed suicide by hanging herself in a hospital bathroom.

Where Did We Come from, Father?

Ever since leaving Shitang, images of my grandparents and our small stony house by the sea had flashed through my mind. I was constantly comparing Wenling to my experiences in the fishing village. There had been a question torturing me for years that I needed answering. One day when I was about nine years old, I managed to pluck up the courage, and went to my father's studio during one of his tea breaks.

'Father, why did Grandfather kill himself?'

My father thought for a few seconds, then said: 'I think he must have felt disillusioned with his life. He had lost hope.' He answered quietly, in his usual reflective tone. I didn't really know what 'disillusioned' meant, but losing hope was something I could understand. 'He was an outsider in Shitang, you know,' my father went on. 'Your grandfather moved from Fujian to Zhejiang. He was Hakka.'

'What's Hakka?' The meaning was literally 'guest family'.

'They were travellers and migrants originally from northern China. But that was long ago and I don't know when your grandfather's family moved to the south. It could easily have been two hundred years ago. He didn't keep any family records, neither did the government.'

I remembered the stationmaster telling me that Grandfather used to live in Zhoushan and had once saved some foreigners from a Japanese boat.

'I heard that Grandfather was a hero and that he saved some big-nosed Westerners who were drowning in the sea. Is that true?'

'Where did you hear that?' my father responded with a frown.

'I heard it from the stationmaster in Shitang. He said the fishermen in Zhoushan rescued lots of foreigners from a Japanese boat.'

'It sounds like the stationmaster was telling lies. Your grandfather wasn't that kind of man.' My father paused, then said: 'But that was a long time ago, no one really knows what happened. I was only a small boy then and I lived with your grandmother in Shitang. Your grandfather often sailed up and down the coast. Sometimes he stayed on his boat for days on end. It is true that there was a huge Japanese boat that tried to transport two thousand prisoners of war to Japan, but the Americans bombed it. I don't think your grandfather saved the drowning foreigners, though. He was a loner, he never joined in on any group activity. And in fact, I don't think he was anywhere near those islands then.'

I was disappointed by my father's words. I had formed an image in my head of my grandfather as a hero fallen on hard times in Shitang. Yes, he had been cruel to my grandmother and had lived a miserable life, but at least this way he had once been brave, adventurous and good, a man who had saved others. But now my father was telling me this wasn't true. Maybe my father was wrong. Before I could speak, my father continued. 'Your grandfather never told me how or why he ended up in Shitang. I think he had spent most of his life sailing up and down the coast before arriving in Zhejiang. Actually, I think he went even further south during the war, past Hainan Island. Then he came north again. Perhaps a typhoon brought him to Shitang, damaged his boat and he stayed. He was a sea nomad. He didn't like to be on land, or to live in a house. He never belonged in Shitang, or got used to the life of a settler.'

My father stopped for a moment. He looked as if he was lost in his thoughts. In that moment, I realised that my grandfather had been as much an outsider as my grandmother. But did she ever know that her husband wasn't a local either? Did they ever talk about their pasts? We fell into a long silence. I had hoped I might now understand more about why my grandfather had killed himself. Maybe the only thing that had gone everywhere with him was his boat, but he had lost it eventually. He had lost everything.

I could see my father was looking at me. Could he feel my sadness? My father was wise and kind. I was sure he understood me. He got up and made a cup of thick Longjing tea. 'Do you know what our family name, Guo, means?' he said.

I shook my head.

'It means "outside the first city wall". In the old days, people built two layers of wall around their cities and Guo is the space between them. An in-between zone. That's what our name means.'

Maybe my grandfather had always felt stuck in an in-between zone. He had no roots, not in Shitang, nor any other town or village. Maybe that's what made him so unhappy that he eventually chose to abandon everything.

'So where were the first Guos from?' I remembered the stationmaster mentioning our family was from the west of China, in central Asia.

'Hmm, good question.' My father gazed at his painting. He had just sketched a troubled sea and a rising moon. He spent most of his days painting the sea, and it seemed to me he wanted to capture its every possible movement. Was he trying to find the answer to my question in his picture?

'I don't think anyone has ever known the real origins of the Guo family, Xiaolu,' my father sighed. 'Our country has one of the longest continuously recorded histories in the world, but the Cultural Revolution destroyed it. They burnt all the history books and destroyed the museums. But I think we can trace the Guos back to the Yuan Dynasty, the period when the Mongols conquered China. Our ancestors were Hui Muslims, but they might also have been Persian Mongols. They were tribes with their own religion and culture. There's really no such clear-cut thing called *the Chinese.*'

I reflected on what my father just had said. No such clear-cut thing called *the Chinese.*

'In recent decades, since the fall of the last imperial dynasty, we have all had to adapt to the customs of the Han Chinese, because they are the majority. Your grandfather had to abandon his Hui Muslim customs in order to fit in with life in the village.'

My father put down his brush, opened one of his drawers and took out an old world map.

'Come here, let me show you this.' He pointed to a large yellowy-brown area circling the border between Iran and Mongolia.

'You see this? That's where we came from. We were outside the city walls. From the borderland. Our ancestors moved all the way down to the south of China.'

I followed my father's finger from Central Asia all the way to the East China Sea. It was a long way from the deepest inland to China's south-east coast. I took another look. There was no water near that yellow-brown patch.

'Maybe that's why Grandfather couldn't swim,' I concluded, thinking that if my ancestors had come from a place without sea or water, then it was no wonder that he had never learned to swim.

'You are right, Xiaolu. Horsemen don't swim. We were originally horsemen. Nomads.'

I was mesmerised by my father's descriptions of our ancestors. Perhaps my grandfather was the last generation to have really known about our family history. But he was dead now. The curse of the amateur genealogist. Did he speak Hakka as a child? Did his family tell him stories of where they had come from? Did his mother wear a headscarf like the Muslim women I had seen in picture books? Then I reflected on my earliest years. My parents had given me away to foster-parents of whom I had no memories at all. If I had stayed with them, would I have ever known about my roots? Would I have one day discovered that my biological father was a painter and my mother a Red Guard? Or perhaps I wouldn't have even bothered finding out, since in those days we just got on with life. Would I instead have been eking out an existence on a barren mountain, feeling as desolate and suicidal as my grandfather? We were really a family of orphans, it seemed to me. Orphans of a nomad tribe. But what if he'd had no tribe to belong to? What kind of life would that have been? I wondered what belonged to me, what I could really call *mine* in the end.

Becoming a Young Pioneer

But I had to belong to something. It was one of the first things I learned about survival in a town like Wenling. Belong to an official work unit, or a school, or an organisation which would give me status. Otherwise I would be the odd one out. I was no longer a peasant in the village. There was no rugged seashore where I could lose myself, no vast expanse of sea to absorb my daydreams. I realised that I had to fit into the social order, a political labyrinth for a child.

I look back on my schooldays in Wenling as a string of anguished memories. I was a late developer, given that my illiterate grandparents had never introduced me to Chinese characters. Nor had I ever gone to kindergarten. I was a taciturn child, fearful, and small for my age. The mere fact of sitting among sixty-five students in one classroom left me feeling at once exposed and constrained. I had been a wild street kid used to wandering around by myself. Days were winding streams. Now I had entered a world of rules and stiff uniforms. I hated it. The uniforms were always too long and too big for me, their colour a dull dark blue. I felt like a dwarf street cleaner – the street cleaners had almost the same blue outfit.

I was bullied by most of my teachers because I couldn't keep up with the other students – I didn't dare tell them that I had very bad eyesight and I couldn't see anything written on the blackboard. They just thought I was an idiot. 'She's retarded,' my maths teacher told my parents. 'She can't even count!' I dreaded maths class. I hated all the strange symbols. I swore that if I ever became a politician I would abolish them all.

I was lost when teachers conducted the class on the blackboard instead of from the pages of our textbooks. But not even
my parents realised the problems were with my eyes; I had my
first eye test at the age of nine. The eye doctor told my parents
that I had severe myopia – both eyes registered minus ten. By
the time I had turned twelve, they measured minus fifteen. But
for some reason, I didn't wear glasses until I was twenty, even
though the myopia had been progressing. I basically lived in a
state of near blindness for most of my childhood and teenage
years. It explained why I always had bruised knees and toes, and
why faces looked like yellow-brown clouds unless they were right
in front of my face.

The teachers in the school spoke Wenling dialect. Only Chinese class was conducted in Mandarin, the official language of
China, itself based on the northern dialects. We use the word
dialect, but really Mandarin was my third language. And Chinese
class was also the only one to focus on our textbooks, rather
than the blackboard, so I could see the characters properly and
was able to follow what was going on. Hence why Chinese was
my favourite and best subject. We were required to learn new
characters every day and compose short essays with the new
characters we had learned. While the other students found Chinese writing too complicated to be enjoyable, I loved it. Maybe
because writing characters for me was like drawing a picture. I
was fascinated by their pictorial nature, the multiple strokes, and
the mysterious meanings that seemed to lie behind each one. I
was never tired of learning new ideograms. For example, the
character for 'bright', 明 (pronounced *ming*), was composed of a
sun symbol on the left, and a moon on the right. Sun plus moon
means bright. I loved how characters could be glued together to

make new meanings. The character for 'dew', 露 (pronounced *lou*), contained the radical for rain on the top and a footpath beneath. Morning dew, rain on a footpath. A beautiful concept even for a young kid. I found ways of creating my own imaginative sentences as well, despite the fact that I had only begun learning Wenling dialect at the age of seven, and Mandarin at nine. I quickly became Teacher Ruan's favourite. He would often get me to read my essays out loud to the whole class.

Apart from Chinese, I also liked world geography. I found the idea of the world beyond China fascinating. Would we ever get to leave this country and see these foreign lands for ourselves? Even travelling beyond our own local region was difficult. I was obsessed by the history of the Mongol Empire. Somehow I still felt that the enigma of my own family history was linked to these wild people who had lived in yurts and ridden horses and stampeded across the plains of central Asia. Our teacher told us that the Mongol Empire had once been the world's largest land empire – twice the size of the Roman one. It had ruled over land stretching from central Europe to southern China. I had a vague idea that Genghis Khan was someone impressive, much like Chairman Mao.

World history caught my attention too, apart from the bit about the Roman Empire. The Roman Empire sounded so remote and strange to me, with all those images of ancient Romans wearing silly clothes looting and fighting across ancient Europe. It didn't seem a very sophisticated empire to me. And frankly, I didn't care. I more or less slept through the chapters on the Middle Ages as well, until we got to the bit about Columbus discovering America. That woke me up again. I still remember the teacher telling us:

'Columbus went to conquer the natives in the name of the Spanish king. He probably never realised that, before him, our great marine explorer Zhenghe had already made seven voyages around the world by 1405, nearly a century before Columbus embarked on his voyage. But unlike Columbus, Zhenghe didn't hurt the natives. Instead, he respected the foreign lands and cultures he encountered. This is the difference between us and the Westerners; they are aggressive and greedy.' It sounded to me like Westerners were evil, at least that was the impression our education system liked to give us.

I was also drawn to the Tang and Song – the great dynasties that ruled China from the seventh to the thirteenth centuries. Their world seemed very poetic, even up to the Qing, when China was attacked by the British and defeated in the Opium Wars. The teacher introduced us to a figure called Hong Xiuquan – the leader of the Taiping Rebellion against the Qing emperor.

'One day, in 1843, Hong Xiuquan claimed that he had seen Jesus Christ in a revelation and he came to realise that he was the Chinese son of God, and the younger brother of Jesus.'

'How many sons does God have?' I asked impatiently.

'That depends on which fairy tale you refer to. As atheists, we don't believe in God and Jesus and all that.' The teacher sounded almost annoyed by my ignorance.

'Maybe that's why Hong Xiuquan didn't inspire people enough to succeed against the Qing emperor, because no one believed in him in China,' I concluded, most pleased with myself.

'Maybe you're right, but he wasn't even recognised in the West. No Western missionary took him seriously. They didn't believe he had anything to do with Jesus,' the teacher explained. Then the tone turned more emotional.

'In my opinion, it was just white people's prejudice against us yellow people. Why can't Jesus have a yellow brother? What's wrong with that?'

We listened quietly in our seats, slightly confused. The teacher had just told us that there was no Jesus or God. So why was he arguing that Jesus might have had a yellow brother? If Jesus could have had a Chinese brother, did that mean God really existed after all? I did the calculation in my head: if Jesus was born two thousand years ago, how could his Chinese brother be born 1,800 years later? It didn't make sense. We are the children of Communists, I told myself once and for all. We don't believe in these religious stories.

It was also because of world-history class that I fell in love with the idealised image of the Yugoslav leader Tito. True, he looked very stern in all the photos, even a little bit scary, but I supposed this was a manifestation of his upright Communist faith. Tito was one of the few foreign figures that the Chinese government decided to promote. Perhaps because he had been keen on the idea of the Non-Aligned Movement against Soviet power, given that the Chinese government hadn't been too happy with Stalin's dominance in the past. In fact, the split between the Chinese Communist Party and Soviets realigned our education more towards the rest of Eastern Europe, with literature and cinema from Poland, Czechoslovakia, as well as the People's Republic of Albania. Tito was our first Western hero, before we discovered Che Guevara and Jim Morrison. The year I turned ten, I was selected to become one of the new Young Pioneers. I assumed my position underneath the red flag of China, alongside a dozen or so other students, as was compulsory in a 1980s Chinese primary school. I raised my right fist and vowed allegiance to the Chinese Communist Party, promising to be a diligent student and a useful citizen, and that I would dedicate my life to the state. After my vow, our headmaster tied a brand-new red kerchief around my neck. I was told to always keep it clean and neatly tied. From that day on, I had officially become a future candidate for Communist Party Membership, a proud *shaoxian duiyuan.*

Life as a Propaganda Painter

My father had spent years in labour camps before I was born, and yet my brother and I never really learned how things had been for him during those long years. We had the feeling that looking into his past was like looking through the thick lenses he wore every day – they glittered but also distorted as much as they revealed. We knew he had worked in mines, built roads and toiled in paddy fields. The Cultural Revolution had done its best to teach him a lesson: peasant values were more important than intellectual ones. But they hadn't understood that my father had always respected physical labour and regarded art as work of the hands.

After Mao died in 1976, the new government began to reform. My father and many others who had been sentenced to hard labour were rehabilitated. The government acknowledged that my father had been a victim of misconduct and the frantic power struggle that spurred on the Cultural Revolution. 'An innocent man and a good comrade' – that was his new label.

From the 1980s onwards, people began to respect him as a talented painter and calligrapher. Shortly after I arrived in Wenling to live with my family, he was promoted to head of the Collective Painters' Team in the Wenling Cultural Bureau. He was given a brand-new studio and a modest monthly salary as a state painter to work on propaganda paintings, although technically he could paint whatever he wanted as well. He remained a landscape painter in the old style, rejecting all colour. There were three types of ink in traditional Chinese painting: dry, wet and green. The green ink was combined with a greenish-blue extract found naturally in some types of stone. My father even produced his own ink by collecting rocks in the surrounding mountains and fields, and then grinding them down with a pestle and mortar. I always thought it looked like a lot of work. Towards the end of the 1980s new fashions began to emerge in Chinese ink painting and my father, too, began to experiment. He mixed green, pink and white Western watercolours. They looked especially transparent on Chinese rice paper, illuminating a subject like the moon beautifully. With his rehabilitation, he was also free to pursue his long-time fascination with French Impressionism – landscapes without peasants or workers. That was my father's way of rejecting the 'social realist' style.

I saw the essential contradiction that troubled my father: in his mind he was a Marxist and believed only Communism would bring prosperity to the people, but in his heart he didn't like using such ideology in his work. Even in his calligraphy and poetry writing, he chose the sensual and apolitical 'obscure' style, itself a rejection of the 'revolutionary poetry' which had been developed during the Cultural Revolution and which still dominated the literary landscape of the 1980s. But as a state artist, he was required to make a certain number of state-assigned propaganda posters and wall paintings every year. These would be used in festivals such as May First Labour Day, Women's Day, Army Day, the October National Holiday. His paintings were even used in service to the One Child Policy. I remember watching him using a selection of Chinese and Western brushes to paint a 'positive' portrait of a happy family flourishing under state-enforced family planning: a chubby laughing baby sat in the arms of his parents under a willow tree by a fishpond. He mainly painted in ink, with only a slight hint of red for the child's clothes. Even the goldfish in the pond were black. Another time, he worked on a large portrait in what we called the 'army and people togetherness' style: soldiers and peasants playing basketball after the harvest. He stayed in his studio for weeks, sleeping there at night.

One day, when I brought him his lunch box, he said to me, 'Chinese ink isn't designed to paint so many intricate little figures . . .' I didn't fully understand what he meant, but I got the sense that he disliked the mishmash of realistic subject matter in traditional inks. Like using Zen Buddhism to analyse the market economy. Certainly, a misuse and abuse of tools! It was unfortunate that social realism had been the only acceptable style in painting, writing, film-making and theatre for so long. By the 1980s things started to relax somehow, but as a state artist my father had serious work to do for the Communist Party, which meant suppressing his own preference for ethereal landscapes devoid of the proletariat.

There was in fact a shift of focus in the propaganda paintings of the 1980s. In the past, they had mainly depicted Mao and his heroic deeds on behalf of the people. But in the Deng Xiaoping era, the authorities were keen to show a clear break from the

Maoist period and so no longer focused on making portraits of our leaders. Most of my father's assignments were to paint peasants, low-ranking soldiers and workers, to sing the praises of the ordinary Chinese. But painting a propaganda poster was never an easy task. In those days, there was no fashion for postmodernism. Indeed, to use such a style would leave yourself open to accusations of both moral and political incorrectness. My father had always been scared of having to paint Mao during the Cultural Revolution in the 1960s, for fear of prosecution on the ground of misrepresenting the Great Leader. Besides, my father had never studied human anatomy. He never felt comfortable with the human form as his subject matter. After all, he painted mountains and seas and drifting clouds. The worship of Mao killed many a painter's imagination.

'It's so wrong that the state classifies painters as intellectuals, rather than physical workers,' my father said to me once, standing before one of his large propaganda pieces. It had taken him at least four weeks of work, day and night, to do a four-square-metre poster, and that was just to get the faces of the leaders looking perfect. 'Each hair had to be just right, or I'd get in trouble,' he told me. 'But the worst part was painting Mao's mole.' Everyone knew the Great Leader had a large, unsightly mole on the left side of his chin, just below the corner of his lower lip. Exactly how this was depicted, without overstating or understating it, was a serious issue.

My brother Dapeng followed my father and studied Chinese ink painting throughout his teenage years. He enrolled at an art school in the province's capital, Hangzhou. He then moved from Hangzhou to Beijing to continue his studies. It seemed as a family we had swapped fishing for painting. My brother was also drawn to abstract, poetic subjects, under the influence of my father. But he turned out to be more progressive, and received proper training in human anatomy and Western geometrical perspective. He knew about 'vanishing points' and 'foreshortening'. Therefore he could paint figures very well. I remember he had piles of art books by his bedside – mostly about Leonardo da Vinci. I once saw my father leafing through them when my brother wasn't there. He studied the images for a long time, raising his eyes every now and again, as if lost in thought. Then he sighed, put the book down and walked slowly back to his studio.

The Blood Eater

Although I was slowly absorbing by a kind of osmosis the lessons of my father's painting studio, life in Wenling was nevertheless centred around one thing: filling my hungry stomach with food. The food was better than in the fishing village, but I was still starving most of the time, and extremely thin. I weighed only three stone four pounds as I turned nine years old, while the other children my age weighed four stone ten pounds. I also had very low blood pressure, so that each time I stood up from a sitting position I felt dizzy and often blacked out. I desperately needed iron, but meat was rarely available in our house. On top of all this, I had tapeworms growing in my belly. I was constantly swallowing pills in a war against the parasites, but they always returned. I needed nutrition. But our monthly quota wasn't enough. At that time, every household was still given *liang piao* (food tickets) distributed by the state annually. Under the quota system, we were allowed to buy a small portion of meat each month, usually pork. But even before it had touched the dining table, my brother alone would have devoured the whole portion. I was as hungry as him, but he was a boy so my mother gave him more. My constant hunger became an obsession, finding food was a compulsion.

Like most of my fellow countrymen, I ate anything I could find or catch: I trapped birds, caught toads, ran after wild chickens, and gnawed on the hard roots of the sugar-cane plant. Catching birds I did alone. I found a rusty birdcage at the back of our compound and hid it behind the communal toilets. Normally I placed a small bowl with grain inside the cage and took it out into the fields. Then I would tie a long string on the cage door and, holding the other end, went behind a tree or some bushes. Once a bird flew inside, I tugged the door shut. In all those long hours of waiting, I succeeded only once, and when I got home with the dead bird in my pocket, my mother shouted and even smacked me for being late. Which meant I didn't get a chance to eat it until the next day, when my parents were at work. The birdcage method was useless, so I continued to experiment. I carried a bucket up into the hills behind our house, where I filled it with water. Seeking out a clump of bushes sure to be home to a flock of birds, I crouched in the undergrowth and waited, my eyes bulging, for a chance to strike. A bird fluttered close; I jumped up and doused it with water. This weighed down the wings and I could grab it before it could fly away. Bird in hand, I wasted no time: I grabbed a rock and smashed its head. Then it was back down the mountain, straight inside, no time to gut it, it was in a wok with leftover rice. I had to spit out the feathers as I ate rapidly. My brother couldn't be allowed to catch me.

But I was still ravenous. Sometimes I was so hungry by bed-time that I couldn't sleep. I needed other sources of sustenance. When it rained, I would be up the next morning to climb the hills in search of newly sprouted bamboo roots. I dug out the whole plant and took them home to share with my family, because they too loved eating young bamboo. It was all I could do to find enough vitamins, but with so little iron, I was struggling to grow.

Then I discovered pig's blood.

One afternoon, I overheard that our next-door neighbour was having a miscarriage. She was pale and thin, and worked at the same silk factory as my mother. It was a sweaty summer morning, and I had been listening to her cries and screams for nearly half an hour. Eventually I went next door. A crowd of women blocked the door, but I squeezed past in order to find out what a miscarriage was. All I saw were trails of blood on the floor, then a pool collected on the bedroom floor. The woman was half crawling in her blood-soaked clothes, her mother and grandmother on either side, trying to get her to stand. Her husband was nowhere to be seen. Perhaps he had been dispatched by the work unit, just as my father was often sent to other towns. That month my father wasn't around either.

Then I heard my mother's voice: 'They slaughtered two pigs this morning in the factory. Should I run to the canteen now?'

Another woman's voice, much more urgent than my mother's: 'Take the bucket! Two buckets!'

Still hiding, I saw my mother and another woman run towards the factory canteen, buckets in their hands. Half an hour later, my mother and the other woman returned, out of breath but carrying two buckets of pig's blood. 'It's still warm!' someone cried.

The mother of the young woman brought a rice bowl from the kitchen and poured some of the pig's blood into it. Then she handed the bowl to her daughter and ordered her to drink.

Another voice spoke up: 'Auntie, can I use some of your ginger? We'll make some blood soup. Let's add some *gouchi* seeds and meat too, if you have it.'

All of a sudden, women were running in and out of the front door, ferrying special herbs and vegetables from their own kitchens as the hens and roosters that were scuttling around the yard were shooed away. In all the excitement I managed to make my way into the woman's bedroom.

Her lips were red with blood, her eyes terrified.

'Look at the veins in your wrist!' her mother cried. 'You can see them expanding!'

I crept closer and looked for myself. Her veins seemed to be darkening and thickening. Was the pig's blood making her veins thicker and stronger?

'Now your blood has fortified with iron, you'll be fine,' an elderly woman near me added.

This was the first time I had heard of such a method for fortifying the blood. Still a bit scared, I watched the activity going on around me. That day, the kitchen was busy with women making all sorts of food containing pig's blood. First, blood soup with shredded meat and ginger. Then the women used coagulated blood to make blood tofu. At the same time, several other women were making blood sausage and mixing it with sticky rice. All the kids were hungry in those years. But we were told not to touch any of the food until the miscarrying woman had eaten her fill and felt better. So we children went out to play by the local pond up in the bamboo hills. But from then on, I started demanding pig's blood sausage, or blood soup. My parents often managed to secure free supplies from the silk factory canteen. After about a year or two, I noticed that I didn't faint as often as I used to in the past, and my face wasn't quite so yellow and sickly as before. I was raised on the blood of pigs, the luckiest and laziest members of every Chinese peasant household. Perhaps I had been half pig all along.

The Four Modernisations

My stomach satisfied, I could begin to focus on my studies. My memories of primary school are played to the accompaniment of political slogans. I must have been shouting them in my dreams, since they were drilled into us by every radio and television programme, phrase by phrase, day in, day out.

Once a child started school in China during the 1970s and 80s, he or she would be instructed to love and learn from a national hero by the name of Lei Feng. Lei Feng had been a young soldier serving in the People's Liberation Army in the early 1960s. He had died when he was twenty-two, we were told. For years he had been the ultimate poster boy for the revolution, always wearing his army uniform and a big smile, a rifle in one hand. *Follow Lei Feng's example; love the party, love socialism, love the people.* We learned how selfless Lei Feng had been, how he had dedicated every single minute of his life to the greater good. That was the ideal; to be entirely selfless, without vanity, and not to daydream. Lei Feng was a great, if not the greatest, example to all children. Of course we took the teacher's words to heart and tried to be as good as Lei Feng. Because at that time we had never heard of *Peter Pan* or *Alice in Wonderland*, or even Disney. We had no other alternatives.

Lei Feng's Diary was first presented to the public by the then vice chairman of the Chinese Communist Party, Lin Biao, in the 'Learn from Lei Feng' propaganda campaigns of 1963. The diary was full of accounts of Lei's admiration for Mao Zedong, his self-sacrificing deeds, and his desire to foment the revolutionary spirit in others. He described sneaking into the house of an old grandmother and doing all her housework, even buying rice for her, then leaving like an invisible man. The 'Learn from Lei Feng' campaign lasted until the mid-1990s. I still remember a *People's Daily* editorial published in 1993, the year I left for Beijing, which said: '*When Lei Feng died in the line of duty, he was only 22, but his short life gives concentrated expression to the noble ideals of a new people, nurtured by the communist spirit, and also to the noble moral integrity and values of the Chinese people in the new China.*' I remember liking that expression 'a new people', even though I didn't want to be one of them myself. I wanted to be 'new' in the sense of free from both Chinese tradition and Communist dogma. I wanted to be a new woman unburdened from domestic housework, as well as the obligation to read lengthy textbooks on 'Mao's Revolutionary Thoughts'. We had to memorise the government slogans, which was stressful. I remember sitting a political studies examination at the age of twelve. We were given an exam paper with twenty questions printed on it. I read the first one:

What exactly are the Four Modernisations to be achieved by the year 2000? Detail the four goals.

I stared at the sheet in front of me, and tried to recollect what the textbook had said. Then I wrote:

The Four Modernisations to be achieved by the year 2000 are in the areas of: 1) agriculture, 2) industry, 3) science and technology, 4) . . .

I couldn't remember the last thing we were supposed to be modernising. I held my pen tight and thought very hard. The sweat from my palm had already soaked into the exam sheet. Oh, what were we supposed to be modernising before the year 2000?!

The cicadas were screaming in the poplar trees outside, and the teacher was pacing up and down, watching us. The other students had their heads buried in answer booklets. I felt thirsty and dizzy. I read my answers over again. *1) agriculture, 2) industry, 3) science and technology . . .* That should be enough. What else did we need to achieve? Nuclear weapons? Spaceships? Conquer the Americans?

I gave up on this first question and moved onto the next one: *Describe the main ideas behind Deng Xiaoping's term 'socialist market economy'. You may use his famous 'white cat, black cat' slogan to demonstrate your point.*

I stared at the words. Oh no! I sort of remembered the white cat, black cat slogan. Our teacher had mentioned it enough times, but I hadn't really learned the principles of the socialist market economy by heart. The answers were clearly written in our textbook but they were pretty complicated for a twelve-year-old to grasp. I couldn't remember, let alone understand, any of them! But I tried with a few sentences:

The outstanding 'socialist market economy' innovation by our great leader Deng Xiaoping points towards a better way to organise our country's money flow, which is to use the marketplace as an economic platform. But it still has socialist characteristics because our party will control the market. And it doesn't matter if the market is

*a black cat or a white cat as long as the cat catches the mouse, that
is to say, as long as the market works for the country and the people.*

A few days later, the teacher sent a note to my parents telling
them that I had failed the political exam. I was ordered to resit it
a week later. If I couldn't pass it in the resit, I would be *liu ji* – that
is, held back a grade. My parents were worried. Because not only
had I failed this exam, but I had done the same for maths and
chemistry. Knowing that my brain didn't function well when
it came to these subjects, they had decided to let me off, but I
couldn't fail political studies. My father chided me.

'You must pass the politics exam. All you need to do is memorise the textbook. You don't need to understand the concepts,
just learn them by heart!'

'But how can I learn something by heart when I don't understand it?'

'Understanding doesn't matter!'

I listened to my father's advice and took the textbook to bed.
I thought about the way my grandmother had learned to recite
the Heart Sutra. Learn by heart! Yes, I could do that, as long as
I could put up with the boredom. But surely a life lived like Lei
Feng had no space for boredom? I set about learning every line
on every page, for a whole week. I was reciting them during
lunch and supper. It was a painful week, but my future relied on
a positive outcome. A week later, I managed to pass the exam. I
even answered the last question about Marx's notion of 'surplus
value' in *Das Kapital* and wrote every word exactly as it appeared
in our textbook:

What is surplus value? Conventionally, it means sales rev-
enue. It should be equal to the sum of gross wage income

and gross profit. But in Marx's theory, he thought that the gigantic increase in wealth and labour population from the 19th century onwards was due to the competitive striving to obtain maximum profit from the employment of labour, resulting in an equally gigantic increase in production and capital resources. Essentially, surplus value is extra profit in an immoral social system.

Just like my grandmother, I didn't understand a word of what I was saying. Even today, I can still recite those lines, though now I have a little more understanding. This method of education wasn't entirely without its uses.

The last year of my primary school was so heavily loaded with homework that there seemed to be little room in my mind for anything else. I often felt like a shrimp stuck in the rice paddy, desperately searching for a way to clean flowing water. I was not yet thirteen, but I barely had any time to play. I was reciting textbooks even during the evening meal. I was a walking, talking study-robot whose lips murmured nothing but meaningless syllables.

There were moments in which I felt like I was penetrating the airtight mud of repetition. I remember one of the rare foreign texts we studied was a section from Shakespeare's *The Merchant of Venice*, including the famous speech in which Portia begs Shylock for mercy.

> *The quality of mercy is not strain'd,*
> *It droppeth as the gentle rain from heaven*
> *Upon the place beneath: it is twice blest;*
> *It blesseth him that gives and him that takes . . .*

We had no idea who Shakespeare was, except that he was the West's most famous writer. The Chinese translation of the original text was quite obscure, but we were given official guidance before even reading the text.

'*The Merchant of Venice* demonstrates the ultimate conflict between money and morality in the early stage of Western capitalism,' the teacher announced, holding the textbook. 'Shakespeare obviously witnessed this first-hand in Elizabethan England. The playwright uses his characters to persuade the rich and powerful of the need for mercy. Does anybody here think that a moneylender could possibly show mercy?'

The teacher stared at us, waiting for an answer. But no one said anything, because we had never read the text and we had no idea what the teacher was talking about.

'Of course not!' the teacher concluded. 'Shakespeare was naive in his grasp of the real nature of capitalists. He would have written the play differently if he had read Marx! Still, all things considered, *The Merchant of Venice* is an anti-capitalist work. It denounces the mercilessness of capitalism!'

We listened on our hard benches and scribbled down what the teacher was telling us in the margins of our textbooks. 'Anti-capitalist' and 'denounces the mercilessness of capitalism'. We knew these were the 'correct' answers, whatever the questions were going to be in the exam.

As I look back on my childhood now, I can see that our proletarian upbringing was anti-capitalist, that is true, but it was also quite merciless. My grandfather beat my grandmother mercilessly every day, but he was only a penniless failed fisherman. His ruthlessness seemed to have no motivation. Mercy is not an automatic human quality, not even between mother and child. My relationship with my mother showed that. I was never more than a secondary concern in her male-dominated world – surplus without value.

But this bleak reality did mix with more optimistic emotions. I memorised the government's simplistic slogans and Four Modernisations, and yet somehow also dared to hope China would make great improvements by the year 2000. This imagined future was largely based on the Western movies and soap operas available in 1980s China. State television dubbed *Falcon Crest* and broadcast the lives of a rich family in the Californian wine industry to the masses. That was where I got my very first introduction to the concepts of modern agriculture and business, as well as the trappings of wealth such as long evening gowns, wine tasting and snappy dialogue. *Falcon Crest* was pure glamour and fancy Californian real estate. In 2000 I would be twenty-seven years old. If we succeeded with the Four Modernisations (especially in industry and science), the results would be amazing. How and where would I live? In a brand-new high-rise in Beijing or Shanghai? With a functioning flushing toilet and a microwave oven? Perhaps I would learn to drink Western wine in long-stemmed glasses like the ladies and gentlemen in *Falcon Crest*, always poised and well groomed and never wrinkled like us peasants.

Had that young girl been able to ride on Time's Arrow all the way to the turn of the millennium, she would have found that the Chinese had achieved more than just the Four Modernisations. Not only did most of us have flushing toilets and microwaves, we had also built modern railways and high-tech factories. We had sent rockets out into space. And yet, despite all that progress in the fields of agriculture, industry, science and military technology, there was still no space for human rights and political freedom.

As it turned out, by the year 2000 China was no longer interested in the Four Modernisations. She had simply forgotten about them and had moved on. Chinese ambitions had grown exponentially. And so had my own ambitions. I wanted to see the world beyond Wenling. I must.

Sex Education

I don't remember my father ever beating me. He slapped me a few times, but nothing more serious. My mother, on the other hand, beat me regularly. I imagine that was how her parents treated her when she was young. In China at that time, every parent hit their children – it was normal. My mother used whatever she could get her hands on: broom, stick, belt, shoes. The frustration was clear to see, and the violence was cathartic. I remember her hitting me particularly hard with a broom once. All because of a misunderstanding about a harmless toy.

My parents always kept a couple of drawers in the bedroom locked, and I frequently checked to see if they had been left open by mistake. One day – I was about eleven at the time – I saw a small key hanging from the keyhole of one of the drawers. My parents must have forgotten to take it. My hands were itching with curiosity. I opened it and found two drooping transparent balloons, three volumes of a book called *The Plum in the Golden Vase*, and a marriage certificate with a photo of my parents smiling towards the camera. I grabbed one of the small balloons and blew it into a big ball. As I was playing with the balloon, I flipped through one of the books, wondering why my parents felt the need to lock away such innocuous items. They didn't look expensive. As I was leafing through the pages of *The Plum in the Golden Vase*, I found some strange illustrations alongside the text. In one picture, a naked man was squatting, facing a naked woman lying on her back; in another picture a naked couple were cuddling together; in another, a naked woman sat on top of a man's belly under some flowering trees. These naked figures were like worms, their bodies were plump and their hairdos like the wealthy characters in a traditional Chinese opera. I tried to read a few lines next to one of the illustrations. But the text was written in old Chinese with lots of added explanations underneath. After struggling with the text for some time, I could roughly make out the following paragraphs:

. . . thereupon, he started to undress, sent the maids out of the room, and proposed to go to bed with Yüeh-niang and seek his pleasure with her.

'If I let you into the kitchen, you'll only make a pig of yourself,' said Yüeh-niang. 'It's concession enough if I allow you into my bed tonight. If you've got anything else in mind, forget it.'

Hsi-men Ch'ing responded by exposing his organ to Yüeh-niang. 'It's all your doing,' he joked. 'You've made him so angry he's having a dumbstruck fit.'

'What do you mean "he's having a dumbstruck fit"?' demanded Yüeh-niang.

'If he's not having a dumbstruck fit,' said Hsi-men Ch'ing, 'how come his eye is bulging so wide, but he can't get a word out?'

'You must be delirious,' responded Yüeh-niang. 'What makes you think I've got even half an eye for the likes of you?'

At this point, without permitting any further explanation, he lifted Yüeh-niang's two fresh white legs onto his shoulders, inserted his organ into her vagina and gave free rein to the oriole's abandon and the butterfly's pursuit. Entranced by the clouds and intoxicated by the rain, they are not yet willing to call a halt.

The last few lines confused me. What were an oriole and butterfly doing there? But I had a vague sense that the book was about sex, or marriage. I tried to read a bit more, but was soon bored with having to read all the notes underneath just to understand what was going on.

I threw the book back into the drawer and took out another two balloons. I took them with me to school and blew them up for my friends to see.

'Where did you get this?' one of the teachers barked, her eyes bulging, when she saw what I was playing with.

'From home,' I said. I didn't understand why she was angry.

'Stop waving them around in public,' she said nervously. 'They aren't *real* balloons!'

I looked at her and then at my two balloons. They were very small, to be sure, but I couldn't see why they weren't real. Why shouldn't I play with them? But still I obeyed her instructions and put them back in my pocket. Later, some of the older kids laughed at me, and told me they were condoms – a sort of medical balloon worn by your parents when they were having sex.

Medical balloons? 'What do you mean, worn by your parents when they're having sex?' I said in a small voice.

'No, worn by *your* parents,' one of the kids giggled, 'not *my* parents!'

My face turned red. I felt ashamed and I didn't want to know any more. The idea of 'having sex' sounded so mean and dirty to me. If sex was a good thing, why did people talk about it in such a secret and nervous manner? I certainly wouldn't do anything like that.

Only a few days later, my parents discovered the missing 'balloons'. By then, my teacher had already sent a letter home, reporting my 'indecent behaviour'. Feeling shamed by the teacher's letter, my mother beat me severely with the spiky broom from our kitchen. I remember the beating lasting the whole afternoon. I screamed and cried and ran out into the compound for help like a rat being pursued by an irate cat. But no one came to help me. Everyone stood and watched me being smacked. Only later in the evening, when my father came home, did it stop, as he dragged my mother away and told me to stop crying. But I had cried for so long that I couldn't breathe properly. I vomited that night and felt sick for days. I hated my mother so much. The weals on my skin were red at first, then became very itchy and hard, until they turned into big purple-coloured patches. I scratched them constantly until they bled. In my bitterness I imagined killing my mother one day. I would strangle her and watch her die. But I needed to be bigger and stronger first, big enough to fight back.

Some years later I realized that the big volumes locked away in my parents' drawer were the most famous erotic novel in Chinese literary history. The book had been banned by the Communist Party as pornography during the Cultural Revolution and was still banned until the late 1980s. No wonder my parents had had to lock it away.

Seeing Grandmother Again

Then the beating got worse. I was clearly a 'useless girl' and 'a food bucket' in my mother's eyes – my existence in the house only meant dwindling food resources. Feeling timid and fearful in her presence, I seemed incapable of making her happy. At that time the One Child Policy had reached its height and we often heard about baby girls being abandoned at bus stops or by the railway tracks. Often these nameless babies were left in shoeboxes. If found alive, they would be taken to an orphanage. Every little Chinese town had at least one or two big ones. It made me think: would it have been better to have been left at the orphanage instead? My father was my only protection at home, but he was often away for work. Really, I would have preferred to have been left in a shoebox. I would have been able to sleep wherever I wanted, and go wherever I pleased.

My brother followed my mother's example, and continued to treat me as his enemy. He and the other children teased me, calling me nasty words such as *sha zi* (little idiot) or *ben dan* (stupid egg). Every day was a humiliation. What was wrong with me? I turned my back to them, and wandered the hillside behind our house alone. There I often sat and found solace. There was a little pond, but all the fish and shrimp were gone. I stared at that lifeless pond with the dead leaves floating on its surface, and even the keys around my neck seemed to whimper with loneliness. In those moments, desolation came and swallowed me. I hadn't had many friends in Shitang either, but still I missed it. I missed the fishing village miserably. I missed seeing the newly caught red snapper and eels jumping in their nets as they were dragged up onto the dock. And I missed my grandmother, alone and hunchbacked, praying to her Guanyin statue. I pictured her hobbling on her small bound feet to the beach in order to buy the cheapest leftovers for her supper.

One evening, I told my father that I wanted to see my grandmother and bring her back from Shitang to live with us. I was determined to realise my plan.

'But where would we put her? We don't have space for her in the house,' my father said, looking around the narrow space between the kitchen and the bedroom. Since my brother and I had to share this tiny four-square-metre corridor next to the kitchen, he wasn't wrong. Not enough space for even a chicken or a dog.

'But she can sleep with me,' I suggested, pointing at my narrow bed squashed against the wall.

My father said he would discuss it with my mother, and he was in fact quite keen on the idea of my grandmother coming to live with us. For years, my parents had been sending small amounts of money for her living expenses, but I knew how difficult it was for her, now that she was alone.

Somehow my suggestion was approved, although I had no idea how and why my mother had agreed to it. The plan was that I would go back to Shitang in my school holidays and bring my grandmother to Wenling. I was so happy that I nearly wept; my grandmother's misery was finally going to come to an end! But before I had packed my things for the journey, I sensed my mother's growing unease. I knew she had never really got on with my grandmother, although in truth she barely knew her, just as she barely knew Shitang. But I didn't care about all that. I was eleven years old, and I felt proud that I would travel alone on a long-distance bus to fetch my grandmother.

The trip back was much shorter this time. The mountain tunnels had been finished and the roads were smoother. It only took five hours to get there, but I had thrown up the contents of my stomach within the first hour. The world was spinning around me and my stomach throbbed from the constant vomiting. Some peasants on the bus offered me water to clean my mouth and handed me tissues to wipe my face. I felt awful, but I had more important things to think about. As the familiar salty air entered my nostrils, I knew I was getting closer and closer to my home. I was in an acute state of anticipation about seeing my grandmother. I visualised the old stone house, and how we would greet each other after so long. Had Shitang changed much? How were Da Bo's four daughters that lived next door doing? Did they go to school like me? I also wanted to see the stationmaster, and luckily the bus would stop exactly where he lived and worked. I wanted to tell him everything that had happened to me over the last five years, since leaving for Wenling.

I jumped down from the bus, my face dirty and my shirt wet from vomiting. I first went to look for my stationmaster. There were some buses waiting to be dispatched and some young drivers who I had never met before. The station looked much cleaner than in my memory, no vomit or sugar-cane peelings on the floor. Somehow the place seemed very small to me. There was a new office building by the front gate. I walked straight over to it and stood on my toes to look inside. I saw a man selling tickets and another behind him, supervising. There was no stationmaster inside. Nor his wife. So I found two bricks on the ground, piled them up by the ticket window and stood on them so that the man inside might see me. I leaned forward and asked in my rusty Shitang dialect: 'Do you know where the stationmaster is?'

The two men looked at me as if I was a small insect. They didn't pay me any attention. I repeated my question, louder this time.

'Which stationmaster?' The man who was doing the supervision glanced at me suspiciously, then added: '*I* am the stationmaster, what's the matter?'

I was a little confused. 'No, the stationmaster who worked here a few years ago. He sold tickets, and drove some of the buses too.'

'Oh, you mean the old stationmaster? He died last year.'

'He died?' I couldn't believe my ears. He wasn't that old, maybe only about my father's age.

'Yes. An accident. The bus crashed into a truck and fell into the sea. You didn't know?'

I was speechless. He died when the bus fell into the sea? He sank to the bottom of the ocean? Were there lots of passengers on the bus? I couldn't bring myself to ask. All the things I had planned to tell him about Wenling and about my parents on the way over were now lost without anywhere to go. I wanted so badly to tell him that my father was a painter and that I loved his work, and that my mother played the part of Iron Plum in the revolutionary opera. And I wanted to tell him that I had missed him, missed his soothing words and his funny jokes. This news left me sad and depressed, so soon after my arrival.

Shitang hadn't changed much; the salty fishy smell from the sea was still just as strong as I remembered. The little alleyways were always wet and slippery from the women doing their washing-up on their doorsteps. The gardenia flowers blasted their powerful scent into my nostrils, and the sea in the near distance churned with brown waves. My footsteps were light and impatient.

I pushed open the door of my grandmother's house; I knew she never locked it. I burst in and saw her, a small hunchbacked figure in the kitchen. It was dark inside. She was kneeling on a straw mat, praying to her statue of Guanyin. It stood in the same place, right above the dining table. I looked over to the stove, and saw rice-porridge leftovers in a bowl, along with a small jar of pickled crab.

I flung out my arms and wrapped them around my grandmother.

'Ah, Xiaolu! Is it really you?' My grandmother had been informed about my visit, but she was still surprised to see me. Her eyes were filled with joy – a rare emotion for her. She put her hands on my arms and I helped her to stand up. I noticed a white discharge around the edge of her eyes.

'I can't see much these days, but I could tell it was Xiaolu before you even entered the room!' she cried. I told her that my parents had asked me to bring her back to Wenling to live with us, so we could take care of her.

'We eat fried pork every day in Wenling!' I lied, trying to convince her. 'And we have a big television. You can watch operas on it,' I said before realising that she probably wouldn't be able to see the screen even if we had it anyway.

She was delighted. But first she asked if I was hungry from the trip. Of course I said yes. She then warmed up some rice porridge and fished out a big spoon of pickled crab. A sadness came over me as I chewed on the astringently salty flesh of the crab and drank the watery porridge. Although this was the food I had grown up with, I had never liked it. Such salty food was barely edible, but it was all we had been able to afford. As I sat at the old dining table, looking around my grandmother's kitchen,

I realised it had all been bitterly salty: salted jellyfish, salted kelp, salted crabs. There had never been any variety in our diet. It was poor people's food. In Wenling, my parents and I ate much better, even though supplies were limited by a quota. No wonder my grandfather couldn't bear this kind of life. But then, how could it have been any different? I watched my grandmother pack as I finished my porridge. As the brine bubbled down into my intestines, I felt even hungrier than I had before the meal.

That night I lay in my grandmother's squeaky bamboo bed, unable to sleep. I listened as my grandmother continued packing her clothes and sorting the house out in the dim light, as well as the sounds coming from upstairs. I hadn't been up there in years, and the thought still frightened me. I wondered whether my grandmother went up there, and sometimes did her prayers.

'Your grandfather's ghost comes to visit me almost every night,' my grandmother remarked, her breathing heavy as she climbed into the bed beside me.

'What does his ghost look like?' I asked.

'Very thin, very pale. Like he has no blood in his body.'

'What does he want from you?'

'He says he wants some money to use in Hell. He needs to buy some meat and rice, and a pair of new shoes too,' my grandmother murmured.

Chinese Hell is made up of eighteen layers. Each layer is ruled by a judge who decides what sort of punishment the dead deserves. The old people had been telling us about it ever since we were little. The ones who killed themselves or killed other people were placed in the bottom layer. I imagined my grandfather squashed inside, unable to breathe or stand up straight. He was probably given rotten food to eat: moss, shit, rubbish, dirt.

And his feet must have hurt, either from the burning-hot stony floor or the icy-cold ground.

'But if my parents heard you say this, they would criticise you and tell you there's no such thing as Hell!' I said, even though I was not entirely sure who was right.

At school, the teachers told us this talk of Hell and Heaven was just stupid superstition, left over from the feudal times, designed to fool and control the masses. And I was inclined to believe them.

My grandmother didn't argue with me. The street outside sank into the darkness. With the sound of the sea and wind echoing around us, we fell asleep.

The next morning, after another ritual bowl of bitter salty crab and porridge, we were ready to leave. I helped my grandmother to carry her shoulder bag of clothes and shoes. Before we left the house, my grandmother prayed one last time to Guanyin, and murmured something I couldn't hear. I was about to suggest she bring the Guanyin statue with her, but I realised that none of the villagers dared to move a god or goddess, let alone take it to another town. That would be the height of disrespect. So we left Guanyin there. As we locked the house, I told my grandmother I wanted to say hello to Da Bo's four daughters. I rushed over and banged on their door. But no one came out. They were probably all working in the new Shitang Frozen Seafood Processing Factory, my grandmother said. Since it was now the summer break, all the local kids would be helping their families on the cold workshop floor, peeling shrimps, cutting fish heads and packing them into boxes. I was disappointed. But I couldn't waste any more time here.

By noon, we were on the bus. I told my grandmother that my parents would be waiting at the other end. She looked slightly worried. I could sense her concern about dealing with my mother. I knew already about the terrible conflicts between Chinese mothers- and daughters-in-law. But everything would work out in our family, I thought.

Mother-in-Law

The bus journey back from Shitang to Wenling felt much faster. And yet, the constant motion of the bus made me feel sick once again, although I managed not to throw up as much, perhaps because I was in a good mood, or because I was so focused on looking after my grandmother, who felt worse than I did.

'It's too far to travel for an old person like me!' my grandmother croaked in a weak voice.

As the fishing village receded further and further away behind us, she grew increasingly uncertain about leaving the village: 'I don't know if I will ever manage to get my old bones back there!' She kept repeating phrases like that as she clung to the rail in front of her seat, her eyes moist and doubtful.

Our napkins were soaked with vomit. We took turns stretching our heads out of the window to let the air on our cheeks restore us. Life was always torture, I thought, even for a young kid. But that particular day, I didn't feel miserable for once. My heart was full of the joy of our reunion. Although I was still very young, I felt the weight of responsibility to improve my grandmother's remaining days. She was already sixty-seven that year, to me an ancient creature, always bent over like a dry, brittle leaf that could be swept away by the wind any second. Finally, the bus arrived at the station in Wenling. My parents and my brother were waiting by the entrance hall, my mother looking anxious, my father relieved, and my brother oblivious. My grandmother was happy to see them. In no time, my father had arranged two electric rickshaws to take us back home.

Daily life in the small apartment of our factory compound wasn't as easy as I had described it to my grandmother. Firstly, it was indeed too small to fit one more person in it. Nevertheless, we managed to set my grandmother up in a corner next to my small bed, placing her small bundle of possessions underneath it. That night, after a family meal, my grandmother and I managed to squeeze in together and sleep. The next morning, I gave her a tour of the compound. She seemed a little disorientated, but I tried to comfort her and make her feel welcome.

Things didn't seem to be going too badly for the first few days. But tension was growing between my mother and my grandmother. My mother felt that the hunchbacked village woman in her smelly rags and her crooked shuffle was always getting in her way. My grandmother simply didn't know where she should hide herself so as not to take up space. Every meal was a torture for her. She had never eaten at the table, especially when there were men around. She felt compelled to make herself invisible. She would hide behind us and sit by the stove to eat like a frightened mouse. For my mother, this only made things worse, because in her eyes, this was just a display of self-effacement, a spectacle of feudalistic female debasement. My mother would demand that she sit with us at the table. She also kept ordering my grandmother about, telling her to place her chair at a particular angle, to mop the table twice but not three times, to wash dishes with a yellow cloth rather than a green one . . . All this made my grandmother deeply stressed. As an illiterate peasant woman born in old China, she had lived her whole life anonymously.

She couldn't bear her humbleness being exposed before everyone's eyes. She felt embarrassed about helping herself to vegetables, or meat on the rare occasions there was some, given how little food there was on our table. My mother scolded her, and told her to stop being so pathetic and weak. In response my grandmother wept, which in turn only drove my mother to curse her more and more, choosing the most horrible words she could imagine. 'Get up from your bench! Don't you dare go drinking poison like your dead husband!' My mother was cursing my grandmother as if she were her class enemy.

My grandmother shook at these vile utterances, her fragile spine shuddering under the formless black of her old widow's clothes. Yet my father didn't intervene, despite his affection for his old mother. Although modern and open-minded in many respects, he too was a slave to convention, and felt powerless against my tyrannical mother. This was between the women and he had no part in it. He sat quietly at the dining table, spooning food into my grandmother's bowl, before retreating to his studio to paint.

As the days went by, I could see my grandmother was feeling more and more lonely. We were out all day at school or at work. No one came home until late. She sat alone on a bench in the yard, with no one to talk to. She couldn't really venture out much further with her twisted, bound feet. And she was worried about getting lost in the town with its hectic traffic and complicated road system.

The tension between the two women was becoming unbearable. My mother wanted my grandmother to help her with the housework because she had to labour in the factory from early morning until late in the evening. But my mother never liked the way my grandmother approached the household tasks. She claimed that the old woman didn't even wash our clothes properly. But my father and I thought that was because of my grandmother's bad eyesight. One day, she chopped a cube of soap into a wok of noodle soup, thinking it was pork fat. The noodle soup bubbled and soon foam started to pour out over the brim and onto the floor. We had to throw away what had promised to be a hearty soup. My mother cursed my grandmother with such toxic hate, as if a wok of noodle soup was more important than my grandmother. Feeling ashamed of her mistake, my grandmother sobbed as she hobbled out into the yard where all the neighbours were watching and gossiping. The next day a doctor came and checked my grandmother's eyes. She had thick membrane cataracts and possible macular degeneration. The old woman was practically blind, he told us. But it wasn't really her eyes that were the problem. She was profoundly depressed. She looked sick and had aged a lot. Her white hair was an unkempt mess. Her black clothes were a patchwork of ingrained dust and brown stains. She needed help just to change her clothes. She was homesick, and missed her Guanyin statue.

One day she announced that she had to go home. My father was in a dilemma: whether to look after his aged mother or appease his wife. He asked her to stay longer. But she refused, not even for one more night than necessary. She cried silently beside me in bed; by morning her pillow was soaked in tears.

She had met my grandfather in Hell and he had asked her to join him. We were all disturbed by her telling us this. After a quiet conversation between myself and my parents, I was given the mission of accompanying my grandmother to the bus. But I wasn't going with her all the way back to Shitang. We packed my grandmother's belongings and walked slowly to the station. Before we separated, she repeated the words she had once said to me as a child:

'Xiaolu, your grandmother's life isn't even the life of a dog. I don't have anything to live for.'

My eyes smarted, my throat grew tight, and I looked away. Then I heard her utter these last words:

'I don't know if I will ever see you again, but I hope that you will be happy and healthy. Obey your parents and study hard in school. One day, when you grow up and are making a living, send me a ten-yuan note to remind me of you.'

Her tears were flowing down her face. She wiped her eyes and took her place on the bus. I managed not to cry. I thought if I started, it would make her feel worse. As the bus disappeared along the dusty new road that led out into the countryside, I turned and walked back home. My heart was still there with my grandmother, but space and time were already tearing our bond apart. And I felt the terrible injustice of her life – her bound feet, the arranged marriage, the daily beatings at the hand of her husband, the fact that she had never learned to read or write, that even in our home she had been denied basic dignity. I couldn't draw her out of her pain, life was a brute force that I had no power to change. The only thing I could hope for was that my fate would not be a repeat of hers. Never, ever!

Farewell, Shitang

Five months later, we received an urgent call from Shitang. It was Da Bo, our next-door neighbour. Come back, as quickly as you can, he said. My grandmother was dying. 'She can barely breathe, but she asked for Xiaolu . . .' he added. My mother didn't say a word, and my father too was silenced. We were told to pack our clothes.

We sat on the bus, all four of us, and didn't speak. The traffic was bad and the bus seemed to be stopping every ten metres. It felt like we would never get there, or that we were going to be too late. My brother had barely spent any time with my grandmother, and he looked on, detached from the situation. I, however, was so worried about my grandmother that I began to cry on the bus. I cried non-stop. I was so afraid that she would die before we reached the village. My weeping made my parents gloomy. Neither of them said anything to me, as we rocked slowly along the congested road. And yet I thought I saw my mother's eyes welling up with tears. Maybe she felt guilty, perhaps even sorry for what she had done to my grandmother. With every jolt in the road, I felt more keenly the inner knot forming in my chest, and although I tried looking out of the window, images of my grandmother coloured my vision. How I dreaded the thought of her body being drained of life. I resented my mother and I despised my father's weakness. If he had been a good son, my grandfather wouldn't have poisoned himself. Nor would I have grown up in that lonely village by a grey sea.

When we finally arrived at my grandmother's house, many of our neighbours were standing around. Da Bo and his wife had been looking after her, and I watched as his daughters ran in and out with soup. My grandmother was lying on the bed, her face the colour of the ocean and her eyes closed. She was barely conscious. My father tried to wake her up.

'Mother, we're here to see you! Mother!'

There was no response. Then my father asked me to try.

I restrained my tears, leaned over the bed and let my words fall upon her grey-white face. 'Grandmother! It's me, Xiaolu! Grandmother, can you hear me?'

My grandmother's eyes fluttered slightly. We stared at her and listened to her faint breathing. Then she opened her eyes and turned to my father with a confused look. Her throat made a noise no one understood. Was it speech? Then she groaned again, this time we discerned the meaning.

'Is that Third Cousin?'

Third Cousin was from her maternal family and he used to visit her in the past, but he had died a while back. My grandmother didn't seem to recognise my father. He leaned in closer: 'Mother, I'm not Third Cousin, I'm your son, Xiuling.'

She rolled her eyes blankly.

My mother tugged on my arm, hinting at me to speak again. Then my grandmother noticed me, and said: 'Is that Jinglin selling crabs in the market?' No one knew who Jinglin was and why she was selling crabs in the market. My grandmother was thoroughly confused, and as if exhausted by our visit, she closed her eyes again. Now my brother was a bit scared. He left and wandered the streets outside. We waited by her bedside for an hour or two but she didn't open her eyes again. Then Da Bo and his wife said maybe we should come to their house to have some noodles and tea if we were not too worried. My father said he would wait with my grandmother. My mother and I returned half an hour later with a bowl of noodle soup for my father, but my grandmother had stopped breathing. My grandmother never realised that her son had been with her when she died.

It turned out that my grandmother had been saving money for years to buy herself a coffin. Da Bo and his wife knew exactly where it was stored, in the backyard of the village coffin maker's workshop. That was behind the village market, as far as I could remember. So my father and Da Bo went to fetch the coffin. Later, I heard that the coffin maker had been complaining for years about not having enough space and that he hoped my grandmother would die soon so he could be rid of it.

Before we laid my grandmother in the coffin, we had to change her clothes. We had a special outfit prepared for her. My parents undressed her and wiped her skin with wet towels. Only then did we see how thin and spindly she had become. She was a skeleton. I was not unfamiliar with my grandmother's naked body, but it was a horrid sight. Being old seemed the most undignified state in the whole world. She looked so ghastly that my parents ordered my brother and me to leave the room.

As I walked around outside, I saw the neighbours gathering and gossiping. Someone thought my grandmother might have starved to death. 'Either she had no money for food, or she couldn't get up to feed herself,' one of the mean-looking women said.

According to tradition, we, her closest family, had to keep my grandmother's body beside us for three nights. 'Hold three days' wake for the soul of the dead,' the villagers said. But my parents had always disliked superstition and feudal customs like these, and they decided to stay awake for one night only. We prepared the candles, and borrowed a sheet from next door to lay upon the coffin. My parents didn't go to sleep, but we children fell into a strange and horrid slumber on the floor, smeared with confusion between the living and the dead. I dreamt my grandmother was talking to me in her usual breathless tone. She'd been running after me. 'Xiaolu, I bought you a sugared ice. Take it!' I reached out and took the wet, dirty handkerchief. The ice was melting and it broke apart. We both looked at it melting in my hand with sadness.

Stop Crying! Every Girl has to Go Through This

My grandmother's death stayed with me for a long time, a grey haze hanging over me. I often dreamt that my body had suddenly aged like hers, skeletal, withered skin like worn white leather, laid out in a coffin, utterly abandoned by the spirit that had once animated it.

Nevertheless, outside of my nightmares, my body was obviously growing larger and stronger. My hair was becoming very long. My body had reached a stage where I was somewhere between childhood and adolescence. Then this interim period was brought to an abrupt end, and all the things a girl was destined to encounter came crashing into me. One after another.

I find it very difficult to reflect on my early sexual experiences; they were frightening and ugly, and I preferred at the time to move on. But pretending they didn't happen has not been useful; and I know how powerful the consequences of trying to escape my past have been on me as a grown woman.

My psychological and physical responses to sex have their roots in those years; they shaped all subsequent relationships with men and with the world. For a young girl in 1980s China, sex was an ordeal endured at first with terror, then with mute disgust and finally numbness. I was twelve when I was first sexually assaulted by a man. It didn't just happen once. The abuse lasted for about two years. When I left primary school to attend middle school, which was located in another part of town, it stopped, for whatever reason. And since then I have never tried to remember or to forget those sexual acts. 'Remembering' is the wrong word to use here, because those moments are embedded in my brain, on my retina, under my skin, in my loins. They don't need to be *remembered*. I can instantly *see* and *feel* them if I want to. Forgetting them would be like forgetting I have two hands or a mouth.

I have never mentioned his name to anyone or in any of my previous writings, but here on these pages I want to say it out loud, exactly as it is spelled, for the simple reason that he was never punished for what he did to me. Hu Wenren. Maybe he did it to many other girls, and we were all too scared to fight back. The son of a communal farming officer in a neighbouring town, Hu Wenren worked as the secretary in my father's office. No one knew why he, a young man without a college degree, was given that position. Perhaps his father had connections. Perhaps it was his skills in calligraphy – he wrote well, which was an important asset in a provincial cultural bureau. His handwriting had a distinctive style, his characters were hard with long, thin strokes.

Hu Wenren knew the route I took from school back home, and to my father's office. He would wait for me. At first I noticed him following me. Then he took me somewhere quiet, and so began the terrible normality of the situation. As my body trembled, he pulled down my pants and played with my clitoris, then he inserted his fingers into me while threatening to beat me if I made any noise. I was shaking all over. I remember looking around and noticing the rubbish and rotting food dumped on the corner. Beneath my feet, patches of chicken shit. A metaphor for my situation, no power, no dignity, no hope. Years later, as I reflected on that beginning (I never liked to think of it), I realised this was where my emotional pattern was formed: fright and shame in the face of physical invasion. The enormous fear and shame effectively silenced me.

Sometimes Hu would force me into the men's toilets, or corner me behind a large truck in some car park, or an unused office room to which he had the key. I remember seeing urine trickling down my legs as he fingered me. Immobilised by distress and horror, I was unable to react in any other way. After a few weeks, he began to have sex with me, threatening me with some horrible consequences if I told anyone about it. I hated him with a burning fury, but I never dared tell anyone. I never showed any signs of the abuse when I got home. I washed my underwear secretly. I hid my gloom. I never talked about what I had done at school, nor did my parents ever ask. I was thus abused, pathetically and hopelessly, like many young girls at that time. I even found myself repeating quietly the words Hu Wenren said to me as he stuffed his penis inside me: 'Stop crying! Every girl has to go through this!'

Every girl had to go through this. Sometimes I thought about my grandmother, who had lived such a sad life and cried so many times in front of me. She never really explained the source of those tears, what exactly had happened to her. She must have

gone through worse, I thought, given that she had been a child
bride and was sold to my grandfather! And probably had many
shocking stories about her treatment by the men in her life, yet
I would never have a chance to ask her now. She took all those
secrets to her grave and we buried them with her. No wonder
Chinese ghost stories know only weeping women looking for
justice in the afterlife.

And what about my mother? Probably the same. She had
never mentioned sex to me, never told me how babies were made.
The teachers at school didn't fill us in on that either. The only
time she spoke to me about the female body was when I got my
first period. I remember seeing blood in my pants one morning
during physical education when we were taught to jump from
one wooden block to another. By the afternoon, they were soaked
in blood. Since no one had ever told me about menstruation, I
automatically assumed I must have hurt myself from jumping.
But the bleeding continued the next day and I was in pain. My
mother saw it. She simply folded some soft cloth into a rectangle
and put it in my underwear, then told me to change and wash the
cloth regularly until the blood disappeared. 'You will have this
once a month, because you are a woman now,' she said simply
and nothing more. I was puzzled by this physical change. What
did it mean that I would have this once a month from now on?
Because I am *a woman* now? How? The prudish Chinese education system taught us nothing of the essential facts of human
biology, nor did my parents give me a clear explanation of this
change. It's so unfair that women have to bleed once a month
and men don't, I thought to myself unhappily. A few years later
I discovered that menstruation was connected to a woman's
fertility. I was horrified when I read lines like 'The period blood

contains dead eggs from the womb' in one of our biology text-books. Us women, we walked around carrying dead and alive eggs in our bodies. Women are like chickens, we are the hens, I thought. Egg-producing animals. No wonder we were treated so badly – humans give no respect to chickens. The only way to end a chicken's misery is to let it die. Better still, to never be hatched in the first place.

All the Aunts

I met my mother's family for the first time when I was fourteen. I knew that she was one of many siblings, but I didn't know they were estranged because she had married my father, a Stinking Number Nine, recently released from a re-education labour camp.

For all these years, my mother didn't visit her family, and her family didn't invite her to any gatherings or celebrations, not even for the most important festival, Chinese New Year. But around 1986 (ten years after the Cultural Revolution had ended), just before the end of the lunar year, my maternal grandmother sent some friendly signals and asked to meet us children. At first, my mother didn't respond, so my grandmother tried again. She even sent us some dragon eye fruit and lychees to soften my mother up. I ate all the dragon eyes at once, and my brother finished the lychees. I was curious to meet the cruel old woman, our own Mother Heaven from *The Weaver Girl and the Cowherd*, who forcefully separated her daughter from her beloved cowherd.

In China, because women marry 'out' of their families and into that of their husband, the maternal grandmother is called *waipo*, literally meaning, 'outer grandmother'. It wasn't strange to have so little connection with your 'outer' family. But this year we were going to our *waipo* for the Chinese New Year banquet.

The morning of the first day of the new year, as fireworks exploded in the sky above us, my brother and I were all dressed up in our new clothes. My mother prepared some ginseng packages to take with us. My father felt awkward about coming, since he had been held to blame by my mother's family for all these years. But he was persuaded, and we took a bicycle rickshaw to the outskirts of the city. The urban landscape gave way to rice fields, buffaloes and horses. As we drew up to my *waipo*'s house, we saw a number of kids screaming and playing out front. My brother and I didn't know who they were, but we soon discovered that they were our cousins. We entered the house, and I was greeted by a room full of women of different ages. There wasn't a single man to be seen. We were introduced to five aunts in total, one after another, which surprised me. I didn't know that my mother had five sisters! They looked much older than my mother, although she was one of the middle sisters. They looked as if their legs had been soaking in the paddy fields since dawn, and they had only just changed into their new city clothes. Their manners and accents were those of simple, rough peasants. They spat directly on the kitchen floor, leaving the white saliva pooling in the dirt.

Then we were led to an old woman. She was in her seventies, but looked very healthy and strong. This, apparently, was our *waipo*. I was a bit scared of her in the beginning, having expected to be scrutinised by a brutal woman with piercing eyes. But she was very charming, kind even. I paid extra attention to her hair. To my disappointment, she didn't have a giant hairpin in the back of her head like Mother Heaven in *The Weaver Girl and the Cowherd*, only short hair neatly trimmed just below the ears. Her clothing was good quality: grey cashmere and dark trousers. She didn't have bound feet, and her feet looked to be a normal size. In any case, she appeared much more modern than my hunchbacked paternal grandmother.

After my brother and I had said the customary pleasantries, we children were immediately given *hong bao* – red envelopes with money. We were in ecstasy. I didn't know about my brother, but this was the first time in my life I had been given money, even if it was mostly small change. Then the five aunts also gave us some smaller *hong bao*. It was an incredible feeling: the first time I came to realise that it was profitable to have a large family. But we could have had this a long time ago! I could have had a very different life if I had been included in this side of the family from the day I was born! Who was to blame?

We were so happy. Instantly my brother went to light fireworks with the other kids, while I stayed and guzzled food from the table. I noticed a pot of shark-fin soup, a symbol of luxury and prosperity. As I drank the gluey soup, I thought about my dead grandmother – my heart's *real* grandmother. She had never experienced a day like this. The singers on the television regularly performed a song called 'Socialism is Great', but my paternal grandmother didn't live long enough to see how great socialism could actually be.

Gradually, I got to learn the stories of my *waipo*'s family. *Waipo* was born in the 1920s, when the Chinese Communist Party was starting to gain a strong foothold in the south with their anti-feudal ideology. So she had never had her feet bound. My maternal grandfather, *waigong*, was a hard-working farmer, but had died when their children were very young, leaving his wife to raise the children by herself on a little patch of farmland. Like her mother, my oldest aunt was also illiterate. She had stopped farming life in the seventies to help *waipo* sell groceries. Her husband, too, had passed away, from liver cancer. They had two girls. My second aunt served in the army and had married a soldier who was sent to North Korea in 1950 to fight the Americans. He had died in battle, making widow number three. My third aunt had been selling vegetables in the market for the last ten years. Her husband wasn't dead, but he was absent from the banquet.

The two younger aunts seemed to have a lighter spirit. They worked in the newly built state department store. 'The best job you can have for women,' they exclaimed proudly during the meal. 'Socialism is truly great,' the youngest aunt said during the meal, and she meant it.

These women were loud and drank a lot. They paid special attention to my father, adding pork and fillets of fish to his bowl. I thought that was partly because he was the only adult man in the house, but also because they had excluded him from the family during the Cultural Revolution and now they felt they had to redeem themselves by showing him particular respect.

It was during that banquet that I learned that my mother and her sisters had 'only one decent man' in their family: their elder brother. But he too had died. He was the only educated one in the whole family. Apparently my aunts as well as my mother had had to give up any thoughts of school so that the family could afford to give my uncle an education. And receive an education he did, earning a college degree in law in the 1970s. He became a lawyer – one of the first in our province. He specialised in women's rights and domestic violence. The choice was apt given that he had come from such a female-orientated family! But their brother didn't get the chance to pay his sisters back for their sacrifice. He had died in his early thirties, of lung cancer.

It didn't make sense to me, that so many women should sacrifice themselves for their only brother. In reality, they had been the ones to support the family after their men died one by one. My mother's chance at an education had been taken away from her. Without that uncle, my mother probably would have gone at least up to middle school. She would have understood why I wanted to write and why I wanted to be an artist! But then, if she had gone to middle school, she probably wouldn't have been my mother at all. And who would I have been? Would I have existed? At that point my mind was swept into a dizzying whirlpool. I gathered up my presents, and ran outside to play in the afternoon sun.

A Poet from America

As a provincial child raised in the Communist education system, I had no concept of America except for the slogans we were taught at school like 'Down with American imperialism'. I didn't know there were 'normal' people living in the USA and that some of them were even Chinese! But one day we received a letter with an American stamp, and it was to be the start of a new fascination for me.

It was autumn when the postman brought us the fancy airmail envelope. My brother collected stamps obsessively, so he grabbed it immediately. He peeled off his foreign prize and opened the letter. A photo dropped out. I picked up the photo and looked at it. It seemed to be a sort of family photo. A good-looking forty-something woman was smiling, her husband on one side and her son on the other. Behind them was a huge foreign-looking building with an American flag on top.

My father took the photo and the letter, and scanned them quickly while my mother observed from behind.

'From America?' my mother enquired.

'Yes, it's from her. Zhang Kang.'

I was perplexed, who was this Zhang Kang? And why were Chinese people sending letters from America?

My mother paused for a second, and then asked: 'What does she say?' My father straightened the two pages and read out loud to my mother. It was all so mysterious.

Dear Old Guo, Dear Xiaomei:

We hope you are healthy and your children are well. It's been a while. Today is Moon Festival but people in America don't celebrate it like we do. Still, I thought I should write. My husband, my son and I just spent a week on the road on holiday. We drove to Washington DC and went to visit the White House. It's so beautiful and so grand. I thought I should send you a photo to show you what it looks like . . .

I didn't have any idea what the White House was, let alone this Washington DC place. Besides, it was strange enough to think they had spent a week driving around for a 'holiday'! In China, only high-ranking officials had cars. And there was no such thing as 'holiday', apart from at Chinese New Year. From then on, we would receive one of these American letters about three times a year from the same woman in Philadelphia. And each time, my father would read it out loud to my mother. The letters offered a window onto a strange but fascinating world: her husband worked in a science laboratory, which provided sandwiches for lunch and free coffee every day. What was a sandwich? It sounded amazing to me. She mentioned buying a lawnmower. That was especially odd – because only peasants in China needed machines to manage their crops. Why would an American family need such an unfashionable tool?

Gradually, however, my parents revealed details and I managed to piece together her story. Zhang Kang lived in America and she was a poet. More importantly, she was someone my father had *loved* in the days before he met my mother. This was the first time I had heard my father use the word 'love', and it was shocking and almost shameful to hear him speak such a raw and strong word.

'She was the daughter of a very important general in the Nationalist Kuomingtang Party, so she had the best education and writes wonderful poems,' my father explained to me. 'She and I were very close because of our common interest in literature and painting. But that was in the early 1950s, and Mao had just defeated the Nationalist Party and taken over. So her family had to flee the country, first to Taiwan, then to America. We wrote to each other although of course our correspondence was interrupted when I was sent to the labour camp. We only started writing again recently.'

'What about Mother? Isn't she angry with you for writing to her?' I whispered, trying not to let my mother hear us from the next room.

'Your mother knows the whole story. We never keep secrets, there's no such thing in marriage. I always read my letters to your mother before posting them, and she gives me comments. It's always been this way.'

No secrets in marriage. Indeed, my mother didn't show any bitterness towards this other woman; if anything, I could detect a twinge of envy over her American life. Although I'm sure my parents were as clueless about America as me. But the photos were amazing enough. I remember once she sent one of her local supermarket, somewhere in the suburbs of Philadelphia. 'Look, Xiaolu,' my father said, 'this is a Western supermarket!' I stared at the glossy photo; what I saw was a large modern building with a row of shiny cars parked outside. Displays of black-coloured cakes were visible through the windows (I didn't know what chocolate was then), as well as shelves of cute, blonde-haired dolls. I was absolutely blown away. A supermarket! It was so beautiful to the eyes of a small-town Chinese child. America must be on one of the Nine Continents the Taoist monk had talked about. I swore I would go there one day.

Misty Poetry with Optimism

As if the American Chinese woman had cast a spell on me, my head started to fill with thoughts about poetry and love. She was a poet, and so had my father been before becoming a painter. And they had *loved* each other. Did they love each other because they were poets? Is that what poets did? Did they still love each other, or had those feelings been killed off during the years of separation when my father was in a labour camp? I was used to reciting Tang

Dynasty poems at school, but I had never really paid attention until then. I couldn't stop thinking about it, and what this thing 'poetry' really was. At some point I started to read all the poetry I could find to try and uncover these supposed magical powers. But perhaps it was because she was in America? American poets? I should read them first. So I went to the biggest bookshop in Wenling looking for American poetry books. Previously banned during the Cultural Revolution, collections like Allen Ginsberg's *Howl*, Sylvia Plath's *Ariel* and Ezra Pound's *Cantos* were suddenly available. I was drawn to these texts, but I was still too young to really understand them. Then I tried to write some poems myself. I was more inclined to write using image and metaphor than narrative. The style I sought to emulate had been given the most dreamy, fantastical name in Chinese: Misty Poetry. It had emerged after the Cultural Revolution and became very popular among the young intellectuals of the 1980s in China. Young writers no longer wanted to be told to write about politics or the Communist Party. They wanted to make the land, the cloud-covered mountains, the foggy sea, ethereal love, the subjects of their writing. And contrary to the strict formal requirements of classical poetry, it did away with rhyme schemes and tonal patterns. It was, in the words of the time, historically free.

I wrote my first Misty Poem at the age of thirteen. It was called 'Autumn', and the first stanza went like this:

> *I walked into the autumn forest*
> *Feeling the touch of a leaf*
> *falling behind my head*
> *I turned around, and*
> *Only found my melancholy*

My father read those first lines and they satisfied him, but he wasn't as convinced by the mournful tone as each stanza developed. The last lines went:

> *I gazed at the dried souls around my feet*
> *And wondered about the difference*
> *between*
> *the death of a leaf, and*
> *the death of a human*

After reading the whole poem, my father turned to me with a deep frown scored across his forehead. 'What do you know about death? You're only thirteen!'

I had witnessed my grandfather's suicide and more recently the death of my grandmother. They had raised me for the first seven years of my life, and now they were no longer here. Why couldn't I write about death? But I was too afraid to answer back.

'It's a very negative perspective on life, even for a poem. You should always look at the positive,' my father announced in a slightly disapproving tone. 'You should always try to give a positive ending, even in a Misty Poem.'

A positive ending. Was that why he never visited us in that dim, depressing house in Shitang? Is that why he ran away from his father's way of life, because it wasn't positive enough? I wondered.

I continued writing poetry and started expanding into the short essay form. I continued using the death metaphors, and sometimes even tackled the subject head on, despite my father's disapproval. With the letters from America and my new passion for writing poetry, my father believed I might become an accomplished poet when I grew up. It even inspired him to take up writing again, and he would show me his lines. His preferred imagery was always linked to the sea, the moon, the mountains, as well as everyday fishermen and villagers. He didn't like the classical style of rigid rules or rhymes either. He was, after all, a modernist. He was a good influence on me, because he encouraged me to do away with restrictions of form and tradition. Since Misty Poetry was very much influenced by Western modernism, my father introduced me to Walt Whitman. He read these lines to me from a translation of *Leaves of Grass*:

> *Not I, nor anyone else can travel that road for you.*
> *You must travel it by yourself.*
> *It is not far. It is within reach.*
> *Perhaps you have been on it since you were born,*
>   *and did not know.*
> *Perhaps it is everywhere – on water and land.*

I repeated in my mind the words, 'You must travel it by yourself'. It sparked a kind of excitement in me, and soon became my mantra. Yes, I will travel the road by myself. I will. The road is everywhere, on water and on land. I will travel it by myself.

Because of *Leaves of Grass*, I began to collect strange-shaped leaves from the almond tree, the Japanese maple, the crying plant, wisteria. I dried each carefully selected leaf and flattened them in between the pages of my diary. Soon my collection had grown so huge that I had to relocate them into the pages of *A Study of the Thoughts of Marx and Lenin*, which I had found on my father's shelf. I relabelled the book with my own title *World Leaf Collection*. It was not much of a 'world' collection. The dried specimens were just fallen autumn leaves picked up from the street corners of Wenling.

I started reading Whitman. I connected more and more with his lyrical style, and with his descriptions of vibrant trees, grasses, mountains and seas. I would learn verses of his poems and recite them to myself as I wandered on the bamboo hills behind our house, searching for my perfect leaves and moulding my heart into Whitman's words. I started to write every day, to do more than just imitate him. And then I started to send the results of my labours to literary magazines. At first I got no response. But one day, my first letter of acceptance arrived. By the age of fourteen, I had published my first poem and received my first *hui kuan* by post (the official payment cheque sent from publisher to author). Over the next year, I managed to publish a few more and even won first prize at the National Young People's Poetry Competition. I was on the road to becoming a poet.

Five Thousand Miles of Coastline Expedition

Just as I spent my days at school, my father spent his days in his studio, painting. But I could see he wasn't happy being a state painter. Once home, he chain-smoked by the kitchen window, frowning and not talking to my mother. The moon above the bamboo hills was often very bright and he used to stare at it intensely, as if meditating on its luminosity.

One day, as we were finishing our evening meal, my father placed his chopsticks on his bowl, and then, after sitting in silence for a few brief moments, turned to my mother.

'Xiaomei, I have to leave.'

My mother looked down at her rice and didn't respond. I could hear her breath deepening. My brother took his chance, and reached for the rest of the dumplings on the serving plate. My father continued in a clear and steady voice. He seemed to have prepared his words, which he reproduced with a certain gravity.

'China has a great coastline, with thousands of bays and beaches. I am a painter of the sea, but I know only this small corner of the world. To continue to develop, I must walk this coastline, to know and feel it deeply and remake myself as an artist. I will make a thousand sketches, in watercolour, ink and pencil, and this will be the new foundation for my work. I have decided the time has come for me to do this. I have to leave home and begin my journey.'

'How long will it take?' my mother said with sadness but evident resignation.

'It won't be a short trip.' Then my father tried to make light of it. 'Ideally, I will go on foot without taking buses or trains. I imagine it will be at least six months . . .' My father's voice was gentle but firm.

'Six months!' my mother exclaimed. 'You're not coming back home for six months?'

We had all stopped eating and were staring at him. Even my brother was visibly concerned about this news. He was already taking lessons in painting and calligraphy from our father, and he was progressing well. He didn't want our father to go away now.

'I have already sent the request to my superior at the Provincial Culture Bureau, asking for their assistance. And they said they would stamp my work unit reference letter. I feel very encouraged,' my father finished.

At that time there were only two types of citizens in China: government officials and the rest of us. An artist needed an official introduction letter from an upper-level governmental department in order to receive assistance when travelling around the country. Without that letter, my father wouldn't have been allowed to stay at hotels in other provinces.

My mother was silent, like a small stone statue, her emotions knotted inside her. We could all feel her growing anger towards my father, but she seemed to be swallowing the bitter taste in her mouth. She was, after all, a woman born in 1940s China. She didn't have her own goals in life, and often felt abandoned by my father. Yet at the same time, she felt it was her obligation to support his work.

So that was it. My father had made up his mind. He wanted to hitchhike along the Chinese coastline to develop his art. And he gave the project the grandest of names: 'Five Thousand Miles of Coastline Sketching Expedition'. He even knew how he was going to present his final report for his superiors – he would put on an exhibition of all his sea-life sketches once he had returned home.

The task my father had set himself was immense. The Chinese coastline is vast, stretching from the North China Sea next to the Bay of Korea and the Sea of Japan, then all the way down to the Yellow Sea, the Taiwan Strait, the East China Sea, the Qiongzhou Strait and finally the South China Sea. It is also dotted with innumerable islands both closer and farther from the mainland. The northern part of the Chinese coastline was going to be the more straightforward part of the trip, he told me. It was mostly blocked by marine bases that he wouldn't be able to enter. But the southern part was more irregular and the landscape here interested him more. Much of the Zhejiang and Fujian coastline, for example, was rocky and steep. People had lived along its edge for thousands of years. Farther south the coast became less rugged: low mountains and hills reached towards the sea gradually, with river deltas and fertile fields meeting the ocean. As my father pointed his finger on the map, my eyes lit up like two lamps. I wished I could go with him. But I couldn't. I had to go to school. I had to wait, until one day when I was an adult and could decide to leave myself.

The morning before my father's departure, large bags blocked the doorway. He was taking one large bag which contained two cameras and many rolls of film, wrapped up in his sweater. Another was filled with his painting materials and sketchbooks. His ambition was clear. Before he left, some government officials came to say goodbye to him. A group of television journalists were going to film his leaving. Somehow his project had become famous in the province. He told my mother that he would write letters to us. And just like that, he went, leaving my mother and us on the roadside. He simply walked off, along the dusty road, lorries and buses bustling past him, battering him with gusts of an indifferent wind. As he disappeared into the haze, a small figure laden with the weight of his painting materials, I felt a tightening in my throat and a moistening of my eyes. I missed him already. I wanted to run after him, to join him on his great quest, and get away from this stale small-town life.

My father had left me something before his departure, however, as if he knew that I would need something to sustain me in his absence. He had left two books on my bed, with a brief note that said: 'I loved these books. Reading them will help you understand why I had to leave. One day you will do the same yourself.'

One of the books was a biographical novel about Van Gogh, *Lust for Life*, and the other was Hemingway's *The Old Man and the Sea*. By the early 1980s, restrictions on Western literature had been loosened and almost everything was available to Chinese readers. That night after my father's departure, I started reading *The Old Man and the Sea*. I was almost fourteen. I had never heard of Hemingway. I had read Western poetry and been dazzled by its directness. But Western narrative fiction was a new thing for me. The story didn't draw me in instantly, although I saw in the image of the old fisherman my grandfather, who had spent most of his life in the same way as the old man in the novel. Both used the most basic kinds of fishing tools. Both murmured to themselves and felt the bitterness of their poverty. I could understand why my father had been drawn to this book.

Some lines did leave a deep impression on me, such as '*Most people were heartless about turtles because a turtle's heart will beat for hours after it has been cut up and butchered. But the old man thought, I have such a heart too.*' These words seemed to touch something within me, though I didn't know quite what it was. Naturally, reading them took me back to Shitang, where I had known the sea and its creatures. The fishermen of my childhood had worshipped turtles. Our steamed rice cakes were always stamped with their image, especially during the festival season. My grandmother had a bench carved in the shape of a turtle, and that was one of the most valuable objects in the house. We knew that the good old sea turtle could live up to 150 years, and a fisherman paid his respects when they caught one by mistake by either letting it go or keeping it as a pet in their house. But Hemingway's old man identified with the turtle and its plight in a way that was new to me. I finished reading the novel within days, but I didn't feel that I had totally understood the book. The Van Gogh one I saved for later.

While Father was Away

During those six months of my father's absence, each one of us left behind faced some sort of a crisis. First, my mother had a serious fall down the stairs, breaking one of her arms and injuring her back. She was hospitalised for weeks. She asked me to write a letter for her to the address on the back of my father's last letter, but got no response. No one really knew where he was, and we only received more details when his next letter arrived.

'*I have just arrived at Qinghuang Island, where the Great Wall plunges into the sea. It's blue and windy here and you cannot help but admire how the army in ancient times managed to build this part of the Great Wall . . .*' More romantic rambling followed in the next paragraph. '*There is a temple dedicated to the Lady of Mengjiang which I visited today. This Lady of Mengjiang, whose husband was sent to build the Great Wall of China, missed her husband so profoundly that her tears flooded the Wall. An impressive story, but even more impressive scenery here!*'

He wrote this to my mother entirely without irony. It could only be a one-way correspondence. We received another letter in which my father had sent a beautifully shaped golden almond leaf for me.

'*This leaf is for Xiaolu's World Leaf Collection – it fell on my shoulders while I was walking through the forest in Hainan Island, at our country's southernmost tip.*'

I had barely any specimens from outside our province in my World Leaf Collection. As I placed it among the others, I imagined a tropical forest in the middle of the South China Sea full of golden leaves. How much I wished I was with him! The letters just made my mother unhappy. Once she was out of hospital, my brother and I had to look after her and cook every day. Sometimes I had to ask for leave from school. I remember seeing her weeping on the bed when I brought in a bowl of noodle soup. But even then, we weren't brought closer together as mother and daughter. It was a burden to look after her and do the household chores. In my heart, I was coming to know what it was like to be a trapped housewife, just like my grandmother. A house made a woman busy with meaningless things. And now it seemed that I too had been swallowed by such a fate, while my father wandered freely.

Then my brother got bored being stuck in the house without much to do. He started associating with some wild teenagers who smoked and engaged in gang fights. He was only sixteen, but he no longer came back home until the early hours of the morning. He was often drunk and stank of cigarette smoke. He started missing class. But since my mother loved him, she felt powerless to change his bad behaviour.

Those six months felt very long and lonely to me. For some reason, though, it was during that time that Hu Wenren stopped following me through the mazes of Wenling's streets, and so for now the sexual abuse ended. But I didn't feel any sense of relief. Instead, I felt unpredictable danger lurking at every corner like a miasma. I had one or two female friends from my class, but I had never mentioned my plight to them, nor anyone else. I couldn't stand living with my mother and brother without my father to temper their behaviour. I didn't feel emotionally attached to them. I was intimidated and frightened by both of them most of the time. My father had been my only protection. One lonely night, two months after my father had left, I remembered the other book he had left me: _Lust for Life_. With an image of my father sitting by some rocky bay, sketching boats and waves, I picked it up and started reading.

I continued reading every night after I had finished washing the dishes and had done my homework. I even read it discreetly during class. I had to use a dictionary occasionally, since quite a few of the characters used in the translation were unknown to me. The first half of the book was so joyful, pure and intense, describing the young Van Gogh's desire to paint, and how much he loved the landscapes that surrounded him in Holland. All this reminded me of my father. It was strange that a painter's eyes should be so different from everyone else's, from all the 'normal' people, but it seemed to be so. A painter's eyes took the familiar dead things around us, and made them come alive again. I was moved by Van Gogh's long letters to his brother Theo, in which he described his absolute attachment to nature. Sentences like these were magical to me, and I read them repeatedly.

When one has walked for hours and hours through that country, one feels that there is really nothing but that infinite earth – that mould of corn or heather, that infinite sky. Horses and men seem no larger than fleas. One is not aware of anything, be it ever so large in itself, one only knows that there is earth and sky.

I was enthralled by the book's depiction of how Van Gogh's love for his brother inspired him in his love of nature. Those letters were like poetry.

And then when twilight fell – imagine the quiet, the peace of it all! Imagine then a little avenue of high poplars with autumn leaves, imagine a broad muddy road, all black mud, with an infinite heath to the right and an endless heath to the left, a few black triangular silhouettes of turf huts, through the little windows of which shines the red light of the little fire . . .

How could anyone write so beautifully? How could I obtain this sort of ability, to be able to look at nature with such an intense love, and also let that love come out in my writing? Instead of the painter, I thought about the writer, the poet, as I came to the end of *Lust for Life*. And such an ending! Reading about his suicide left me mournful. What really killed him? Poverty? Loneliness? Losing faith? Madness? I thought about my grandfather again, and for the next few days I was consumed by my melancholy solitude. I walked to school on my own in the morning and back home again in the evening. I ate in silence. I went to bed without saying a word. I had taken the poison, my stomach ached at night and I woke up in tears. My father probably never knew how much that book had affected me.

After what felt like an eternity, my father returned home. A beard obscured his face; he was scruffy and his clothes were torn, the heels on his shoes wrecked, the sleeves of his jacket were ripped and the zips on his bags were broken. But he was in high spirits. He had filled every page of his five sketchbooks with drawings and watercolours. He had taken plenty of photographs, too. The trip had restored his energy, and my mother was relieved to have him back. She was recovered now and didn't tell my father how hard it had been. Instead, she took to cooking chicken soup. But after finishing two bowls and a glass of hard liquor, my father went straight into his painting studio and disappeared for the next few weeks, coming out only when he was hungry or needed a proper sleep. He was inspired and in a hurry to complete some large paintings for his official solo exhibition. He had to repay the government with new work, he said. 'I want everyone in our province to see how wild and beautiful our coastline is. I want everyone to realise that the sea is our mother,' he said with a great earnestness as he devoured a plate of pork dumplings.

Adolescence

My adolescence was spent under the influence of Hong Kong pop music and Western literature. I particularly liked reading anything sentimental, as long as it didn't have too much official Communist talk in it. Apart from Whitman, one of the very first Western poems I read was Frank O'Hara's 'Why I Am Not a Painter.' It's a very simple poem, especially for us Chinese who grew up studying the Chinese classics and Soviet literature, but it had a great impact on my thinking. It had lines like:

> . . . *One day I am thinking of*
> *a color: orange. I write a line*
> *about orange. Pretty soon it is a*
> *whole page of words, not lines.*

Then another page. There should be
so much more, not of orange, of
words, of how terrible orange is
and life. Days go by. It is even in
prose, I am a real poet. My poem
is finished and I haven't mentioned
orange yet. . . .

Why could Westerners write something like that, but not us Chinese? I was startled by its clarity and straightforwardness. It was especially striking for a child like me, given that we had to go through the pain of memorising hundreds of highly complex and metaphorical Tang and Song Dynasty poems. O'Hara's words were a kind of untrammelled freedom the like of which I had never before encountered.

I was reading this poetry around the time I first fell in love. Our teacher Mr Lin was in his late twenties and taught us science. I was drawn to him from the very beginning, maybe because his manner was so gentle, even slightly feminine. Most of the adult men I had encountered were macho, rough and insensitive. They treated girls like second-class humans. But Mr Lin had none of that attitude. He rode to school on his bike, kept himself to himself and took breaks by walking calmly around the campus on his own. In the late afternoon he would ride his bike back home again and we wouldn't see him until the following morning. He was mysterious.

He walked into the classroom and introduced himself, then said nothing more. He turned to the blackboard and drew something, which I could only roughly make out due to my weak eyes: a man pushing a long stick with a circle on the end of it. Then, in

a soft voice, he announced: 'The Greek mathematician and philosopher Archimedes said: "Give me a lever and a place to stand
on and I will move the Earth." What did Archimedes mean?'

We were about thirteen or fourteen years old, and in the
first year of middle school. Such a bold opening astonished us.
What kind of lecture was this? I was impressed. I wasn't good at
physics, and spent most of Mr Lin's classes reading my Chinese
literature textbook, doodling, or sleeping. But I took to following
him around the campus, to try to attract his attention. In China,
schoolchildren are forbidden from entering relationships with
each other, let alone with a teacher. But I only had two kinds of
interactions with men, either sexually or not at all. One day Mr
Lin and I walked back home together; I had discovered he lived
nearby. But instead of going back to the compound, I followed
him to his apartment. He lived alone, which was not unusual
then for an unmarried man. He explained that his parents were
farmers and they still lived in the village. I wandered around his
apartment, looking at his books and the small sculptures he had
made. He seemed to spend his spare time carving little wooden
animals: horses, cats, fish, chicken and other trinkets. He was
pretty good, I thought. My father would have approved.

It was late afternoon and I didn't want to go home. An idea
had formed in my fourteen-year-old head: I was going to be with
him. I was going to be his girlfriend. Without even a kiss or an
embrace, I lay on his bed and undressed myself. There was no
foreplay. We made love for the first time, although there wasn't
much lovemaking really. He had removed his clothes and gone
through the whole thing so clumsily that I realised Mr Lin must
have been a virgin, despite being fifteen years older than me.
He was rather timid and even frightened by our naked bodies

touching. His body was trembling as I watched his hardening penis slip out from his underwear.

We continued our affair in secret. He understood my loneliness. Every night, it felt like a torture as I lay on my small bed, listening to the sounds of the television in my parents' room. I wanted to escape the monotony. I wanted to be beside Mr Lin. I could no longer sleep alone. I thought about running away with him. We could live together in a little hut, grow vegetables and go fishing. Like the forbidden lovers the Weaver Girl and the Cowherd, like Madame White Snake and the medicine man Xuxian, we could live outside society. But in those stories, there was always an evil character who would chase after the lovers and punish them for their transgression, and in our case that person would be my mother. She would savage me if she found out about our affair. I couldn't sleep from the anxiety, and the situation made me feel even more lonely. Some nights, I waited in the dark until I could hear the sound of snoring coming from my parents' room, before getting up and stuffing some clothes under the duvet to give the impression of a sleeping body, and sneaking out the door. But I had to return before six, so as not to get caught. A game that dangerous couldn't last long. Early one morning, I pushed open the door discreetly and slipped inside. That's when I saw her, a dark shadow sitting at the kitchen table, waiting. I was petrified. My mother's face was blue-grey with a frosty anger.

'Don't you have any shame?!' she hissed at me like a snake, her eyes red like a hungry wolf in the night.

I was shaking all over.

'You're up to no good. Are you going to tell me where you were?'

'I . . . I slept over at my classmate's house,' I muttered, my teeth chattering from the morning chill. Or perhaps I was just scared.

'A classmate? Take me there now!' My mother stood up and began smacking me, her chubby palms landing on the back of my head. This time, she slapped me so hard that my eyes hurt. I cried out and tried to run away. But at that moment, my father came in and stopped my mother.

'You always spoil her!' my mother said, turning to my father, her left arm still raised above my head. It hung there, threatening me. 'Your daughter is about to become the biggest scandal in Wenling! All the neighbours will laugh at us. There is no decency left in this house any more!'

She was furious at my father's interference. She pushed him out of the kitchen and resumed the beating. My brother was now up too, leaning against the doorway and watching everything.

'You're not going to school today if you don't tell me where you were last night!'

My mother locked me inside the bedroom.

I didn't get out that day. My brother went to school and my parents left for work. I had no one to help me. I wondered if Mr Lin noticed I wasn't in class, and worried whether my mother would find out the truth. I was stuck under my mother's autocratic rule. I hated her. I secretly wished she would die in an accident, be mangled in a car crash or be swept away by a natural disaster. I cursed her every second of that day and swore to myself in desperation. Then I made a plan. I was going to get out of Wenling forever.

The day gradually passed, but it was one of the longest of my life. And the greyest. In the evening, I heard my parents returning home. I heard them talking. My father was distressed to see me still locked up. He told my mother to let me out. They argued. Then came the sound of the key in the lock and I was out. My mother ignored me for the rest of the evening. I was her enemy, she detested me. The feeling was mutual.

Abortion

My mother couldn't stop me and I managed to keep my secret. Nobody knew I was with Mr Lin, not even my classmates. I had always been a good pretender. The affair lasted for a year or two, our bodies entangling together many evenings. At some point, my mother gave up on me.

The affair also resulted in my first pregnancy at the age of fifteen. My parents didn't know anything about it, and I was in deep distress. It was clear that if people knew I was pregnant, I would be finished. I heard somewhere that a woman could bring on a miscarriage by jumping up and down non-stop until the foetus dropped out between her legs and onto the ground. So, whenever we had a break between classes I would find a quiet corner of the school and jump up and down wildly. My stomach ached, but nothing came out from in between my legs. I tried in my bare feet in the middle of the night when I couldn't sleep. But still nothing. The nausea continued and I could taste a metallic bitterness on my tongue. I had also heard that a mouthful of ash caused a miscarriage. So I snuck into the canteen of my mother's factory and filled my pockets with the remnants of the coal fire. I gathered my courage and swallowed a mouthful. It was so terrible that I choked and coughed, but in my desperation, swallowed some more. It was deranged. But still there was no effect. Knowing it would be a big scandal if we were discovered, Teacher Lin began to contact places. He found an abortion clinic in another town. He raised the money and told me to use a fake name when registering. We made something up, something so ordinary that I had forgotten it by the next day. He also found some womanly-looking shoes with a medium-high heel for me to wear on the day of the operation, so I would look a bit older than I actually was. I had long straight hair back then. Maybe I should curl it so I didn't look so much like a schoolgirl? But I didn't have the chance, I didn't want my parents or anyone else to see and grow suspicious. On the day, Teacher Lin left school before me and waited for me at the bus station. I left class at noon and met him there. After about an hour and a half on the bus we arrived at the isolated clinic. It was dirty, nothing more than a country hospital with very basic facilities. I remember seeing piles of rusty metal waste at the back of the hospital. And further in the distance, buffaloes grazing on a patch of grass in front of an expanse of paddy fields. In the 1980s, abortions performed in the countryside barely involved any anaesthetics. Teacher Lin told me I would just have to endure the pain. The two female doctors led me into a separate room, apparently not noticing my real age. Their job was to operate on me as efficiently as they could. They didn't even ask me how long I had been pregnant. Abortion must have been a doctor's most common surgical procedure in 1980s China, the high point of the One Child Policy, and perhaps affected more women than any other operation too. Including young girls like me.

The operation room was shabby and bare. The walls were painted green, but looked as if someone had vomited on them.

Teacher Lin wasn't allowed in. They asked me to remove my underpants and lie down on the operation table. One of the doctors had strong arms. She forced my trembling legs open and placed them up in the stirrups. I felt so dreadful, so shameful that I couldn't bear to ask what was about to happen to me. I would rather have died in that moment than be treated like this. Then they turned on all the lights in the room. With tears flowing down my cheeks, I shut my eyes. Then came the sound of clinking metal, like medical scissors or a knife. The doctors made some irrelevant conversation. I was told to take a deep breath. Suddenly I felt a freezing cold tool enter my lower body, some sort of suction pump. Then came the most horrifying pain as the sharp tools worked in and out between my legs. I have no idea how long it went on for, but just as suddenly, it was done. They had sucked the foetus from my womb.

When the operation was over, the doctor supported my back and tried to get me to sit up, as Mr Lin was still not allowed to come in. I will never forget that moment when she pointed at the little chunk of flesh in a bucket by the bed and said in the most ordinary tone:

'There it is.'

Terrified and still recovering from the agonising pain, I leaned over the operation table and took a quick glance at the little ball wrapped in blood. It was an utterly inexpressible feeling to see my supposed baby, having just been cut from my body. Close but separate. So little, this *thing*! But already as big as a chicken's egg. Yes. There it was, lying in a cold white bucket. Dead, or maybe it was dying, not dead yet. There it was, a consequence of love, the poisoned fruit of my relationship with my teacher.

The whole thing left me numb. It occurred to me that there was only one truth to being a woman, and I had seen it confirmed again and again – being born this way was a curse. The worst thing in the world. We were doomed by the fact of our woman-hood. The only thing we had any control over was pregnancy. Never again, I swore to myself as I lay on that hospital table, never again would I get pregnant. I walked out of the operation room, pale and hollow, and fell into the arms of my teacher.

The affair didn't last much longer – I began to remove myself from our emotional entanglement and found I didn't even want to see him. Everything that had been so wonderful about him was now so very boring. Now, I just found him pathetic. My heart grew more ambitious and my eyes were focused somewhere higher, somewhere bigger. He started dating another woman not long after we split up. I later heard that they were getting married. One part of me felt hurt and betrayed by this news. But the other, stronger part was already done with Teacher Lin. The abortion had freed my body, but it had also freed my heart. I knew that I was supposed to make a mark on a much larger canvas of life.

Confucianism vs Feminism

I was fifteen and a half, it was the first day of autumn term, and we were sitting in the classroom reading out loud from Confucius' *Analects*. The weather in early September is the worst; the air was steaming hot like a proper post-typhoon day and our white shirts were soaked through and stank from sweat. Trying hard not to fall asleep, I joined in with the collective murmur: *Fu mu zai, bu yuan you, you bi you fang* – The Master said, 'While his parents are alive, the son may not venture far abroad. If he does go abroad, he must have a fixed place of abode.'

Abroad was a huge and heavy concept for most Chinese people, especially if they came from remote provinces and small towns. But my new heroes, such as Hemingway and Whitman, all came from abroad. Not only that, but Hemingway himself was always venturing away from his home town. And Whitman spent all day wandering around the wilderness, naked and singing about love. Going abroad seemed to be the very definition of freedom. Contrary to Confucius' wisdom, I was determined to travel the Nine Continents whether my parents were alive or not! And once you'd made it out, who cared if you had a home to go back to – that home would be travelling with you! Life flows like a river. Home is for old people. I secretly cursed this worship of Confucianism. The more I studied what Confucius had said, the more I loathed this ancient man and his rotten words. It was a philosophy as depressing as the fates of my suicidal grandfather and my hunchbacked grandmother. I felt bored and imprisoned at school, and wondered how such a book had managed to root itself so fundamentally in the lives of the Chinese people for the last 2,400 years, even in the Communist so-called New China!

Wei nu zi yu xiao ren nan yang – '*Of all people, women and petty servants are the most difficult to deal with. If you are close to them, they lose their humbleness. If you maintain a reserve towards them, they grow discontented and complain.*'

The boys often quoted this at the girls in my class. I detested those lines, but they had been used as weapons like this for over two millennia. No wonder women had been so brutally treated and nonconformists so relentlessly prosecuted. Years later, I was to find solace in the words of Juliet Mitchell's 1971 book *Women's Estate*. She talked about how the traditional family structure has built upon the systematic exploitation and suppression of women, and how a patriotic society was based on the sacrifice of women's freedom. This lady must have studied *The Analects* and found that passage, I remember thinking. At that age, I didn't know such oppression was common in both East and West. I didn't even know that in many advanced Western countries, abortion was still illegal.

For me, the life Confucius had led seemed much more interesting than his dogmas. The details remained obscure, and so much about him sounded fictional. For example, it is said he died when he was seventy-two. But it is also said that he had seventy-two disciples. Was that a coincidence? If Confucius had indeed made it to seventy-two, he lived to be a very old man for someone born around 2,500 years ago. A miraculous survival even, considering the tigers and lions that roamed the land. But maybe it was only improbable, not impossible. I found it hard to trust much of our notorious historical archive; besides, so much of it had been burnt in the 1960s during the Cultural Revolution. Another thing that troubled me was this idea that Confucius was a great politician. Clearly nonsense; he was a failure. He may have been an important minister in the state of Lu, but he exercised no military power. The official version went that his career was interrupted by a power struggle within the court, partly caused by the conflicts of the warring kingdoms. Confucius left the state of Lu and went into exile, spending the rest of his days wandering from one kingdom to another, looking for a ruler who might employ him. So he was just another desperate longterm-unemployed man. Since no one took him on, he had to inflict his knowledge on the young, amassing his seventy-two disciples. It seems his main concern was to exercise authority over others. In that respect he was like all the other power-seekers. Seen in this light, it's pretty obvious why Confucianism has been so favoured by the emperors of China, including leaders of the Communist Party. Chinese autocracy clothes itself in the core teachings of the Master with these lines: '*The mind of the superior man is conversant with righteousness; the mind of the mean man is conversant with gain.*' Pretty good for an emperor who wants to bolster his right to rule.

My Chinese class now left me feeling flat, deadened and slightly drowsy. It was as if life had been squeezed out of me. I needed to read something I loved to re-energise myself. I would quickly return to my beloved Beat Generation poets, such as Allen Ginsberg and Frank O'Hara. They had been introduced to Chinese readers with a very modern translation and were wildly popular among the educated young. I loved how direct and simple a Western poem could be, and I sought to make my own writing in its image. I wanted my words to capture the rawness of life. Yes I wanted to be a poet, but not a dead Tang Dynasty intellectual, nor a disciple of Confucius. I wanted to use a real-life language, one with absolute modernity. And I was serious. While the other students played sports after school, I hid myself in corners and imitated the Western poetry I was reading.

1989

1989 was an eventful, anguished year. I was sixteen, and I remember it began with the news that the new American President George H. W. Bush would visit our leader Deng Xiaoping in Beijing. The television repeated footage of their meetings as well as the state banquet held in the president's honour. Change was in the air, and it seemed like everyone was paying extra attention to politics in the capital.

That May, news came that students across China had taken to the streets in many of its largest cities, reciting poetry and delivering carefully composed speeches demanding an end to corruption. In Beijing, the leaders of the movement shouted their slogans in front of Mao's mausoleum, addressing the then general secretary, Zhao Ziyang. This protest had been going on for a month when the hunger strikes began. Watching the news with my parents, I secretly wished I could go to Beijing and be a part of the revolution. As Mao said, 'History is an empty book waiting for us to fill its pages.' But Beijing was a long way away from my home town, three days by bus and train to be precise. My parents would never allow me to go, though my brother, now eighteen, was studying fine art there. He phoned home a week before the massacre, throat dry and voice high.

'Yes, of course I've joined the revolution! I have been on the square shouting slogans for weeks now!'

He talked in a breathless torrent and hung up before my father could respond. So we sat and watched it unfold on the television, until the violence of 4 June erupted. Deng Xiaoping ordered an end to the whole thing. The party declared martial law and mobilised 300,000 troops from the People's Liberation Army. That day, we watched soldiers with machine guns storm the square. Then the tanks appeared. They were rolling into the crowds of students. Before our eyes, the movement turned into a massacre. The state channels denounced the movement as a 'counter-revolutionary riot', and the shooting began. People were screaming and running from the gunfire. A few hours later, that glorious square fell silent. Bodies lay sprawled on the ground, blood stained the paving stones, tanks burned, banners lay destroyed, and the wave of students had receded.

We had lost contact with my brother. The last images we had seen were of tanks rolling into the square. My parents panicked. There were no mobile phones and no Internet in those days. I remember my mother crying one morning, standing by the phone. She was terrified of what was about to come. Three days later, my brother called, his voice almost inaudible.

'I'm fine, just hungry.' He was calling from a roadside stall near the university. Classes had been cancelled as the professors were being hauled in for investigation, he said as he swallowed a mouthful of noodles. He had lost his voice from screaming slogans. 'Don't worry about me,' he said and hung up, just as my father was trying to prise the phone from my mother's tight grip.

A few months later, we heard that some of the student leaders had been imprisoned: Wang Dan from Beijing University had been sentenced to four years, and political activists Chen Zimin and Wang Juntao to thirteen years. Some had fled China for the West. Students like my brother ended up having to write weekly self-criticisms. Public gatherings were banned. And the universities added extra hours across all departments for political studies classes focused on 'Chinese Socialist Democracy', and what made it distinct from Western democracy.

After the massacre we learned that Zhao Ziyang, our much respected general secretary of the Chinese Communist Party, had been sacked by Deng Xiaoping for his sympathetic stance towards the students. He spent the next fifteen years under house arrest until his death in 2005. It felt as if the Cultural Revolution had returned. Although my brother played no significant role in the events, and had never been threatened with state punishment, it cast a cloud of worry over my family. For the sake of our future, they never mentioned to anyone that my brother had been on Tiananmen Square that spring.

Things changed at school, even in Wenling. Teachers started leading readings of *People's Daily* editorials every Wednesday afternoon, lecturing us endlessly in carping tones about Beijing government policy. My already dull Wednesday afternoons were transformed into exercises in stultification. I sat in the heat and sweat along with sixty other classmates, packed into one room, thinking: what is this all for? Just like my schoolmates, I would never read a copy of *People's Daily* of my own volition. And I doubted I would ever do so in the future. It was just pages of dead language. To read it was to feel your mind shutting down and space closing in until you were sealed inside a tomb. I could see that the other students were also melting in the deadening boredom. One thing was clear: after 1989, young people became noticeably politically indifferent and pragmatic. Everyone wanted to just get on with life, to finish their studies, find a stable job and survive.

Ticket to the Film World

Gradually I began to feel that I could reinvent myself. I was eighteen but I had already published a dozen or so poems in literary magazines. In one of them, entitled 'Red', I imitated Frank O'Hara. Its opening lines went:

> *The day that my mother died, I passed a peasant selling*
> *   red nectarines.*
> *I bought one from him and said my mother had died.*
> *He answered: Have this one for free.*
> *I ate it in the street, and found it had a worm.*

Of course, I didn't dare show this poem to my mother. Another, entitled 'Nomad Heart', ended with:

> *I don't like living in a house:*
> *A kitchen with four stiff chairs around a square table*
> *A bedroom with a damp mattress and a spittoon*
> *A corridor full of muddy shoes and broken umbrellas*
> *A wind blows in one door and out the other*
> *The dust of time collects on the windowsills*
> *A house is not a place for a nomad heart*
> *Only the road can be its home*
> *Only the bare fields its abode*

My father read the poem. He seemed to like it. 'Sometimes I feel the same way.' That was his only comment, but for me, it was enough. It was like some sort of secret code between father and daughter: we understood each other, though we didn't want to debase this understanding with words. Besides, my mother would hear us if we launched into a conversation about why we didn't like living in this house, a house largely constructed by her.

I also managed to publish a few short stories. One of the stories was called 'Far Away, that Aimless River'. I imagined myself as a university student in Beijing, a bohemian in the capital. But I had no real ending for my character, perhaps because I couldn't picture my own future – she was lost in a flow of aimless actions, a life going nowhere.

Writing had been one of my closest spiritual companions, but I wanted to do something new, and my feet were itching to get out and away from the south. When the national exams came around, I didn't apply to study literature, but set my sights instead on film, at the Beijing Film Academy. Why film? everyone asked me. Films seemed to belong to a fantasy world, like an astronaut flying his spaceship to the moon. We had never met anyone in Wenling who made films. It was a decision that surprised even my father. But in my head, one thing was clear: I wanted to be part of *the new*. I needed to study something artistic, something of which I had no knowledge or access. In the early 1990s, film-making was the most modern art form in China, the newest media format. We watched Russian dubbed films such as *Brothers Karamazov*, *Wartime Romance* and *Moscow Does Not Believe in Tears*. I thought they were great, and to me cinema had an immediacy and direct power unavailable to literature. I was desperate to break into that mysterious, seductive world.

But passing the exams for the film school would be an enormous challenge. At that time the only film school in China was the Beijing Film Academy. You had to physically go to Beijing and stay there for two weeks: they tested us on subjects ranging from screenwriting, film history and theatre to visual and sound aesthetics, as well as general artistic aptitude. Although I didn't know anything about the history of cinema, I managed to gather nearly all the books about cinema in Wenling Library and began to prepare. My mother didn't support my ambitions. For her, paying the train fare to and from Beijing, plus the hotel, was a waste of money. But my father supported me and said he would accompany me to the capital. In the meantime, I was totally consumed by my reading. One of the more annoying aspects of my chosen field was having to memorise the names of famous foreign directors – John Ford and Billy Wilder – along with the titles of their films. Chinese translates foreign names phonetically into characters, so John Ford became *Yue Han Fu Te* – 约翰福特, and Billy Wilder became *Bi Li Wang Er De* – 比利怀尔德. My head felt like it was splitting in two as I attempted to commit these odd and artificial names to memory. But I was determined to do it even if it felt like driving nails into my skull. I spent weeks like this, my face fixed ten centimetres away from the page.

When the time for the exams came, my father and I embarked on the journey. We would have an eight-hour bus ride to Hangzhou, the capital city of our province, and from Hangzhou we would have a two-day train ride to Beijing. I saw nothing outside the train window nor any of the sights of Beijing, because every minute was given over to my books.

During those manic two weeks, my father rented a cheap basement hotel room in Beijing. Our room cost eight yuan a night and had no windows, no toilet and no shower. All it contained were two hard single beds, each with a sunken pillow, and a naked bulb that hung from the damp ceiling. On the morning of the first exam, my father and I got up early and ate four pork buns each at a roadside store. Then we wiped our mouths clean and entered the campus like soldiers going into battle. It was six o'clock in the morning, but thousands of people were gathered, hopeful youngsters like me accompanied by parents and even grandparents. There was a strained intensity in everyone's body language. We were overwhelmed by the scene and I instantly fell into a panic. Then, at eight o'clock sharp, two exam officers stood up on a ladder, and one yelled out across the sea of people:

'Everyone participating in the exam will be given a number! Please look for your number on the chalkboard over there!'

The officer pointed and the mass moved like an oceanic wave towards the supposed chalkboard. My father dragged me through the mayhem and we found it. Standing on our tiptoes, we searched through a great array of numbers and names, until we spotted 'Guo Xiaolu' followed by my date of birth. Number 5001. Out of six thousand. I didn't know there would be six thousand students participating in the two-week-long ordeal. All for seven available places in five departments! That morning, the six thousand participants were distributed across different rooms in the campus for the first exam. Parents and grandparents had to wait outside. We were handed our exam papers – a stack of sheets with questions such as: *How did the Hollywood film industry rejuvenate its creativity by adopting the methods of European cinema? Give one or two examples to demonstrate your point.* Every night, the teachers whittled down the numbers and announced who would be called back the next morning. We may have been used to our highly competitive social system, but still, we were like rats running through the streets in a headless panic. I survived the first three days of written examinations. On the fourth day, the lecturers began face-to-face interviews, which would enable them to get an impression of everyone's personality. During one of those sessions, I was told I was out of the game. I had failed the 'Theatre Study' exam because I hadn't known who Stanislavski was, and what 'Method Acting' meant. I walked out and went to find my father. He was as disappointed as me. As some teachers called out the next numbers, a film professor came up to us. He patted me on the shoulder. 'Don't be too sad, number 5001,' he said in perfect Mandarin, 'you were doing well in the other subjects. You can come back to try again next year!'

What? Next year! My heart was bursting. I couldn't just go back to Wenling. My mother would now feel justified in undermining my ambitions completely. Besides, what about the cost of the hotel, our meals and the train tickets? Who would pay for those next time? I was so hurt by the result that I burst into tears before the professor. My father took me downstairs. Once outside, we took one last glance at my number, 5001, slightly faded after being up on the chalkboard for four days. As we left, I saw several other young people my age, also in tears, their grey-faced parents beside them.

But my father wasn't defeated. He took me to a bookshop near the film school and bought a dozen books about cinema and art for me, including a copy of Stanislavski's biography. Ah, now I've got you – Konstantin Sergeyevich Stanislavski – you arrogant Russian imperialist! How I hate you! I swore in my heart. Soon I will conquer you! As I put the heavy books into my bag, I realised that they were a luxury for a provincial kid like me. 'We will be back next year, when you've finished reading all those books!' my father said.

We slept for most of the journey back to the south. We were utterly worn out. But once we were back in Wenling, my will grew even stronger. I spent days and nights studying. My father got his friends to gather any available books on film and theatre they could find – I read about Bertolt Brecht and Orson Welles. I had never seen any productions of their work, but I set myself the task of becoming 'an expert' nevertheless. I could recite the plot of *The Good Woman of Sichuan*, even though I was very confused as to why a German playwright had written a story set in the Chinese province of Sichuan. Then I memorised 'The Tragedy of Kane: Individualism under Laissez-Faire Capitalism', a Chinese academic study of *Citizen Kane* by a professor called Wang Jingsheng. I even overcame my aversion to Stanislavski, making connections between his theory of method acting and my mother's revolutionary opera performances. First-hand knowledge was not important. An unstoppable stream of regurgitated detail would, I hoped, more than satisfy the examiners.

Another year passed with my face buried in the books. Against my mother's will, my father once again accompanied me to Beijing. We stayed in the same basement hotel room. Yet again, I saw nothing of the city. I endured the same almost unbearable tension of daily exams and results. But this time, my number, 3777, kept reappearing on the chalkboard. The total number of applicants had increased to 7,100; one thousand more would fail this year than last. But I managed to stay in contention until the very end. Once the exams and interviews were over, we were told to go home and to wait two more months until the professors had made their final selection.

During those two months, my father was as nervous as me, because he knew this would be my last chance. He couldn't afford another trip. If I failed this time, I would have to become a factory worker, just like my mother. But on that fateful early-summer morning, when my father took the letter from my shaking hands and opened it, he erupted with relief and joy. I had gained one of eleven places in the Film and Literature Department of the Beijing Film Academy. I was in ecstasy. I had managed to beat seven thousand candidates from across China and had earned my place at the best art school in the country.

Leaving the South

August 1993 was the last summer I spent in the sweaty, drowsy south. Term started on 1 September. I could hardly wait any longer. My body was still part of the heavy, brown earth but my mind had already flown to the moon. I listened to news of Beijing and the outside world, and felt I no longer belonged to this mass in Wenling. It seemed to me that important things, momentous things, were happening that year, but no one in Wenling gave a damn about them. Months earlier, Beijing had welcomed our new president Jiang Zemin, who appeared so very grand on television, despite being much less popular than our previous president, Deng Xiaoping. But the people of Wenling hadn't even realised there had been a change of leadership in Beijing. That same month, the moon had passed at its closest distance to Earth in recent history, and thus was at its fullest phase of the lunar cycle. Scientists said that it would appear 14 per cent bigger and 30 per cent brighter than any recent moon. That special night in March, my father and I climbed up into the bamboo-covered hills behind our house and took in the brightest moon we had ever seen.

It was so large we could make out its shadowy, cratered surface. Just as we were about to leave, I stood on the hilltop and screamed to the world beneath: 'Can you see the moon tonight? It's brighter and bigger than it's ever been!' My father laughed in response. But the world below was oblivious to my cry. The town of Wenling had been numbed by the throbbing sound of factory machines, traffic, chatter, all the mundanity of material life.

On the day I was leaving for Beijing my parents walked me to the local long-distance bus station. My mother had sewn three hundred yuan into the inner pocket of my sweater the night before, and my father was carrying two bags for me. I had a long trip ahead of me, and this time I would be alone. With mosquitoes biting at my skin, my hair knotted and tangled, I grabbed the bags from my father's hands and jumped onto the bus. Then I heard my mother yell behind me: 'Make sure you eat plenty of lamb and garlic in Beijing, and drink blood soup!'

I looked at my mother and nodded as I hurried into my seat. Despite everything, my mother was proud of me. At least she cared about some aspects of my future. She knew that I suffered from low blood pressure. Lamb, blood and garlic were supposed to be good for a skinny girl like me. It was some sort of farewell at least, from the mother I had never loved. She was practical, that was all I could say about her.

Then my father waved through the bus window and called: 'Write to me!' Yes, of course, I said in my heart. Of course I would write to my father. He was the only person I would think of writing to in the whole world. No one else. He was the only man I trusted. My parents sent me off without the merest 'Study hard', the standard farewell for most Chinese parents. They knew they didn't need to say it. I was too ambitious to waste this opportunity. I had always wanted to be number one, I was an aggressive competitor. And this brutal competitiveness was probably rooted in the harshness of my childhood.

I was nineteen and a half when I finally left my home town for Beijing. The three-day journey to the capital was emotionally taxing. I was travelling into the unknown and into my adult life. It was with relief that I left behind my distressed teenage years. After the eight-hour bus ride, I sat for another seventeen hours on the train, absorbed in the world rushing past the window. This time I didn't read any books – I could barely sit still. I felt only like writing, a poem to China's rivers and plains. The landscape slowly evolved from the poetic to the utilitarian. Although, in reality, China in 1993 was more like an enormous construction site full of grey concrete foundations and rising factories. By dawn's early light, the train crossed the Yangtze River and stopped at the city of Nanjing. I got up from my seat, stretched my neck and looked down at the muddy yellow water. The Yangtze, the great border between north and south China, the longest river in Asia, the very river Chairman Mao had chosen to swim across, a river that had carried with it a thousand legends east to the sea. 'I've made it!' I cried out. 'Fuck! I got out! Beijing, I'm coming! Independence! Freedom!'

I arrived and delved straight into plates and plates of lamb, blood tofu and garlic. I had taken my mother's words to heart. I felt strong. I wanted to become someone big, in a big capital of a big country. I didn't miss anything about Wenling, even though I often dreamt that I was walking through its bamboo forests, trying to find the fishpond where we used to play as children. The laughter rang so loud and vivid in those nightly visions, and the bamboo shimmered in the steamy summer air. But I was never to see that landscape in person again, it lived now only in my sleep.

My parents, on a mountainside near Wenling, 1980s

PART III | Beijing: The Whirlpool of Life

The pilgrim team led by the master monk Xuangzang had been trudging for eighteen months on the long Silk Road. They had made their way through uninhabited land with deep gorges and high mountains, fearsomely difficult to cross. Only the monkey, Wukong, the Emptiness Knower, was not deterred by these difficulties. Through the energy that had accumulated in his body over centuries, Wukong possessed an immense amount of strength. He was able to lift objects many times his own weight. He was also extremely fast – with one somersault he could spring across a gorge. He could transform into seventy-two different shapes, which allowed him to take on the form of any animal, plant life or object. Yet the monkey was not always reliable. His cunning and trickster personality would get his companions into trouble and he was frequently distracted from the path of virtue along the road.

On one occasion, while the group was crossing the border into Afghanistan, Wukong saw a forest of ripe peaches in the distance and fell into an ecstasy. He flew off and disappeared into the peach forest for three days, devouring the fruits and playing with wild animals he found there, leaving his companions on a bare mountain path to starve and freeze. The monkey was also violent. He would brutally kill small innocent creatures for fun and would not feel the slightest mercy in his heart.

Xuanzang, the master monk, understood that the creature was too wild to be disciplined and he decided to find a way to control *him. So he made a magical, invisible headband for the monkey to wear, which could never be removed. With a special chant, the headband would tighten and tighten around Wukong's head, and cause unbearable pain. With the magical band on his head, the monkey would lose his immense power while the master chanted. Wukong, the Emptiness Knower, had no choice but to obey his master's authority. Thus the journey continued.*

My first year at Beijing Film Academy, 1993

Away From Home

I left the south for Beijing in 1993. I was turning twenty. In my young eyes, the great northern capital had little to do with the Forbidden City or imperial palaces. Beijing for me meant the avant-garde. It was the only place in China where you could see Western art and European cinema. Since up to now I had spent all my time studying the old, here in the capital all I wanted was to study the *new*. I wanted to go beyond all tradition, conservatism and its history. I would cut away the past and become someone else.

My journey ended at Beijing South Train Station. It was early morning on the last day of a steaming hot August. First I saw yellow chrysanthemum flowers blooming in pots along the station platform. Then I saw the university flags being waved by the students tasked with welcoming us newbies. They all wore bright white hats to distinguish themselves from the general throng of travellers. I spotted a blue-and-white flag with the Beijing Film Academy emblem on it, and I dragged my luggage towards the animated-looking figure beneath it.

As the film-school bus moved through a congested Beijing morning, I immediately noticed the different light in the capital. It was much sharper, carving out each thing more precisely. Everything was in soft focus in the south. Or was it the new glasses I was wearing, bought for me by my father before I had left Wenling? In any case, for me, only this kind of light could inspire revolutionary acts. I was sure I could feel myself beginning to transform already. What would I become? I asked myself. I was going to be an artist, but what kind of artist? A film director? A cinematographer? A screenwriter?

We arrived at the film school and I checked in to my dormitory. It was a massive building. Boys and girls were separated on different floors. Each room was shared by four students on two bunk beds. Everyone was given five objects by our dorm supervisor: a quilt, a pillow, a small desk, a wooden chair and a bookshelf. No one was allowed to bring in any extra furniture due to the limited living space. My room-mates had not arrived yet. I chose a lower bunk by the window and proceeded to set up with my meagre possessions. I had brought with me my father's books, *Lust for Life* and Whitman's *Leaves of Grass* which I put on the bookshelf.

Class started two days later. We were introduced to our professors and I met my ten classmates – the lucky eleven finally gathered in one room. Among us was a young man called Jia Zhangke, who would later become one of China's most famous directors of independent films. The professor who welcomed us said: 'Always remember, you have been chosen from thousands of applicants. Don't waste this opportunity, which you have won by your hard work. You will be the future of Chinese cinema!' We looked back at him solemnly. My heart was racing. I nodded my head earnestly.

And yet, I could not really get into my studies right away, because I didn't have any experience with cinema in general. I remember vividly the film we watched on that first day. It was the black-and-white French film *Last Year in Marienbad*, directed by Alain Resnais and written by Alain Robbe-Grillet. The film was undubbed and without subtitles, so we were provided with a simultaneous oral translation read by a lecturer sitting below the screen. He read the dialogue as well as the voice-over in a sleepy monotone. It was a bizarre experience, especially for our poor young minds from the provinces, having no idea what the film was about and what the obscure voice-over was supposed to mean. Besides, class was in the afternoon, straight after a considerable lunch. I had probably eaten two bowls of pork noodles plus a plate of dumplings before entering the darkened cinema. Eating had always been an obsession, ever since I was a child. And here in Beijing, with the dirt cheap student canteen, I would be able to indulge this obsession on an epic scale.

Stomachs suitably loaded, we listened to the lecturer murmur through a microphone:

'*Ah, you never seem to be waiting for me, but we kept meeting at every turn of the path. Behind every bush, at the foot of each statue, near every pond. It is as if it had been only you and I in all that garden. No, I have never met you, no, I was not waiting for you . . .*'

It sounded poetic, although it was also like listening to an old man suffering from dementia. Sunk deep in my seat, I could only guess wildly what the characters were saying. The people on the screen walked around in one scene like zombies. Marienbad was a kind of geometrical mausoleum with a garden of dark, frozen trees. How had the two main characters, the man and the woman, got there? And who were these people walking around this dimly lit, expensive-looking hotel with endless corridors and waiting rooms as if in a trance and talking to themselves? As the noodles made their way through my digestive system, my eyelids grew heavier and heavier. Soothed by the lullaby of the lecturer's voice, I drifted off. I dreamt I was lost in the corridors of Beijing's own Summer Palace, with a large golden-walled room that exited onto a rocky shoreline of the kind we had in my fishing village. I seemed to melt into the sea. Sometime later, I woke up and found the students around me were also asleep. Some were snoring loudly. The lecturer was still reading the transcript in his heavy peasant accent by the light of a little lamp. His Hunan intonation was just like Chairman Mao's. In my dozy semi-consciousness, I imagined Mao's ghost had returned to provide voice-overs for *nouvelle vague* cinema. Somehow that seemed appropriate. Mao had been a poet and a revolutionary. But even this startling thought was unable to jolt me awake, and I surrendered fully to my unconscious, just as the dream-like characters of the film.

So that was my introduction to the next seven years at film school – not that I disapprove of it now. In fact, it was the beginning of a growing sense in me that cinema didn't actually have that much to do with telling stories; it is a visual art form, and yet many people mistreat cinema as a mere engine of story. And of course, one should never see a film after a large lunch.

Over the next weeks, we sat through a long procession of classics of European and early American cinema, from the first film in history by the Lumière Brothers, to Cecil B. DeMille's silent films. Then D. W. Griffith's *Birth of a Nation*, the films of Charlie Chaplin and Buster Keaton, Vertov's *Man with a Movie Camera*, Murnau's *Nosferatu*, Eisenstein's *Battleship Potemkin*. Normally, these films would never have made it past the censorship laws. (At that time, the China Film Censorship Bureau would only allow eight foreign films per year to be distributed into Chinese cinemas. And without a doubt, these would never have been deemed sufficiently 'full of the positive spirit of human life' in the way that *Forrest Gump* or Disney's *Lion King* were.) But we had certain privileges; we had access to them for 'research purposes'. Through them, and old Chinese films from the 1930s, we studied technique, *mise en scène*, close-up and tracking shots, and the dizzying montage effect first realised with success on the Odessa steps by Eisenstein. Before coming to Beijing, I had only ever seen what was available in my local cinema in Wenling, with its steady stream of war dramas and martial arts films, as well as the state television. The visual world opening up to me was beyond my imagination. My days at the Beijing Film Academy became one long dream made up of thousands of black-and-white images.

Beijing

The capital was manic in those days, building ring roads and inner-city highways. The Third Ring Road outside the Second Ring Road, then the Fourth Ring Road outside the Third. Each project involved armies of cheap labour. And yet amid all the dust of the construction work, the old ways carried on: tea houses and quiet parks with people playing mah-jong and practising tai chi; food stalls scattered along the streets both day and night; snaking *hutong* alleys with families squashed inside date-tree-covered courtyards. Life was rough and basic. Winters were long and hard. The shelves of the state-run department stores stocked only three kinds of vegetables: leeks, bai choi and potatoes. Meat was not always available. At night, we secretly burned our small spirit stove with a little cooking pot on top. It was forbidden in the dormitory as it might cause fires. But we were adding bai choi to instant noodles in an attempt to fill our stomachs before sleep.

When spring came, the sandstorms from the Gobi Desert blasted the city with such a force that no one wanted to stay outside. Even though the government planted millions of paulownia trees between Beijing and Inner Mongolia, the skies of Beijing were still a permanent grey-brown and speckled with sand and dust. Then came the hot summer, the forty-degree heat melting the asphalt outside. It was a hard city, *comfort* was not a part of our daily vocabulary. But for a village person like me, I couldn't have cared less. I spent my days in the film school reading about Godard and Duras and watching every film in the library. I was thirsty for knowledge. When I looked around at my fellow schoolmates, all urban kids, I realised that this was my re-education camp, a place to wash out my peasant origins.

In the 1990s Beijing was full of 'body artists' as we called them, making shocking and grotesque performances in public out of their naked forms. The Chinese for performance art, *xing wei yi shu*, literarily translates as 'behaviour art', and it fitted with what was extreme behaviour for post-Mao China. Some people also referred to it as 'shock art'. But whatever the name, those works laid bare a tension between the individual and the state at that time. I loved those crazy performances. But they were illegal, because so many of them involved nudity and sexual acts and attracted foreign expats as their main audience. On many occasions, the artists and police played 'hide-and-seek', though the game was not much fun for either side.

Yellow Pavilion was a coffee bar near the film school where poets and film-makers would hang out. I went there often, spending my Saturday afternoons reading novels or getting used to the taste of Nescafé instant coffee, which was a new discovery for me. One day, in the bar, I heard that a collective of body artists would be performing on the Great Wall at the weekend. The exact time had not yet been announced. It depended on the police. So I moved my chair towards the conversation and asked if I could join them. They looked at me, and nodded.

On the morning of the show, we bought some fruit and red-bean buns and left the city by bus. We thought we'd better get to the Wall as early as possible so we wouldn't miss anything. It was my first time there, and my heart was bursting with excitement. The white, papery wild grass that grew up through the cracks between the bricks, the ancient stone paths, the distant powdery-blue mountains, the eagles circling in the sky above our heads, and the capital in the distance, all added to my feelings of expectation.

As we arrived at the place where the performance was to take place, we saw some long-haired young artists roaming around in the raw spring wind. A few Western journalists were waiting with their cameras for something to happen. We didn't see any sign of the police, but there could have been undercover officers there without us knowing. Perhaps standing around smoking, making notes to report back later.

Suddenly, without fanfare, the first artist appeared. He produced his ID card and read every detail printed on it in a solemn and majestic voice; the fifteen-digit ID number became a Tang Dynasty poem. Then he used an ink brush and painted his ID number all over his body, including his face. But this was only a prelude. He then sat down and, with help from another artist, tattooed the string of numbers on his belly. Since there were fifteen numbers, it took some time. We watched the blood dripping down his skin. One young girl in the crowd screamed and fainted on the thousand-year-old stones. Two of her friends had to carry her down the hill. The artist was undeterred. Once finished, he stood before us, a numbered pig on the collective farm ready to be dispatched to slaughter the next day.

'Our bodies no longer belong to ourselves,' he declared. 'We are nothing but slaves of the state.' He pointed to the tattooed numbers on his skin. 'Our identity number is the only valid thing that follows us through life. We are reduced to nothing but a string of fucking numbers.'

Most of us agreed with what he was saying, but remained silent out of respect.

The second performance involved an artist eating a placenta. He announced that the placenta had been taken straight from the hospital – from an aborted baby. He set up a table in front of everyone with a small stove and a wok. He then chopped the placenta into small pieces and stir-fried them. He added soy sauce, salt and pepper like he was cooking pork chops. Two members of the audience whispered something in disapproval, which the artist heard.

'If the state can violently and legally abort a mother's unborn baby, why can't I eat the placenta? Which one is more obscene?'

No one dared challenge him. We just stood there and watched him ritualistically finish the whole plate.

The third performance was just as startling. A long-haired young man suddenly presented himself. He wore heavy make-up: white face powder, blue eyeshadow and scarlet lips. He stripped bare, revealing his penis: it was painted red. He then threw himself on the ground and began humping it like an animal. He called this piece 'Fuck China's Extraordinary History'. After a few minutes of thrusting and moaning, he launched himself into a mad, nude sprint. Like a tribal man, he ran along the Great Wall, his red penis swaying violently. He screamed and howled. The journalists raised their cameras – surely this could make the cover of *Time* magazine.

But just at that moment, we suddenly found ourselves surrounded by cops. Someone must have reported the activities to the authorities while we were too busy being transfixed by the artist's public lovemaking. The police didn't look terribly threatening. They seemed to be following protocol, asking everyone to show their ID cards or passports. So there we were, as the artist was running naked along the Wall, our details being taken down one by one. Everybody stood, solemn and obedient. No one fought back, and the police didn't think it necessary to make a show of power. The running penis would be back soon enough and they would get his ID number too.

Then we heard laughing.

'You see?' It was the first artist with the new tattoo. 'Even the police agree with me! We are all nothing but a string of numbers!'

We watched as two policemen took out their electric batons. My heart trembled. Everyone was instantly silent.

A few weeks later, I was summoned to speak to the discipline department of the film school. They asked if I had participated in an illegal gathering on the Great Wall recently. Yes, I said, and explained that I wanted to have a real artistic experience rather than only watch French new wave films with sexy actresses in them. The head of the discipline department smiled, noting down what I had said. His deputy came in with a lunch box of pork buns, and he let me go.

By a Waterfall, There Are Swimmers . . .

By a waterfall, I'm calling you.
We can share it all beneath a ceiling of blue.
We'll spend a heavenly day
Here where the whispering waters play.
There's a whipper will that's calling you.
By a waterfall, he's dreaming too.
There's a magic melody
Mother Nature sings to me
Beside a waterfall with you.

The song was from an old Hollywood musical, *Footlight Parade*, which we were watching in our set-production class one morning. It was a black-and-white film from 1933. The school had only a very scratchy videotape with blurry images, but for a provincial kid like me, it was mesmerising. I was astonished to see attractive, half-naked Western girls filmed from all sorts of fancy angles swimming and dancing in great pools. Then the film's most famous scene arrived: hundreds of seemingly free-spirited female bodies formed a human waterfall. The choreographer was a celebrated director called Busby Berkeley, the teacher said, and he liked to create visual fantasies out of hundreds of showgirls. We watched another of his films, *Gold Diggers of 1933*, and I was again amazed by the beautiful bodies and unbridled freedom of the dancers.

I had never been the kind of girl who had much awareness of her own physical being. I barely paid attention to my body. The mirrors in our house in Wenling were always too high for me to catch a glimpse of myself, anyway. During puberty, shame was my overwhelming feeling: I associated menstruation and growing breasts with aches and pains. I covered my chest with oversized jackets, usually passed down from my brother. Nor did I pay any attention to my hair, my face or the look of my legs. I had never bought myself cosmetics. But when I came to Beijing, I started looking in the mirror more often. Every morning, as I regarded my face in the dormitory mirror, I saw my mother. How much I loathed that face, the face of ignorance and violent, brusque manners. It was hers: my mother's peasant cheekbones and rude eyebrows, as well as her short neck. I wanted my own, I wanted to be met in the mirror by someone else every morning. I always knew I was far from being a so-called beauty. But this new environment, and the fantastic musicals we saw at film school, filled my head with plans and a new-found faith. I wanted to know my body. I also wanted to learn to swim. I wanted to wear a sexy bikini, jump into a pool and open myself up like a water lily. Thanks to Busby Berkeley, I finally, at the age of twenty-one, lowered my body into the chlorinated water and discovered my own physical being.

Before that summer in Beijing, I had never tried to learn to swim. The only sport I grew up playing was ping-pong on make-shift brick tables. Ping-pong was considered the game of the people at that time.

In Beijing, I bought myself an old-fashioned one-piece swimsuit, as in those days the state-owned department stores didn't sell Western-style two-piece bikinis. The week after watching *Footlight Parade* and *Gold Digger*, my schoolmates and I jumped on our bikes and like a flock of gulls swooped down on the newly built pool at the University of Science and Technology.

There I was, standing in the shallow end of the pool, too scared to go any deeper. Nearby, a swimming teacher was yelling instructions to a group of young children.

'Don't be so scared! Chairman Mao swam across the Yangtze River when he was seventy-two years old!' He splashed water onto a boy's dry chest. 'If a seventy-two-year-old man can swim across such a big river, a young boy like you should be able to swim across an ocean!'

The boy looked visibly ashamed. 'But he was Chairman Mao!' he stammered.

But before he could even finish, the teacher had thrown him into the water. The boy shrieked with terror and I felt sorry for him. If we always had to measure ourselves against the Chairman, we would give up before trying. No one could compare with Mao, even though he had died fifteen years previously. He was our Superman, of course he could overcome any challenge, apart from death perhaps. I still remember one of the propaganda posters my parents had on their wall. It showed Mao wearing a bathrobe, having completed his heroic swim. *Follow Chairman Mao and Conquer the Wind and Waves!* The seventy-two-year-old had swum fifteen kilometres in sixty-five minutes it was reported. Even if I could swim, I thought, I could never imagine myself in the water like Chairman Mao surrounded by hundreds of young, wet Red Guards.

As I stood in the shallows, it struck me that the experience wasn't exactly turning out to be as glamorous as I had imagined; we weren't swimming under any waterfalls, nor being worshipped by adoring, singing men. I ducked my head quickly into the water, and started choking. Struggling like a dying chicken, I came up again. I needed time, time to understand the relationship between my body and the water, I told myself.

A week later, we were sitting in our film-theory class, discussing 'female presentation in Hollywood cinema'. Our teacher, a renowned professor named Dai Jinghua, showed us some clips of Rita Hayworth and Marilyn Monroe. We were admiring the pneumatic breasts and plunging necklines, the shimmering wavy hair, and the sculptured legs polished like porcelain on high heels. But then Professor Dai introduced us to the British feminist film theorist Laura Mulvey's essay 'Visual Pleasure and Narrative Cinema'. She muted the Rita Hayworth film, and read out aloud from the essay: 'mainstream film coded the erotic into the language of the dominant patriarchal order . . .' She paused and looked at us to see our response. But none of us said anything. Then she asked: 'What does Laura Mulvey mean when she says the sex of the camera is male, not female?'

I turned to the screen, where Marilyn Monroe was swinging her miniskirt with a shake of her perfect waistline, and smiling at the camera seductively.

Timidly, I raised my hand and answered with another quotation from Mulvey: 'She meant that *women are the image and men are the bearer of the look*. So women are the sexual objects of Hollywood films.'

'Yes, absolutely,' Professor Dai nodded. 'Most conventional Hollywood films are just like *Playboy* magazine, but with a bit of narrative.'

Playboy magazine. So far we'd never had the chance to see one for ourselves. Before the days of the Internet, Western magazines were definitely not available in China. I could only guess what it might be like. In truth, I longed to own a copy of *Play-boy*! It would at least prove that I knew a thing or two about the West. I couldn't help but wonder if Western girls were also subjected to the constant sexual harassment we Chinese girls in the countryside were. We didn't wear miniskirts or sexy dresses to seduce men, but we were abused by them nevertheless. In what sort of society had Rita Hayworth and Marilyn Monroe lived? Was it anything like ours, or completely different? These were the questions I took away with me after that class.

It was sunny and warm outside, and I suddenly felt light and free. I went to my dorm and put my swimming costume and a pair of slippers in my bag. Jumping on my bike, I once again headed towards my newly discovered swimming pool. As I rode through the old *hutongs*, no one seemed to notice me and I didn't mind at all. I actually enjoyed this seeming invisibility, the feeling of the wind stroking my skin, and the bubble of quietness around me in the midst of the congestion. When I got to the swimming pool, I saw the usual assortment of people. Some were doing laps with a military dedication, some were floating like seals, their black swimming caps bobbing in the shallows. What would my mother think of me now? I thought, as I entered the delicious water. She had never swum in a pool in her life. I tried for a moment to imagine her in a swimming costume, and wondered how she might have felt about her own body. Could she have allowed herself to experience this freedom from shame, for her body to feel so gloriously alive for even just a moment? I didn't answer my own question. Instead, I slipped below the rippling surface and slid through the blue-green water.

Girls in the Dark

One of the films we watched repeatedly at the Beijing Film Academy was *La Chinoise*. Jean-Luc Godard made the film in 1967, a year after the start of the Chinese Cultural Revolution. Godard's films were compulsory viewing, but there were many reasons why *La Chinoise* had been particularly singled out. For example, in the editing course, we analysed its 'jump cut' method and how Godard used montage to create a dynamic rhythm – in China then, we only edited from a traditional narrative point of view, making cinema something closer to a theatrical format. In production class, we were told to draw a storyboard for the film, or to produce a sketch of Godard's set; a fake Parisian apartment with open doors and connecting corridors, all decorated with white furnishings and lamps in primary colours to match the lead actress's bright clothing. In sound we discussed the use of music, which was interrupted like punctuation between scenes. The one thing we never, or barely, touched on, however, was its politics, which was surprising, given that it was supposed to be influenced by Maoist ideology! Maybe the teachers thought it too obvious to mention.

I felt strange and uncomfortable watching the film, not only because the glamorous French actress Anne Wiazemsky (a real Russian princess) and the funny-looking Jean-Pierre Leaud didn't look like they knew much about Mao, but because their revolutionary acts also felt so out of context. Paris seemed to bore them and so their actions seemed more akin to the Baader–Meinhof Gang, rather than 'a mass revolution of the proletariat' as we called it in China. It just felt silly watching Westerners pretend

they were taking part in the Chinese revolution. I wondered what
my father would have said about it. He probably would have been
angry and said something like: 'Westerners will never understand
the Chinese unless they too go through the misery and poverty
we did.' Or: 'If this French film-maker's parents had been sent
to a labour camp and had died there, he would never have made
a film with such a ridiculous tone.' Of course my father didn't
know that Godard was in fact from a wealthy Swiss family. Nor
did he know that there was a distinct difference between being
a French intellectual and a Chinese intellectual.

But the film made an impression on others in my class, especially a girl in the production department called Mengmeng. She
styled herself exactly like the lead actress: a navy-blue dress and
a 1960s fringe that skirted her eyebrows.

Mengmeng lived in the same room as me on campus. We
were on the sixth floor, four girls from different departments
squeezed into twenty-five square metres. Mengmeng slept in the
bunk above me. If she tossed around, my bed would shake as
if in an earthquake. If I said anything in my dreams, she would
cover her ears with her blanket. At that time, university dormi-
tories were like military camps; lots of rules and restrictions. A
loudspeaker had been set in the ceiling over the door, and it was
always announcing something, only shutting up at night. Most
of the time, it was merely repeating the school rules, with a male
voice in the morning and a female voice in the afternoon. But we
managed to bypass most of the decrees. We hid our guitars and
small sewing machines under our beds. At eleven in the evening,
the electricity was cut so that we would be forced to sleep. We lit
candles instead. It was the start of the witching hour; the dorm
descended into mayhem. Riots in the common washrooms and

toilets, chaos in the corridors and bedrooms. No one was in bed. People were washing, reading, chatting and playing music. Then in no time, the dorm supervisor would appear with his torch. Panic unleashed, a stampede from the bathrooms, along the narrow corridors back to our beds. We were like rats in the dark. The dorm supervisor kept a record of each room's level of night-time activity, and our grades would suffer if he found too much noise or mess. But once he was gone, we would rise again, lighting yet more candles or switching on a torch to read, or just lying in the dark and chatting.

The girls' dormitory was the first place I felt I wasn't alone, especially after one night in particular, when I told them about the sexual abuse I had suffered as a young girl.

'I can't exactly remember what happened to me. All I remember is the fear, the enormous fear and terror when his hands touched my body and fingered me,' I murmured, lying in my bunk in the dark, my eyes wide open.

'Same here.' I heard Mengmeng sitting up on her bunk. 'I know exactly what you mean. I hated the man who abused me and I still hate him, intensely. He lived next door. He was always coming into our house when my parents were away and groping me. He threatened to cut out my tongue if I told my parents. I wanted to kill him.' Her tone was furious, disgusted, as if it had happened only yesterday.

'You did better than me! At least you dared to hate the man, and not just feel scared,' another girl on the bed next to mine spoke up.

'Not really. I was too scared to tell my parents. It continued for a year or two until my father moved us away for business reasons. I don't know what would have become of me if we had remained in that house. I probably would have got pregnant or else become a murderer. Every day I prayed that man would die the worst kind of death. I imagined him falling naked on a razor-wire fence and his penis being sliced through in the most painful way.'

As the dormitory building grew quieter after midnight, we lay in the dark and waited for sleep to come. But it didn't. With an unspoken, but almost collective feeling, we girls were dreading these memories would return to us in our dreams. Mengmeng told me she experienced nightmares often. She described the images to me: an obscure space, a male hand, a vulgar gesture, an icy intrusion, breathing, all devoid of faces or narrative. Then she would wake up in a cold sweat, still trembling, her limbs paralysed. How familiar all this was! I couldn't have described it better! It seemed that all of us had experienced similar ordeals. Stories that remained untold except in the darkness of the girls' dormitory.

When I think back on those days now, it seems obvious that many Chinese girls then suffered such abuse, and so regard love as the opposite of sex: sex only represents the abusive and violent relationships between men and women, whereas love goes far beyond sex, and should really be asexual.

Mengmeng was always stylish and had good taste in fashion. Elegant, pale-skinned with long black hair, you would think that she came from a wealthy, urban family. But she was in fact a peasant's daughter from Shanxi, the home of coal and brown yams. Her family had ploughed fields for years and held no great hopes for their daughter's future. But Mengmeng had always been fascinated with cinema. Her parents must have loved her, since she seemed very attached to them. I noticed how they posted her food packages and clothes parcels, which only increased the disappointment I felt towards my own family. My parents barely ever sent me anything from Wenling.

Mengmeng's father visited once, bringing kilos of dried pork sausage which fed our room of four for a month. He seemed to be one of the smartest peasants in the country. Instead of tending to vegetables under the scorching sun and freezing rain, he began buying and selling. At the end of the 1990s, President Jiang Zemin created the Forum on China–Africa Cooperation and allocated big sums of money to the African development fund. Mengmeng's father bravely left China for Zambia because 'the land is very cheap in Africa'. It didn't matter much to him where he went – Zambia, Nigeria or any other African country were all the same to him, as he had no interest in the history or culture of the continent.

'My father went to Africa alone, leaving us behind. He worked very hard, even harder than he had in China,' Mengmeng told me. 'But within a year, he had managed to buy a huge piece of land in Zambia. It was an abandoned colonial farm. He hired locals to plant sugar cane, tea and tobacco. Imagine that!'

I was intrigued: how does a Chinese man who can't speak any foreign languages create such a large business in Africa? No one I knew then had ever been to Africa, it was simply beyond most people's imaginations. My only reference was the film *Out of Africa* by Sydney Pollack starring Robert Redford and Meryl Streep. It didn't look like the white people had a happy time there. And I couldn't imagine that us yellow people would fare any better, we were so clueless about the place.

'Isn't your father lonely, all the way over there without your mother?' I asked Mengmeng.

'My mother would rather die than go to Africa. I feel the same way . . .' Mengmeng paused, and didn't want to go on. Then she continued, her voice unsteady: 'My father probably has a mistress there. Last time my mother called him, a woman answered the phone. She sounded very young, with a Sichuan accent . . .'

I imagined this middle-aged Chinese man on his farm in Africa. A global peasant! How did the whole thing work? I was intrigued by how being a peasant could be combined with being a global business man.

'Anyway, now my father wants my brother to join him, to help run the business.'

'Does he want to go?'

'Are you kidding? He doesn't even know where Africa is! Africa is a step down for him, it's not America. But to be honest, he couldn't care less. He's bored with his current job and just wants to have some fun. But you can't have much fun in China. Too many rules!'

Yes, that was true, in China we didn't have much fun. Rigid rules trapped everyone. I always had thought Mengmeng a wise person, she was always coming out with wise statements like this. But in my case, being able to leave my stifling home town and study film in the capital was already freedom enough. I would also have liked to have more fun if only I knew how!

East Village

The performance on the Great Wall was only the beginning of my fascination with the underground art scene. I wanted desperately to be part of it, despite the fact that I was only a yokel from the countryside. At that time, all non-official art activities were banned by the state, everything from abstract painting to rock music. Typically the young rebels had long hair, wore hippyish clothes and lived in Beijing without a Beijing residence permit. The police raided residential areas and arrested people living in the city illegally. As a result, the artists went underground and hid themselves in small hamlets on the outskirts of Beijing.

I don't really know where the name East Village came from. It might have been inspired by New York's East Village. But Beijing's version was originally called Dashanzhuan, literally 'Big Hill Hamlet'. It was located in the eastern part of the city, between the third and fourth ring roads. In the 1990s, artists just casually referred to it as East Village, distinguishing it from the other artists' colony, West Village, near the Summer Palace.

The underground was what attracted me – I certainly wasn't going to become one of those state artists like my father. This was my generational statement. So, when in my second year at film school we were asked to produce a short film, I decided to make a documentary about the East Village artists. That way, I could make friends with them.

One May weekend, I carried a heavy video camera (one of those early Beta cameras from the lab in the film school) on various buses out east. I got off at the end of the bus route and looked around. The area was scruffy and downtrodden, the road like hundreds of thousands in other Chinese villages, with stray dogs running about. Buffalo shit replaced paving stones, and the poplar trees looked wilder and older than the ones in the city centre. Date trees were common in Beijing in those days, and here too they absorbed the spring sunlight to mature their still-raw fruits. Yellowing sorghum and wheat fields edged both sides of the bumpy road, along which came the occasional horse cart driven by a local peasant. This was 1994, when the outskirts of Beijing still looked very rural and felt poor. As I approached the village proper, shabby clay houses were dotted randomly in the landscape, their windows broken and papered over with old newspaper and cardboard to block the wind and sandstorms. There were no shops, let alone proper streets. Only broken beer bottles and scraps of metal. It was basically a slum, even by the standards of a village girl like me.

Yet the people were intimidating. I was only twenty-one years old. The camera was a shield, but I barely knew how to operate it. I passed a peasant carrying a hot pan on his bike, off to sell baked sweet potatoes in the market. I stopped and bought one, so that I could ask him whether he knew of any artists living in the area.

'Artists?' The sweet-potato seller raised his eyebrows, staring at me as if I were an alien: 'What artists?'

'You know, those people who paint and play very loud music.' I bit into the soft, piping-hot potato which had been wrapped in an ancient copy of *People's Daily*. It was crusty and very sweet.

'You mean those fucking mad young people who never cut their hair and walk around naked? They are like insane grasshoppers in the winter looking for rotten shit. They're always making a noise, drinking, and up to no good. They came knocking on our door in the middle of the night once, asking to borrow a big wok.'

The peasant was keen to get to market to sell his potatoes.

'Why did they want to borrow a wok?' I asked.

'What do you think, girl? They shot a fucking wild goat and skinned it in the middle of the night. They wanted to make a stew with our wok. They're always hungry, their eyes are like bulging frog-eyes! Just like a pack of wolves who haven't eaten for days! Crazy fuckers! But I have to say, they don't bother us too much. As long as they don't steal our animals, we don't have anything to do with them. It doesn't bother me if they sleep with each other's women!'

In those days, peasants were very much under the influence of the government's propaganda about moral conduct. Hard work and chastity were the ideal, being lazy or committing adultery the definition of depravity itself. If not wanton, the artists must have appeared mad in the eyes of the surrounding peasants. As our conversation came to an end, the sweet-potato seller pointed towards a few houses further down the road, and off he went.

It was already noon, but still too early for the artists to have started their day. I stood outside one of the little houses and knocked timidly on its door. No one answered. I moved on to another house, where I watched two sparrows jump around and suck drops of liquid from beer bottles scattered around the yard. Poor sparrows, I bet even they were starving!

Suddenly the door behind me burst open and a young man wearing only a pair of shorts came out. His hair was tied up in a ponytail and a straggly beard dressed his face – almost a trademark look for avant-garde artists back then. He glanced at me for less than two seconds then, swinging his arms and kicking his hairy legs, he strode briskly past me towards a little house in the near distance.

'Are you a painter?' I followed him closely, clutching my camera to my chest. 'They told me you are a painter.'

But he was not in the mood to talk. He seemed to be in a hurry. Intuition told me he would make the perfect subject for my documentary. So I followed him all the way to a little makeshift shed, around which several ragged, unkempt men were chatting. When we drew closer, I realised that he was heading for a public toilet – perhaps the only toilet in the village. At that time, these simple dwellings typical of suburban Beijing had neither heating nor proper plumbing. I stood and waited as the ponytailed man disappeared inside. I felt slightly embarrassed, but in no time my attention turned to the conversation between the two men beside me.

'We'd drunk a whole fucking bottle of Erguotou by dawn, but the Swiss dealer wouldn't give up. He began bringing out bottles of wine from his car and we finished them too with the leftover pig's trotters.'

'So the Swiss dude bought some paintings from you after all?'

'I did a bulk sale! I even palmed off the ones I did in art school! He gave me a thousand yuan for eight pieces: four big, four small. I was selling paintings like those peasants sell cabbages in the market. I said: "Just take the whole bag! Don't worry about the change!" He was delighted and opened another bottle!'

A thousand yuan at that time was a reasonable sum, given the rent for those small houses was only around eighty yuan per month, so that kind of money meant you were covered for a whole year's rent in the village. It was a good deal – if you didn't expect that ten or fifteen years later those very same paintings would be auctioned at New York's Whitney Gallery or London's Sotheby's for four to six million dollars a piece.

As I was standing around with my ears pricked for any gossip from the village, I realised I too needed the toilet. So I went to the women's side, hoping I would catch the ponytailed man when I came out. But as soon as I entered, I saw that it was fully occupied. Six women were squatting above six holes, chatting to each other in between their bowel movements. The toilet

stank and flies were buzzing like a live electrical wire. All kinds
of bodily fluid decorated the concrete floor and I couldn't find a
clean spot for my feet to stand on. Even our communal toilet in
the compound back in Wenling never got this bad. I wondered if
the Swiss art collector had relieved himself here after consuming
so many beers and shots of liquor. As I was waiting my turn, I
tried not to puke from the stench.

When I finally escaped I saw the ponytailed painter light a
cigarette as he stood talking with two other artists in front of the
toilet block. A few more men arrived. They looked bedraggled
and beat, their jeans splattered with paint. Their chatter was
spiced with frequent swear words, as if they had known each
other for years. I gathered that this was the place – the public
toilet – this was the real social hub of East Village, and I should
use it as my base.

From that day on, I went back to the village regularly and
carried on filming. One of the painters I met was Yue Minjun.
Years later, he became very famous for his series of *Laughing
Man* portraits. He was painting them when I met him, those
crazy-looking figures with the laughing faces – grimacing open
mouths, gaping like pits, fringed with immaculate white teeth.
In my eyes, Yue's work was the result of compulsion. He painted
those pink male faces over and over again. Their wide mouths
and tightly shut eyes, with a strain of a frozen hilarity, reminded
me of Chinese peasants crying over their doomed futures as the
government continued to seize their land for industrial projects.
Yes, that laughter was a bitter cry.

For Western consumers of art, the Chinese avant-garde of
this period is 'magic realist' or 'hyperrealist'. They are absurdist
works that rejected reality in favour of some other stratosphere

of the imagination. But in fact, the artists of East Village were social realists. Their material was the village itself and the people in it. The best work of the period was an utterly realist piece. The putrid, crowded public toilet became a major performance project for Zhuang Huan, who later went to New York and became one of the most celebrated international Chinese artists of our generation. I was lucky enough to witness his performance in that very toilet, a piece entitled *12 Square Metres*. Zhuang Huan covered his body in a visceral liquid of fish and honey to attract the flies. He then squatted down, letting the flies attack his flesh for hours. That day, the toilet was even more crowded than usual with hordes of spectators circulating outside, commenting and taking photos, including journalists from Reuters and the *New York Times*. I was one of the photographers, squeezed in by the entrance to the toilet. But after ten minutes of being crawled on by those awful local flies – who were probably dirtier than any other I had ever encountered – I had to escape from this atrocity, this battle between man and insect.

Away from the crowd and the stench, I put down my camera and took a break. As I sat on the dirt, I thought: yes, these artists are fascinating, but I'm not sure if I could become one of them, or use this mode to express myself. Somehow, I always found their artistic language to be very male. It was too macho and too blunt, to put it simply. What these artists did was give their middle finger to the official talk of the *People's Daily*. But we young people didn't give a damn about the *People's Daily* or any other official media outlets. Not even the middle-class Chinese wasted their time paying attention to the party's propaganda these days. Only the officials did. Times had changed. This was no longer the 1970s or 80s. So what were these artists trying to prove really? As an aspiring young artist myself, I composed a vision of my future – instead of representing the things no one believed in, I would concentrate on the things we did. At least, I would try with my future films and books.

But my filming in East Village was abruptly stopped a month after I started. One sunny day in June, the police stormed the village and arrested some of the artists while one of them, Ma Liuming, was in the middle of a performance in the yard of *Fen – Ma Liuming's Lunch*. Ma Liuming had an androgynous male/female persona, and sat completely naked, sucking a plastic tube attached to his penis. But I was an inexperienced film-maker then. I had used up all my tapes before he had even started the actual sucking, so I didn't capture any of the real action. Some villagers reported the obscene scene to the police, or maybe the police were already monitoring the village's activities that day. In any case, suddenly the police surrounded us. They demanded that all the spectators show their ID cards and Beijing residence permits. Those who failed to show their papers were arrested. My papers were good, so I was allowed to leave without incident, but Ma Liuming was put in jail for two months for his infamous penis-sucking lunch. The other remaining artists fled the village and relocated to other parts of Beijing. Soon after that, a newly built Fourth Ring Road cut through the area and the village was wiped from the map of Beijing. I kept all the footage I filmed during my Beijing years, but during the course of my Western nomadic wanderings, I lost the material from East Village, just as I lost contact with those artist comrades and our time of expressive exuberance. What makes this all the more poignant is that the time of underground artists is now well and truly over in China. These days, artists are either state-sanctioned, in prison, or exiled in the West. We have lost our collective energy, lost our once strong underground identity.

Smells Like Teen Spirit

It was late, after midnight. I had just returned to my dorm from a concert in an airless basement in the Haidian district of the city. Words were forming in my mind and I had an urge to write. So I sat down at my desk and opened my notebook. But my head was still throbbing with the deep pulse of the bass guitar and the clash of the drums, as if an electric current had lodged itself in my body, impossible to calm.

The concert, performed by several of Beijing's young rock'n'roll bands, had been organised to commemorate the death of Kurt Cobain, the lead singer of Nirvana, about whom I knew nothing, save for his suicide two days previously, a fact I had only just learned. At the end of the concert, an original recording of Nirvana's hit 'Smells Like Teen Spirit' – which I had never heard before – was blasted out over the speakers. I heard the lines '*With the lights out it's less dangerous, here we are now*' and felt deeply affected by the desperation in Cobain's dry, throaty voice. Instead of feeling depressed about the musician's death, everyone at the concert seemed energised and excited by it. That was because in the China of 1994, Western rock and punk were so exotic that even a suicide made us feel 'cool' and united in the 'free spirit'. We didn't care about '*All workers of the world unite*', we were now galvanised by '*All angry punk youth of the world unite*'.

When the song finished, I squeezed out of the steamy-hot basement, and into the cold April night. I walked alone, all the way back to the film school. The idea of 'teen spirit' spoke to me in a very personal way. I wanted to write about a rebellious teenager in China, chasing after everything that glittered. So that night, I sat down in my dorm and began to write the first page of my very first novel:

My life began when I was twenty-one. At least, that's when I decided it began. That was when I started to think that of all those shiny things in life, some of them might possibly be for me.

I wrote by candlelight, as the dorm's electricity was already off for the night. But the building was still abuzz with the drone of chatting, washing, coughing, laughing and guitar playing. Our usual manic hour after midnight. No one wanted to go to sleep yet. The multiplicity of sounds was only ever squashed when the dorm supervisor showed up on each floor to shut everyone up. But I was writing, because I had known my character, this young woman called Fenfang, for so long and I wanted more than anything to tell her story. I needed another candle to continue. The three other girls in the room were now sleeping. I stole one from Mengmeng's desk and pulled a makeshift curtain tight around mine. I could hear the dorm supervisor out in the corridor. But I wasn't going to sleep. Sleep was merely a form of time-wasting, I would do all my sleeping after I had lain down in my grave. I wanted to be awake in the electrifying night of my thoughts, and let them pour from my pen.

From then on, I spent almost every night writing Fenfang's story: the country girl who ran away from home for Beijing and tried to become an artist. I worked on the manuscript for the next seven months. Despite knowing Fenfang intimately, I didn't know how to write a novel. I had written poems, but they had never been narrative. The novel was still a very new format for us Chinese, since the dominant literary forms then were poetry, essays and short stories. Books were reserved for historical accounts, academic subjects and reportage. The novel – we called it *xiaoshuo*, meaning 'little talk' – was alien to the Chinese literary tradition. To write a book of 'little talk' with a continuous narrative arc seemed very Western and modern to me. The main examples that I had by my desk were Salingeresque books, slim but with vivid first-person narratives. And the novels I had loved before coming to Beijing had been Marguerite Duras's *The Lover* and *The Sea Wall*. For all these reasons, from the very moment of starting my novel, I knew that I couldn't escape first-person narration. I only felt comfortable when the narrator was speaking in my voice. So I let that almost primitive urge take over. By the end of the seventh month, I had finished writing Fenfang's story. A year later, *20 Fragments of a Ravenous Youth* was published by a young house in Beijing, with a first edition of 20,000 copies. I called my parents to tell them it was coming out. My father was very happy and asked me to send at least twenty copies so he could give it to his friends as presents. My mother, as usual, was suspicious about my writing. 'I hope they've paid you enough to live off. Otherwise what's the point?' I didn't report that it was far from enough, but it was sufficient encouragement for me to go on as a writer.

The day the book was launched in the bookshops, the publisher (who was also a member of the Communist Party) told me: 'We can't make money from your type of novel. It has no story! But we hope your next novel will be *right* for us!'

I nodded and thanked him for his support. Then, in all sincerity, I asked: 'What kind of novel would be "right", in your view?'

'Right? It should have some good murders, some sexual encounters and a great romance. You know, something like *Dr Zhivago*.'

His eyes lit up as he spoke. I nodded again, but felt confused. *Dr Zhivago* was all about the brutality of the Soviet system. I couldn't write a book about the brutality of the Chinese Communist system, even if I added loads of murders and love affairs. Such a book could never live in China. Nor could such an author.

The Western Boyfriend

During my first year at film school, I had little time for men. In fact, I lacked the self-confidence even to consider the men around me as potential lovers. But about the time that I discovered swimming, I also began to thaw, as if the water had woken up some part of me, drawing me to romance. I started tentatively to date some boys in Beijing, but I hadn't settled on anyone in particular.

There was a boy called Jiang who was studying in the film production department. He was a year younger than me, but tall and broad with a northern build. He knew Beijing like the back of his hand and I found the way he talked about the city really attractive. He told me about his great-grandparents who had been servants at the Qing Dynasty court, and how his father was some high-ranking army official. His family had been living in the Beijing army base before moving to their current high-rise. I remember he wore a waterproof army watch on his wrist, inherited from his grandfather, but clearly a symbol of privilege. I only had a simple pager beeping in my pocket to tell the time. How typical, that I should be drawn to someone who represented the city and the culture I wanted so desperately to be a part of. He was the embodiment of the thing I desired most and that was my great mistake, as I discovered later.

Our love affair began when Jiang took me to where his family lived, around the Drum Tower in central Beijing. We went to the top, and he told me how it had been built during the reign of Kublai Khan in the thirteenth century. Since then, each emperor had climbed up just like we had to look out across the city and beyond. I was impressed, of course. Once down again, we were submerged in the intensity of life around that area, with its sizzling eateries that lined the road like the ash trees did the streets and alleyways. As we cycled along the street, the white blossoms on the trees gently showered us. I loved being there with this northern boy. Unlike the compound I had grown up in, this was a street of change and importance, filled with the ebb and flow of life. I adopted Jiang's Beijing accent, too, though I found the slang a bit rude and very male. But the vanity of youth had sucked me into the illusion of sounding cool like a hard-headed northerner.

A year after we met, I moved into his family home. His father, true to his army officer status, never spoke a word to me. Indeed, he hardly ever said anything to his son or wife. I felt rather oppressed in Jiang's house. It soon changed the nature of our relationship. Somehow I became a sort of voiceless daughter-in-law in his family. And I certainly didn't like that feeling. I wanted to move back to the dormitory where I could regain my freedom. And I wanted to talk to and see other boys too. But Jiang was a very jealous person. Very quickly, we began to fight, and he showed his vicious temperament by punching me in the face. The beatings soon became a regular occurrence, turning everything sour. Sometimes I fought back, but most of the time I had no strength to resist. I let him hit me and all I could do was wish he would die. One day, he convinced himself that I was dating another boy and beat me badly with his army belt. My nose was bleeding. His father didn't intervene and his mother stood in the kitchen listening to my cries without protest. I imagined Jiang's father must have behaved the same way to his wife and son. Shortly after that, I ran away. But I was frightened, and didn't want to go back to the dorm. So I rented a small, cheap apartment near the film school, and divided my time between the flat and my dorm.

In those days, white boys were rare in China. And they were very popular with local girls as they represented Western civilisation. I was very attracted to them, especially to their coffee-drinking, party-going and what seemed to me a glamorous hotel lifestyle. I met some Western men in the bars and cafes frequented by artists and ex-pats. Paul was one of them. He was a film-maker. In my eyes he spoke and acted with a kind of freedom and curiosity that you couldn't find in a Chinese man. I decided to go out with him on the first night we met. An impulsive decision, in part a reaction to my violent Beijing boyfriend.

When we talk about youth we often use clichéd phrases like 'wild at heart' or 'walk on the wild side', but actually, young and hungry people live in clichés. At least, that was the kind of person I was. When I met Paul, it was obvious that I wanted to *give* myself to him. *Give* is a word that a young Chinese woman would 'naturally' use. Paul was the only one in his group who could speak some Chinese and he was a young, unknown film-maker from Los Angeles with many wild, artistic visions. He seemed to embrace everything new he came across: he used to chat to taxi drivers about his best and worst experiences; to Chinese waiters about their home towns and education; to cooks about how they should make French fries for their customers.

The only surprising thing to me was that he didn't like Godard very much, especially the film we were constantly studying in film school.

'Really? You don't like *La Chinoise*? Why?'

'It's silly, don't you think?' He shook his head. 'It's not because I'm an American. I just don't see the point of the film. Is it supposed to be educational? Or a parody? Or just comic? It's not even funny.'

I didn't want to embark on a discourse on Mao's revolution or intellectual film-making. I was much more interested in Paul's life, in the West of which I had imagined hundreds of times through literature and cinema.

'What about you? Which American film-makers do you like, Franny?' Paul asked.

At that time, I had adopted the Western name Franny, taken from Salinger's book *Franny and Zooey*. It was a vain and pretentious choice, of course, and totally revealed my obsession with the West. I thought the name would make me just like Salinger's character.

'I like many American film-makers,' I said. I mentioned names like Billy Wilder, Coppola and Kubrick.

'What's your favourite Kubrick?' Paul asked with a smile. He had this very warm presence that made me feel comfortable in his company.

'Hmm, maybe *Dr. Strangelove*,' I answered.

He laughed. 'I love that one too! It's Peter Sellers's best role! But I also love *2001: A Space Odyssey*, don't you?'

Then he mentioned some new names I didn't know. It was the mid-nineties and Tarantino had just scored a big hit with *Pulp Fiction*, which I had found exhilarating.

Everyone else started to leave but we remained in the bar and looked meaningfully at each other across the table. Then Paul asked: 'Do you want to come back to my place?'

I nodded. We jumped into a taxi. It was a cold rainy night. I found myself in a little brick *hutong* house with no heating or bathroom. He had rented it from a local because he thought the old alleyways of Beijing were more interesting to live in. There was not much said between us, we just lay in the dark and made love. He was the first Western man I had ever been with, but I didn't know if I was his first Chinese girl. I didn't want to know. Our lovemaking was spontaneous. Somehow my body had a different personality with a foreign man beside me. All the old habits from a past built up with Chinese men disappeared. And I felt new. It was the first time in my life I thought love and sex could live together without becoming each other's enemy.

My pager beeped an accompaniment non-stop through the night. I knew it was my boyfriend, Jiang, but I didn't care.

'I'm leaving Beijing next Wednesday,' Paul said to me early the next morning, as soon as we woke up.

'When are you coming back?' I asked.

'Not sure. I'm only here because of this film project. I'll be quite busy once I return to California.'

I felt awful and sad. Although I had only met this man a few hours before, I had an absolute conviction that I should *belong* to him. In traditional Chinese culture, women *belong* to their beloveds. In my conscious mind, schooled by modern communist ideas about women, there was meant to be no place for it. We had been taught such thinking was utterly feudal and against feminism. Nevertheless, there it was, bubbling up from some inner recess of my psyche. The hidden memory of my body was much stronger than the frequently recited ideas in my head. Tradition, as a kind of deeper, underlying skin, was now in charge. I was convinced that Paul would be the man to show me the world, the enchanting America that I had heard so much about for so long. But this dream of devotion and adventure was quickly shattered.

'There is some chance that I might go to Hong Kong next year for a film,' he said, as if this information should soothe me.

'But you know that we mainland Chinese are not allowed to go to Hong Kong,' I told him, with a sense of desolation.

The next few days, Paul and I stayed together in bed, absorbed in each other's bodies. Emotionally I found myself tumbling into a new kind of space. It was a kind of love that I had never felt before. I had never known such sensuous surrender. But it was clear that the American was just taking what was here and now. He didn't expect anything further or deeper with me.

I skipped two days of film school, pretending I was ill. The day I went back, Jiang caught me after class and threatened me.

'I know what you've been up to for the last few days!'

I didn't take him seriously. What could he know about Paul and me?

'I'll chop him to pieces! He'll never get out of China alive!' Enraged, he grabbed my arm and it hurt.

I was frightened. He looked as if he was going to slap me, but at that moment a teacher appeared in the corridor and passed us. Jiang let go of my wrist.

'What a fucking slut! You think you can play me for a fool like that? You think I don't know you were sleeping with that American producer? I know his name and I know his flight's departure time. He won't get out of Beijing, I tell you! Either he dies or me.' Jiang spat his words out. 'Just wait, he'll be a corpse the next time you see him!'

I was scared about what might happen to me. As I went back to the dormitory, I decided to hide from this crazed man by not going to the canteen or anywhere else he might be. That evening, as I was leaving the school, I received a call from Jiang's mother. I was very surprised as she had never called me before. Her voice was anxious and urgent. Apparently, she had been preparing pancakes in the kitchen that afternoon, but couldn't find the knife she used for chopping pork anywhere in the house. One of those typical Chinese meat cleavers, broad and heavy. Her immediate thought was that her son might have taken it, because he had tried to chop off someone's arm with it in the past.

'Did you see him at the school? Did you see him with the knife this afternoon?'

My mind was filled with the most terrible images.

'You two were always fighting. He said something a few days ago about you having a new boyfriend. If that's true, he might have taken the knife . . .'

I was shaken by her phone call. I knew Paul would be flying the following morning from Beijing airport; I was supposed to meet him that night to say goodbye.

I jumped into a taxi and rushed to Paul's place. He was packing and cleaning up the house. I told him about the knife and
my crazy boyfriend. Paul was surprised, but calm.

'I knew you had a boyfriend, from those pager messages you
kept getting. But I didn't want to interfere, Franny,' he said. 'I'm
only passing through. I don't know when I'll see you again, or if
I ever will see you again.'

I was in tears. These words were an absolute rejection. And I
really didn't want to hear them, even though I knew in my heart
that we were not going to be together again.

'But how do I come to California to see you? Don't you want
me to come to see you?' I begged.

'I don't think we have a future together,' Paul replied. Hearing
no response from me, he added, 'We lead totally different lives.
Don't you think?'

My heart was pierced with pain. I wept. I suddenly hated
everything about this short-lived relationship. Fragments of our
intense, night-time love and deep morning embraces were running through my mind. Did it mean nothing to him? Perhaps for
Paul it was just sex. Pure sexual pleasure. Nothing else. I was one
of his sexual adventures in China. That was all. Suddenly, I imagined myself as Madam Butterfly, cutting her throat in front of
her heartless American lover. How cheap and stupid I had been.

The night passed dreadfully, with me worrying that my Chinese boyfriend might break the door down any second, wielding
his knife. Paul and I made love again, but our entanglement had
become desolate. There was no real tenderness in our embrace,
our kisses only brought out my tears. His *hutong* house was so
cold that Paul tried to warm my frozen feet during the night, but
there was no warmth left in my body. We got up early the next

morning. He started gathering his luggage. 'Let's go, please.' He locked the door. Then he added, 'You really don't have to come with me to the airport. Really. I'll be fine.'

For some reason, I didn't get into his taxi. I felt so grey and dead. I had lost the love of my life. As Paul's taxi disappeared in the dawn light, I felt utterly abandoned, and wandered aimlessly through the cold. I wondered if Jiang would be there, waiting at the airport with his knife.

I never heard from Paul again, nor were there any news reports of a murder at Beijing airport. Was there a confrontation that day? Or did they miss each other by luck? I don't know. Nor do I know what happened to Jiang's knife, or want to know. Jiang and I barely spoke after that, and I never returned to that house that was always under the cold, military gaze of his father. I never dated another Chinese man.

The Revisit

One afternoon as I returned to my dormitory from class, our door lady handed me a handwritten note. She said that a man had waited an hour for me before leaving the note. I read it. I recognised his writing, stiff, with long, thin strokes. How could I have forgotten him even after all these years? I began to tremble. It was him, the secretary from my father's office who had molested me for two years from the age of twelve. The note simply said: *It's me, Hu Wenren. I am in Beijing and I want to see you.*

There was a telephone number for me to call.

I couldn't bring myself to believe this was happening! It was my third year at the Beijing Film Academy and I was twenty-two.

Had he followed me here to the capital? What did he want from me? Did he really think he could just take me to a street corner again and rub his hands all over my body? Did he think he could resume all that, unaware that it had been a gross invasion of my body? He had been a poison in my life, staining my body and soul with his pathetic impulses. What made it infinitely sadder was that he appeared not to recognise the pain he had inflicted on me.

I folded the piece of paper and put it in my pocket. Silently, I slipped into my room. My room-mates were having lunch, drowning in a sea of patriotic songs being blasted from the loud-speaker attached to the ceiling. Mengmeng was sitting on her bunk bed, eating from a lunch box. Her legs dangling over the bedside above me.

My heart heavy, I climbed into bed without offering any greeting.

'What are you doing, Xiaolu?' Mengmeng came down from her bunk and sat beside me: 'Have you had lunch?'

'No.' I was in no mood to chat.

'What's wrong?' She sensed my distress. 'Are you sick?'

I shook my head, and instead reached for my plastic food container and went to the canteen to buy lunch. On the way back to the dormitory, I felt unable to move my legs. I was scared. Scared that Hu would be waiting for me outside the dormitory, looking for me. Even though I was now much stronger and taller and we were out in public, the old fear returned to haunt me again.

I managed to get back to my room, but the other girls had now gone, only Mengmeng was still sitting on her bed. I decided to tell Mengmeng about Hu's return, since she knew the story.

I showed her the note. She read it, and jumped up.

'You mean this is the same man from your father's office? How dare that piece of shit contact you again after all these years!' I remained silent. Mengmeng continued: 'You know we have to punish him!'

'What do you mean? Tell the police? They're just going to laugh at us . . .' I said weakly.

'No! We'll give him a call, and tell him to meet us at the Yellow Pavilion.' Anger flickered in her eyes. 'There'll be someone there we know who can help if we get into trouble.'

'And then?'

'Then we meet him and curse him for what he has done to you and we spit on him.'

'That's it? What will that do? Why would he care?'

I was not after any sort of revenge. Why couldn't I just forget about the note and move on, as we all did with the bad things in our life? But Mengmeng insisted. 'You know, this dirty bastard has to learn a lesson. He probably doesn't know girls can be tough too! And he asked for it!'

So she called, instead of me. She was connected to a hotel somewhere in Beijing. Hu was not there. She left a message, saying that I would be meeting him the following day at the Yellow Pavilion cafe near the film school.

The next day, Mengmeng and I dressed in our most non-feminine clothes – black jeans and baggy sweaters and big jackets. I tied my long hair into a bun. Although I was extremely nervous about this weird meeting, I knew I had my best friend with me and nothing could go wrong. So, at the appointed time, we arrived at the cafe.

There he was, the man from those dingy Wenling street corners covered in chicken excrement. I had been twelve, a small, skinny girl. He had been very tall. But now, he suddenly appeared much shorter, older and more feeble than a normal man of his age. He could only have been in his forties, but he was unkempt, weary and grey-haired. I couldn't believe that the last ten years had turned him into such a wreck of a man. When our eyes met, I shot him a spiteful look and I could tell that he felt my repulsion.

We sat in front of him. The waiters came, but Mengmeng sent them away. The man sensed our hostility and avoided our gaze. I felt a mixture of feelings: anger, disgust and, above all, embarrassment. But Mengmeng took charge.

'Are you planning to molest some young girls here in Beijing? I thought you only dared abuse local girls,' she snarled.

Mengmeng set off a nuclear explosion. Everyone in the bar looked over at us. Hu's face was shocked and stupefied. This provocation seemed to hit him like a blunt instrument. Even I was unprepared for the aggression of her verbal attack. I couldn't think of anything to say at that moment. All I could do was sit by her side and watch the unfolding scene like I was an outsider to it.

'We know what you've done. And it's not only you. We know quite a few pathetic men like you and we're going to teach all of you a lesson. Just be aware that the police know where you are now.'

She then stood up, and tugged my sleeve. Brisk and dignified, we walked out of the cafe, leaving him there.

That was the last time I saw him. Two months later, the Yellow Pavilion was pulled down. The little cafe disappeared overnight, the spot was swallowed up by a brand-new motorway. Every time I walked past the old spot, I paused for a few seconds. But there was nothing left to see, only the endlessly moving traffic, like life itself.

The Quiet American Again

I was working on my second book, *Village of Stone*, a novel based on Shitang and my Beijing life. Inspired by the idea of applying the montage method from European cinema to novel writing, I began to use a structure of parallel narratives. I was so immersed in writing and my other work that I hadn't written to my father in months. Finally, a letter arrived, asking me how I was. *'How are your film studies going? We have not heard from you for so long. I hope you still like Beijing and have made some friends. Your mother wanted me to ask you about your blood pressure. Is it better now? Are you eating enough blood soup and spinach?'*

I replied and told him my blood pressure was fine, and yes, I had made some good friends in Beijing. Which was a lie. The reality was, I had made barely any, apart from my dorm-mate Mengmeng. My schoolwork and night-time writing left little time for socialising. Besides, I was busy seeing an American man called Andy. Of course I didn't tell my parents about my Western boyfriends. In fact, we barely talked about my love life at all.

After the episode with Paul, Jiang and the missing knife, I was more cautious about embarking on any serious relationship. I didn't know if it was a coincidence that Andy was also an American, but one thing was clear to me: I didn't want to date another Chinese man ever again. It's not that I was against Chinese men and couldn't see that some were attractive, intelligent or interesting. I wasn't that superficial. It was the culture of masculinity in China that I was revolting against, a fact that was inextricably linked to all my bad experiences with the old traditions. I didn't formulate my disgust with it so clearly, but my violent ex-boyfriend had been the distillation of it.

Andy was from Massachusetts and had come to China to study Chinese, before trying to start a business in Asia. I don't remember how Andy and I really met or got together, but I do recall I was drawn to his quietness – something atypical for a young American man, at least in my experience. Quietness suggested a kind of interiority that I found attractive. I couldn't help but associate him with a film I had watched in our screenwriting class – an old black-and-white classic called *The Quiet American*. Although the main character, Pyle, was not a good man, there was still something about his innocence, the foreigner in Asia, that intrigued me. As for Andy, he was totally apolitical. He never thought about it. I remember him making only one statement on the matter: 'I think Communism did so much for China, it's amazing.' This remark of course interested me greatly. It sounded nearly like something my father would say. So we found ourselves starting a relationship.

During my summer break from school, Andy and I decided to travel around China together to the north-east seaports of Qingdao and Dalian.

Qingdao was bathed in a light rain when we arrived. The red-roofed German-style buildings – relics from a long-gone colonial time – were quiet. The port reached out into the green-grey water of China's Yellow Sea. It was a beautiful city. In the early nineteenth century, the Qing imperial court decided to make it into a naval base, and built fortifications around the natural harbour. But at some point during the Opium Wars, German troops seized the town and occupied the surrounding area. The city was under German administration until the Japanese took over during the First World War. As we walked around, we saw little signs of Japanese influence. Yet the parks, the shore, and houses were more European in their elegance. We stayed for two nights before travelling on to Dalian.

The city of Dalian used to have a Russian name – Port Arthur – and a Japanese name – Ryojun City. One hundred years earlier, it had been nothing more than a fishing village, and now it had a population of six million. There were very few people out in the streets. It was unusual for a Chinese city to have such a sombre feel. As Andy and I were taking some photos by the sea, a police jeep suddenly stopped beside us. A policeman jumped out and started yelling.

'You two! Get into the car!'

'What's wrong?' I asked fearfully.

'Get into the car! You're going to tell me what's wrong when we arrive at the station.'

The station! He obviously meant the police station. Andy was worried. He tried to argue that he was just a tourist. But his Chinese was no use here. His efforts to speak only added to their suspicions.

We were forced into the back of the jeep and they locked the door. They drove us for some time before we finally found ourselves at the gate to the police station. The jeep stopped just inside. The two police officers jumped out and covered our eyes with blindfolds. Then they drove us another ten minutes, making repeated turns and reversals. I was growing ever more frightened. What would happen to us? A beating? Imprisonment? Labour camp confinement? In China one could be imprisoned without being officially charged. Then the vehicle stopped and we were dragged out. Still unable to see, we were led into a room, and told to sit down on a bench. Only then were the blindfolds removed.

The sight that greeted us was a bare room with a desk and two chairs. A telephone and a pile of papers sat on the desk. A map of China had been glued to the wall. As I glanced at Andy, I saw his legs shaking. I felt awful. This was the first time I had been in such a serious and dreadful situation, but we had done nothing wrong. We had to see what the policemen really wanted.

After taking down our details, including Andy's American address, the police began to ask me to report everything we had done in Dalian, including the names of every street we had walked along and which restaurants we had eaten in, etc. Unfortunately, Andy was being too honest: he mentioned the Navy Museum we had visited that morning.

'The Navy Museum? What did you see there?' The policemen were now very grim, looking from me to Andy and back again.

'Oh, we walked about, looked at old photos of Dalian from about one hundred years ago,' I said, trying to make light of everything.

'Did you take any notes? Photos?' One of the policemen turned to Andy.

We shook our heads. Then we watched them search our bags. We weren't carrying much: a tour guide in English, a bottle of mineral water and Andy's camera. Instantly, they snatched Andy's camera. In no time, the interrogation was over, and one of the policemen announced:

'You will be under arrest for three to five days for entering a Chinese military zone, until our investigation proves you are not here as spies or have stolen information from the navy base and communicated findings with anyone outside China. Until then, you will have to stay here.'

We began to argue, trying to explain we really were just tourists. But apparently, we were told, no foreigners were allowed in Chinese naval bases without permission.

'But there was no noticeboard telling us that we weren't allowed to enter the street. We were only walking around,' I argued again, my legs trembling and my voice beginning to quaver.

'Don't you feel ashamed, as a Chinese citizen, to be ignorant of the fact that foreigners are not permitted in military zones? Where is your patriotism? Hmm?' One of the policemen stood up and, pointing to the map of China on the wall, gave us a brief lecture. 'The coastline is our defensive border against all foreign nations. Every seaport has a naval base to ensure we will never again be attacked by foreign forces. How can you not know this? Huh? You are a university student? What a joke!' He choked on the smoke of his cigarette – he had been chainsmoking through the whole interview.

Since we had left our passports and ID cards in the hotel, the police dialled the hotel number and told the receptionist to get our details. While they did this, Andy and I fell into a deeper panic. My future was ruined. I would probably end up in prison, and Andy would be thrown out of the country. I tried to think who, in this cursed city, might be able to help me. Suddenly, I recalled a wealthy Dalian tycoon I had met at the Beijing Film Academy. His name was Lu Something. He had been looking for a screenwriter in Beijing two months previously in order to make a film about his rise to the top as a real estate developer and head of an instant noodle company. He had made that year's 'Top 100 Chinese Entrepreneurs' list, we had been told. I had saved his number on my pager when he had invited me for dinner.

My hand reached into my pocket. But wait, I thought. Once the police left the room, locking the door behind them, I fished it out, found his number and sent a quick message.

'*I'm in trouble, locked in Dalian police station.*'

In no time, he replied: '*Will call the boss. Wait.*'

About ten minutes later, the same police officer who had interrogated us came back into the room. This time his attitude was completely different, and he gave us two cups of steaming green tea. What a mistake, we shouldn't have been brought here, he said. He would drive us all the way back to our hotel. Apologies followed. Andy's camera was returned, and his hand was shaken, with profuse apologies.

We were surprised by this sharp turn of events, but I realised just how effective my tycoon friend's phone call had been. He must have been a real big name in Dalian. Not even the police dared offend him.

We were back into the same jeep and being driven by the policeman back to our hotel. Now he was cracking jokes. Andy was obviously still in shock.

'That's my first experience of the power of corruption in China,' he whispered, knowing that our companions didn't understand English.

'Corruption. Yes, but on this occasion we have to say thank heavens for corruption!' I replied, as we stepped into the lobby.

We turned and waved goodbye to the jeep and the smiling officers. I too had to obey the unspoken laws of corruption, I realised, and repay the tycoon by helping him with his film ambitions. I would now have to call him properly, and make a date to express my formal gratitude. After all these years of film-school training, I had finally found some use for my knowledge. In an interrogation room, rather than some fancy Hollywood studio, admittedly. Well, nothing ever goes to waste.

Truffaut Legacy

I always thought Mengmeng was a much stronger-willed person than me. She seemed not to get caught up in emotional entanglements. She had advised me not to get too involved with Andy, and she was right. The relationship ended when Andy left China for Taiwan. But I had noticed some changes in her recently. She had grown sullen and withdrawn. At night, she spent her time reading on her bed, and writing in her diary. She wanted to be left alone. I observed, but didn't want to pester her with my questions.

The news that Mengmeng had 'fallen' from our dormitory windows shocked everyone at the film school. The night she 'fell' from a third-floor balcony we were all back in our room. It was around eight, and I had just returned from the canteen after finishing my dinner. I didn't see Mengmeng. Her table lamp was on and her lunch box lay on her desk, but there was no food in it. I thought she might be having a shower or was downstairs making telephone calls. Then, all of sudden, I heard some students screaming outside. It was always loud around the dormitory building at night, so I didn't pay much attention to it at first. But the cries were growing louder. I opened the window and peered out, only to see a body splayed on the pavement. People were crying and shouting. Students rushed up to our dorm.

'Did she fall from this window?' they cried.

I had no idea what they were talking about. 'Is that Mengmeng lying on the ground?' I asked in shock.

'Yes!'

The ambulance arrived as we were running back downstairs. They carried her to the vehicle. I saw some of our teachers jump into the ambulance too, including our dorm supervisor.

That night, a few teachers came to our room and asked us many questions. But we had no idea what to tell them. I told them that I felt something had been bothering Mengmeng for a few weeks, but I didn't know what it was. Besides, I didn't know if I should be talking about her with everyone like this. I always believed that Mengmeng treated me as her a special confidante, and I acted on that belief. People searched through her belongings on her bed and desk, until they found a letter under her pillow. A farewell letter. It mentioned our French-film lecturer's name, and her obsession with him. She described the unbearable pain she had suffered after his rejection of her. 'He drew me down into the turbulence. Then he left me alone in the whirlpool.' These were the last lines.

It was clear. Everyone went silent. At eleven, the electricity was cut. The others left, dejected. In the dark, I heard activity in the building, just like every other night. But our dorm supervisor didn't come up with his torch to silence everyone that night. He had gone with the ambulance to the hospital and had yet to return. In the dull surroundings, I sat on my bed and didn't know what to think. I felt frightened. I couldn't imagine that my best friend in Beijing had died, or was dying, as I sat alone with my thoughts. My two other roommates were in a state of shock and were unable to articulate anything much.

I started to reflect on what had happened. I knew that Mengmeng had fallen in love some months ago. She had told me about it. The object of her desire was our lecturer who taught French cinema. He was a handsome intellectual man in his thirties, and had studied French in Paris a few years earlier. He was very popular with the female students. Perhaps some of them were also secretly in love with him. He had this charming air reminiscent of François Truffaut, and his analysis of *Jules et Jim* stuck with me:

'What is the shared theme of both *Jules et Jim* and *The Last Metro*? It is that of the *love triangle*. That's what Truffaut was interested in exploring. He didn't believe in monogamy. If there was a logic for monogamy, it was only economic. Love only manifests its threatening power when it involves three people. You cannot just love one person. That's not love, that's religion, morality, or economics.'

Mengmeng was so affected by this statement that she spent the next few days in a kind of trance. I wasn't sure if that was the moment she fell in love with him. But everyone knew that he was married and had a child. And I didn't think he was a disciple of Truffaut's love triangle philosophy personally.

Mengmeng had been attending nearly all of his classes, even when he was teaching in other departments. As with her previous obsession with *La Chinoise*, she watched the whole of Truffaut's oeuvre. And she was especially fond of the ones with love triangles, such as *Love on the Run* and *Two English Girls*, men falling in love with two or three women at the same time. The turning point for Mengmeng, I guessed, was when she expressed her love to the lecturer and he rejected her outright. It must have been a very brutal experience. He was, she later told me, her first real love.

I think she chose to throw herself out of the storage-room window because she knew no one would disturb her there. But her life was saved by a pile of rubbish bags on the pavement. They softened her fall. She broke one of her legs and some bones in her back.

We didn't see Mengmeng for a few months. She was hospitalised and her mother came to look after her. Then her mother took her back to her home town for another month. She was, we were told, emotionally unstable. During that time, when she was absent from school, the dorm supervisor asked us questions and one day he came and took all the notebooks that were left on her table. They wanted more clues. But for me, it was clear enough. She had had her heart broken.

I still remember a conversation we had after watching *Jules et Jim*. It was past midnight and we were lying in the dark on our bunk beds. In such moments we liked to discuss love or, more frequently, the confused feelings about love we were experiencing.

'I still don't understand it fully,' Mengmeng said. 'Why did the woman in *Jules et Jim* kill herself in the end?'

'Her madness. Don't you think?' I murmured, hearing the light snoring of the other girls in the room. But I wasn't entirely convinced by my answer. Catherine – Jeanne Moreau – left her husband Jules, then suffered a miscarriage with Jim. Jim then left her and her pride was hurt. But then again, most of the women in Truffaut's and Godard's films were presented as dangerous and crazy. Suicide was a romantic act, an easy solution to emotional turmoil, at least in fictional form.

For a while, we said nothing. I was about to drift off, when I heard Mengmeng speak as if she was talking in her sleep: 'I think the answer to her death was in the moment when Jeanne Moreau sang that song "Le Tourbillon de la Vie".'

'Le Tourbillon de la Vie' ('The Whirlpool of Life') was such a beautiful song. I couldn't remember the lyrics, but I knew Mengmeng had been reading a translation of them. Then she began singing, softly:

> *She had eyes, eyes like opal*
> *that fascinated me, that fascinated me*
> *The oval of her pale face*
> *of a femme fatale who was fatal to me*
>
> *We met, and then*
> *we lost sight of each other*
> *We met again, we warmed up each other*
> *then we separated*
>
> *Each one is gone*
> *in the whirlpool of life*
> *I've seen her one day at night, oh*
> *it's been a long time now*

I listened as her voice went quiet. And then I fell asleep. Now, as I recalled that night, it occurred to me that Mengmeng had been cast under the film's spell – the fact that she had fallen in love with the lecturer was her way of connecting with the spirit of Truffaut's fiction. She didn't realise that her life bore no similarity to the characters in *Jules et Jim*, that she was no Catherine, caught between two men. But for sure, this was the first time in her life she had felt an intense love. And she hadn't been able to cope with the rejection. Would I have done something similar if I had been in her situation? I wondered.

I couldn't imagine myself jumping from a building for a man who was not in love with me. The last man I really loved was Paul, not Andy. Paul and I had shared an intense physical connection, which was not something Mengmeng could say for our film lecturer. Despite that, I hadn't let myself be destroyed by Paul's leaving for America. I had learned a little about saving myself from men.

From a practical point of view, life had been difficult up until now. The examination to get to Beijing had been the last step in a series of tough challenges. At this stage of my life, I wasn't going to sacrifice my artistic ambition and surrender myself totally to a man.

But this reasoning was really only a superficial explanation. There was something else, something much deeper going on in my psyche, that went way back as far as I could remember. Back to Shitang and what I had had to do to survive. It came with me to Wenling, with my disrupted puberty and sexual awakening. It had shaped my entire thinking about men. Masculinity for me was a kind of foreign occupation, which I could take temporarily. But once that force had taken over my body and mind, I was stripped of any sense of reality, and left in a fearful state of confusion. More than this, a granite hardness had grown inside me since I was a child. I was not an unfeeling stone, but at some level, my psyche had formed a hard knot or core that couldn't be loosened. I had dimly felt this hardness the day my grandfather committed suicide. It was there, and made even harder, when Hu Wenren fingered me in those dark toilets and on the shabby street corners covered in chicken shit. And it was so vividly felt on the operation table after my secret abortion at the age of fifteen. I had carried it with me until now. It would never be softened or melted by some handsome man offering himself as an object of my love. On the one hand this stone in my heart gave me strength, on the other it left a deadness at the centre of my emotional life.

I went to visit Mengmeng a few times in hospital with some of our classmates. Her upper body was connected to all sorts of tubes, while the bones in her lower body were basically destroyed. She could only roll her eyes. Some months later, she was back in the dormitory, but in a wheelchair. She was gloomy, and had clearly lost her youthful spirit. She no longer went to any classes the French-film lecturer was teaching. Nor did we mention him in front of her. He continued teaching French cinema, and philosophising on Truffaut's thoughts about love. 'Love triangle.' He kept saying those words, as if he was unaware that a girl had jumped from a third-floor window because she had fallen in love with a married man.

Post-University Life and Censorship

On New Year's Eve, just minutes before the twenty-first century was due to begin, we gathered in the film school's canteen and awaited the final countdown. As the clock ticked its final gong, the Rolling Stones's 'I Can't Get No Satisfaction' blasted from eight loudspeakers placed around the large room. It was our new propaganda slogan: *I can't get no satisfaction, but I try and I try and I try.* We celebrated the arrival of the year 2000 with an inexplicable sense of anxiety and expectation. Some cried in the haze of flickering candlelight and ear-piercingly loud music. A strange depression came over me. I couldn't understand what it was. We had entered the third millennium, and our future was completely uncertain.

After graduating from film school, I was possessed by a fever of enthusiasm to write film scripts. Some of the ideas had been circling in my mind for a long time and I wanted to get them out, realised, and ultimately on-screen. I also got commissions to write scripts from established film makers, mostly from so-called Sixth Generation directors (ones born in the 1960s during the Cultural Revolution). I didn't really care about how much I was being paid as I knew that, being a young woman in the industry, I had to become a professional and experienced screenwriter before I could become a film-maker. I worked on draft after draft of countless scripts, but almost all of them came rushing out of my computer and immediately slammed into a great wall, otherwise known as the Chinese Film Censorship Bureau.

In China, each literary work goes through different stages of censorship. We writers have been bitterly joking about the process for years. We use *a hard rock* and *a small round pebble* as metaphors. If a book or a film manages to survive all stages of censorship, the rock's original sharp, jagged edges will have disappeared and it will have been transformed into a small, smooth pebble. One film script I wrote was about a ten-year love affair between a young man and a young woman: they begin as teenagers, study at the same university together, and after graduation try to survive in the real world but ultimately fail to meet each other's expectations and eventually separate. I wrote this story after witnessing the gap between the expectations developed at university and the realities of post-university life. Before applying for a production permit, I submitted the script to the Censorship Bureau. A few weeks later, the bureau sent me back ten pages of revision notes, and informed me the script was not yet ready to be passed. I still have those notes today. Here are a few extracts:

1. Why do the young lovers live together in the same house without ever getting married? Although in reality such inappropriate behaviour does occur, it shouldn't be encouraged in film. We strongly advise that a scene be added showing that the young lovers are responsibly married.

2. The couple live in an old-fashioned *hutong* house without a toilet. In the night the girl gets up and curses the *hutong* for its lack of sanitary facilities. But the *hutong* is a great traditional Chinese architectural style. A character cannot be allowed to denigrate this jewel of our Chinese heritage. This would only encourage negative feelings in the audience. This scene must be deleted.

3. It seems the girlfriend only studies English in her spare time and does not undertake any other worthy activity. The impression consequently given is that this young woman is only interested in the West. You have to add some scenes to show she also engages in Chinese activities benefiting ordinary people.

4. In the karaoke scene, the girl sings the song 'Wild Flower' with a few other male characters. It suggests that she is disposed towards prostitution or loose morals. This scene should be cut.

5. The script has an overall sickly, melancholic tone. It would not be overstating it if we were to say you have submitted a depressing project. This is its biggest problem. The writer and the film-maker have to work on raising the spirit of the story, infusing it with optimism and hopeful realism. If such positivity is not shown and felt, the script will not receive a permit for production.

The rest were stern statements about various details and the content of the dialogue.

Yet I was willing to revise the script in order to make a film. So I worked hard and tried to add positive elements here and there. But I was being naive: my mind wouldn't conform to the Chinese Communist Party way of thinking. My generation is different to that of my parents, I thought. The script was resubmitted three more times and each time it came back with more notes and a stamp of rejection.

Months passed and all my other scripts similarly failed. One night, sitting with my latest rejection note and contemplating the growing pile of unproduced scripts, a new idea entered my mind. I should give up and just forget about trying to get funding. What would I do instead? I would make underground films! These would be low or no budget. Any budget would come from my own pocket or from a generous friend who wanted to be part of the action. Suddenly I remembered all those underground performance artists on the Great Wall and in East Village who had taken this path, and had fought for artistic freedom with their own bodies. Maybe I wouldn't go so far as to run naked along the Great Wall with my genitals painted in various colours, but I wanted to be authentic and stay true to my own vision.

'You're a real *fenqing* now,' my film-maker friends joked during one of our extended dinners. A bitter mood had suffused the evening, as we savoured the succulent spices of our hotpot meal: chilli crabs and crayfish, frozen-blood tofu and pig intestines. *Fenqing* literally means angry youth – a reference to the 1990s generation with their roots in the 1989 Tiananmen movement. For them – for us – there was no way to penetrate the ironclad system of politics and society. To be an independent film-maker meant going underground, becoming an illegal artist, embracing an angry identity. I was ready for it.

In the heat of the steamy hotpot restaurant, my friend Rao Wei asked me an important question: 'So where are you going to get money to make your films?'

'Good question. I'm not sure I know.'

'A young female *fenqing* has only two choices. Either you can sleep with a rich man . . .'

I didn't like this option so I asked him for the alternative.

'Or you can get drunk with a few rich men, and *then* sleep with them!'

Everyone laughed. I knew some female artists worked their way up the career ladder using this method, but it didn't really guarantee a production budget at the end of it.

I also realised that, for a woman, it seemed easier to become a writer than a film-maker. Writing for me required only solitude and imagination, but film-making demanded everything. And money was its driving force. Where *was* I going to get money to make underground films? I was already in danger of being disillusioned from my failures so far. Way back in film school, when I first read Luis Buñuel's autobiography, *My Last Breath*, I had been so inspired by the world this Spanish film-maker lived in, and that of the other artists of his generation like Dalí, Cocteau and Orson Welles. At least they had enjoyed some basic freedoms, despite having lived through wars. We in China had undergone a proletarian revolution under Mao, and yet there was barely a free thought allowed in our heads. The layers of self-censorship we had to engage in before the official censorship came to get us had already strangled any creative work. In China, creativity meant compromise. Creativity no longer bore its original and intended meaning. Creativity under a Communist regime requires the struggle to survive under such rigid rules, and for all creative thoughts to be kept to oneself.

Becoming a Soap Opera Writer

Exactly twenty years after the day I watched a black-and-white television set being carried into our communal living space in Wenling, I began to write television scripts. At the age of eight, I had already understood that the television was a propaganda box, and that's why it had been placed in the centre of our evening life in the collective. But I never imagined that one day I would produce stories to feed to the masses after dinner. I had learned a lot about life in those intervening years, especially about ordinary, day-to-day misery. It was not my first choice as an outlet for my creativity, but film censorship had led me to despair. I was also desperately in need of the money. After graduation, I had been living on three packs of instant noodles a day. My novels barely earned me any money and I had received no financial support from my parents for some years now. Some of my university classmates had already begun writing for television, so when asked if I wanted to lend a hand, I said yes.

At that time, every province was home to numerous TV channels that all produced their own lengthy soap operas. Demand was huge, and every family loved watching them after dinner. As a result, I got a considerable amount of work. Usually scripts were commissioned, with titles such as *The Tale of Third Aunt's Marriage*, or *The Loves and Sorrows of the Family Liu*. All I needed to do was to write page after page of combat-style dialogue between, say, a husband and a wife, a mother and a daughter, or a grandmother and her daughter-in-law. No political discussions, plenty of discourses on marriage and romance; in other words, typical kitchen-sink dramas with Chinese socialist themes thrown in for good measure. There would be no despair, no hopeless alienation or critiques of the political class. Everything would work out in the end, and the sun would shine down on the factory or neighbourhood block. I surprised myself that I could actually write these scripts so easily once I was in the mood.

In order to give the dialogue some authenticity, I decided to write my scripts in cheap restaurants, so that I could note down amusing conversations going on around me. I especially loved hearing customers' complaints about the bill or dirty jokes about their office secretaries. As soon as I heard anyone arguing, I would put down my chopsticks and feverishly make notes in my notebook. I wrote fast and ate a lot.

I remember the first time I received a chunk of cash from a television producer after delivering a script. Twelve thousand yuan. Enough to cover a whole year's rent, also to buy clothes and eat out every night. Over the previous few months, I had been listening to music on my Walkman through headphones, but now with cash in hand, the first thing I wanted to buy was a new stereo. My beloved Walkman went into retirement and I could listen to music properly. I bought the works of great Western classical composers: Chopin, Schubert, Beethoven, Mahler. I was listening purely for educational purposes. I needed to understand why we Chinese didn't produce this type of music.

As I put a recording of Mahler's Fifth Symphony on the CD player, I somehow thought of my grandmother. 'Xiaolu,' she would often say to me after her daily prayer to Guanyin, 'one day, when you are able to make a living, do send your grandmother a ten- or twenty-yuan note every now and then. I would love that. But I don't think I will live to see the day.' I could have sent her quite a lot of notes now, even a few hundred-yuan notes with Mao's smiling face on it. But where would I send it? To an address in Hell? In which of the eighteen levels did she dwell? I hoped the Demon King had placed her on an upper level. Surely that was where she belonged, seeing as she had never hurt or killed anyone in her life. Why was there no Heaven for dead Chinese people? It struck me as odd. People in my village never questioned this lot, every dead fisherman and his dead wife ended up in Hell, including my grandparents. I thought about Shitang and my grandparents often in those days, but 'miss' would be the wrong word. I had left behind that period of my life, my orphaned existence, and the whole scattered assortment of souls who dwelt in that windswept, rocky village.

Cancer

From now on there would be no more underground film-making or experimental novel writing: TV soap operas were my work. I spent most of my days alone in a rented one-bedroom apartment on the fifteenth floor in Beijing's Wudaokou. I lived in a world of cheap dialogue, petty rivalries, shallow materialism and middle-class aspirations.

I became very efficient at producing this kind of work. I was a one-woman factory. I wrote on a first-generation Chinese PC called 'Great Wall' which only had one function, Chinese character input software for Word. I could write a solid and decent three thousand words every day, sending them to the television producer as I went. He was usually quite happy with what I wrote. I imagined myself as a female version of Woody Allen, writing television comedies before becoming a real film-maker. There was hope, I thought, leaving aside the censorship issues.

But this work flow was to be interrupted. One morning, I received a call from my mother requesting that I return home immediately. 'Your father has been diagnosed with terminal throat cancer. Stop everything you are doing and come back!'

I agreed, of course, the guilt of not having visited my parents in years weighing on me. I bought a ticket and flew back to Zhejiang, which now had a brand-new airport near my home-town. As I sat on the plane, I began to feel very stressed by the dilemma I faced. From a Confucian point of view, I was not a good daughter. I hadn't put much focus on fulfilling my filial duty up to that point. The demand to be a dutiful daughter or wife was purely an ideological tool for the suppression of women, I thought. Just think of my grandmother! On the other hand, my father was the only person in my family I respected, and I would probably stay if he asked me to. But for how long? I was already missing my Beijing life. I didn't want to sacrifice my freedom and my future for the sake of my family.

The air in Wenling had that familiar moist, slightly stale, subtropical feel. The dialect I heard in the streets somehow seemed much coarser and more primitive than I remembered. I hadn't spoken Wenling dialect for some years now, since in Beijing I spoke Mandarin. And I was not sure if I really wanted to make those sounds again. Time slowed down.

When I finally got to the hospital, I saw my mother's frantic, bloodshot eyes and my brother's sallow, depressed face. I knew then it was bad.

That night, my father underwent a seven-hour operation. The cancer had spread to his neck and lymph nodes. They had to remove his larynx entirely. We waited outside the operation room for what felt like a delayed death sentence. The next morning, when my father woke up, it became apparent to both us and him that he would never be able to speak again; nor would he be able to swallow water, urinate unaided, or engage in the simplest physical tasks. It was a shocking realization. He lay on his bed, staring blankly at the tube that passed food through his nose and into his stomach.

My father lay in that hospital bed for three weeks. He shared his room with four other cancer patients. During that time we saw two of them die in front of us. The nurses came to remove their bodies. It was an efficient procedure; first an old bedding sheet was spread out under the dead body and then it was wrapped like a sausage roll. Off they went, leaving the bed bare and empty. One of the patients was a very young girl of maybe only ten. She, too, had had throat cancer. My father had given her an apple the day before her operation. Two days later, she was dead. When the girl's family wept in devastation, I saw my father burst into tears. My father, who had always believed the mind stronger than the body. He thought the will controlled our physical being, that it would prevail over any physical weakness. This came from Mao. But the cancer ward taught him a heavy lesson. The mind is powerless when it comes to certain illnesses.

My mother tried everything to improve my father's health. Apart from the usual mix of Western pills and traditional herbal medicines, she regularly brought him turtle. Chinese people believe that eating turtle will promote longevity, as they regularly live for hundreds of years. First she cooked turtle soup with all sorts of herbs. Then she ground the shell into powder, and fed him the mixture. I've never been sure whether it worked, but with all the radiotherapy that followed, he survived for another thirteen years.

I was quite disturbed by what we witnessed in that hospital ward. The sheer number of patients was shocking, and it seemed to take all sorts indiscriminately: rich businessmen, poor farmers, young migrant workers, middle-aged women as well as small children. Most of them were diagnosed too late and were already deemed terminal. Some were actually dying in their beds. The wards were full: new patients had to sleep on makeshift beds in the corridors. Even the narrow space between staircases was crammed with chair-beds. The sick puked, coughed and howled, seemingly without respite. Nurses and doctors were bombarded by demands from patients and their families. The place was a living hell. There was no such thing as human dignity in this provincial hospital.

Women and children who had never smoked in their lives were dying of lung cancer. Most likely because of the pollution – Zhejiang was a fast-developing industrial province with countless large-scale factories. There had been lots of talk about water and soil pollution, and rumours that factories were releasing heavy chemical waste into the rivers. But no one was conducting any thorough investigations, since proving the link between such catastrophic pollution and human health would be too damaging: all the big factories were state-controlled. The people on the bottom rungs of society had no power to demand changes in regulation.

My father's cancer was the catalyst that got me thinking about the fragility of human health in relation to our environment. His sickness gave me an increasing sense of foreboding, indeed gloom, about China in particular. So much of what the 'New China' is about is getting rich at any cost. And what's waiting for us? Cancer, on a national level. Yes, cancer is eating us up, even as another industrial zone is built and another power station constructed. Perhaps I would leave Beijing and become an environmentalist. How many years would it take me to make amends, after all that meat-eating and relentless energy consumption? Ten years? Twenty? I could only hope that I might live to see that day come.

Leaving China

From 2001 onwards, Beijing was consumed with preparations for the 2008 Olympics. Everywhere you went, there was construction going on. Every bus route had to be redirected. Every building was covered in scaffolding. Highways were springing up around Beijing like thick noodles oozing from the ground, with complicated U-turns and roundabouts. Suddenly, many old residential houses were marooned in the middle of six-lane highways or under snaking flyovers. The city was perpetually surrounded by a moonscape of construction sites. Living in Beijing had become a visual and logistical torture. It was also becoming artistically impossible. There were increasing restraints put on my books and film scripts. I was desperately looking for a way out. This time, it had to be for real. It wasn't just my fishing village Taoist monk's supernatural imagination working through my subconscious, sending up its obscure vibrations. It finally made sense to leave. The lines that my father read to me from *Leaves of Grass* when I was fourteen had turned into a mantra inside my head: *Not I, nor anyone else can travel that road for you. You must travel it by yourself.*

Yes. I must travel it by myself. No one else would be with me, and no one would do it for me. Just like my father's 5,000-mile seashore expedition which he had done alone, I had to travel the Nine Continents, wherever they might be. My father had never made it abroad, even though he had been the one to introduce me to Whitman and Hemingway. I knew he would support me in my resolve to go. It was just a question of how and when and perhaps where.

The opportunity came sooner than I could have hoped. I heard that the Chevening Scholarship and the British Council were looking for talent in China. I had never heard of 'Chevening'. Someone told me it was a large historical mansion in Kent, England. This was as good as anything abroad, so why not? To apply for a residency in a large mansion in England would be interesting. My mind was instantly filled with images from *The Forsyte Saga* – one of the most watched English television programmes on the Chinese Internet. The wealthy housewives of Beijing in particular loved the fancy houses and rich people dressed in elegant costumes riding about on white horses. So I applied as a film-maker. Eight months later, after many stressful exams, the British Council in Beijing called me in. 'Congratulations! You are one of three people in China this year who've won the scholarship! You beat five hundred other candidates!' The English lady brought me a cup of tea with a big smile. She also handed me back my passport with a UK visa in it.

'Oh, thank you so much,' I said, flipping through the pages to check. I couldn't really believe that I had received a year-long UK visa, the first visa ever in my Chinese passport. 'So what should I do now?' I asked in disbelief.

Somehow, I was comfortable as soldier and warrior, but I was unable to function when the 'war' was over. Especially when I had been the victor.

'Oh. You know the purpose of the Chevening Scholarship, don't you?' The lady was a bit surprised.

'Actually, no,' I answered. 'To be honest, I only studied the subjects the exams required, such as film-making skills, English literature, etc. But I don't know what Chevening is. Is it a large mansion house where I will be staying in England? In Kent, I heard.'

The English lady started to laugh. She laughed for so long, that I began to laugh too. I now thought that I might be at risk of losing the scholarship because of my ignorance.

'You're actually not too wrong about Chevening! It *is* a mansion in England, but I'm afraid you won't be living there. It's the official residence of our Foreign Secretary in the UK. Sorry!' She gave me a wry look, then added more seriously: 'But you should really know what a Chevening Scholarship is.'

Now I felt slightly ashamed. I should have never mentioned the mansion. She would think that I was a greedy Chinese who wanted to kick out the British Foreign Secretary from his home. But the woman seemed to have forgiven me and went on: 'The Chevening Scholarship is a British government award for future leaders from all over the world. We select young, global talent with leadership qualities, then we bring them to Britain so that they will have the opportunity to develop their vision and international skills. And the money you receive will enable you to focus on your work.'

'Oh, really?' I looked at the official letter she had just given me. Fifteen thousand pounds for a year's film study in England. 'Who gave me this money?'

'It's funded by the Foreign and Commonwealth Office of the UK.'

Commonwealth. This was a strange word for a mainland Chinese to hear. We are not part of any Commonwealth. We have never been under British rule, except for Hong Kong which had only recently been returned to the mainland at that point. So if I was not a British subject, how could I receive this scholarship?

I didn't dare ask the nice lady these questions. I knew I was ignorant about global politics, which only showed I was not really the future leadership material they were looking for. I thanked her repeatedly, took my passport and the official letters from the UK government, and walked outside.

Beijing was its usual mess of construction. Every inch of earth and wall was being penetrated with ear-piercing drilling and banging. Crane drivers were shouting down at me to get out of their way, and barely a layer of scaffolding protected the pedestrians below. I looked up in distress. A few tall cranes were hovering above like spacecraft from *Star Wars*, shifting tons of building material and turning in all kinds of directions. There was nowhere for me to sit down or think in peace. I ran into the nearest McDonald's, which had some empty seats, and I sat and studied my passport and the mysterious-looking visa. I had to get used to this, I told myself. Leaving aside the ridiculous 'future global leader' stuff, I realised that I had to tell my parents the news at once.

They were rather surprised but both thought it sounded like a great opportunity. My father couldn't talk, but he wrote his words on a piece of paper and my mother repeated them to me down the phone.

'Your father says he is very proud of you! All your years of studying now make sense.' Then she added: 'You said the scholarship is from England. Do you mean Great Britain?'

'Yes. Great Britain,' I confirmed.

'That's great. Greater than United States, right?' my mother said, drawing her conclusions from her Maoist education of the 1960s. But I knew that she had no idea about either Britain or America. The only thing she knew about those countries was that they were in the West. 'You should take a rice cooker with you. I heard that Westerners don't use rice cookers.'

I didn't respond to such a trivial suggestion. I was thinking about my father's cancer. How long would he last? But I wouldn't let this thought trouble and delay me. I just wanted to leave the country now.

I remember very well the day I left China. It was 1 April, and the notorious Beijing sandstorm season had begun. At noon the sky above Beijing was still blue. But within minutes an ominous yellow billowing sheet enveloped the tall buildings and a crazy wind whipped at my hair. I dragged my luggage towards the subway, choking in the sandy soup. This was my chance to escape the world I had grown up in. But that world was trying one last time to keep me. I will be walking under a gentle and moist English sky soon, I said to myself. It nurtures rather than hinders its inhabitants. I will breathe in the purest Atlantic sea air and live on an island called Britain. All this was destined to be nothing more than a memory.

This is to certify that

Ms Guo Xiaolu

was awarded a Chevening Scholarship by the Foreign and Commonwealth Office to study for an Advanced Programme at the National Film and Television School from 2002-2003.

Her Britannic Majesty's Ambassador
for the Secretary of State
For Foreign and Commonwealth Affairs

It was on the back of receiving this scholarship that I managed to leave China for the first time

Part IV | Europe: In the Land of Nomads

After another eighteen months, the pilgrims arrived in India. Although they had heard legends about India's fabulous wealth, instead they found poverty brought on by drought: the rivers had dried up and the vegetation had shrivelled to scrub. There was no water in the wells and no food in the markets. A bushel of wheat cost a hundred pieces of silver; a bundle of firewood cost even more. Girls of five were sold for three pints of rice; boys of two were being given to whoever would take them. Everywhere they went, they saw human suffering. Under his master's influence, Wukong the monkey began to see and feel the misery and injustice of the human world.

For the next thirteen years, they travelled through the subcontinent, visiting Buddhist pilgrimage sites and studying at the ancient universities. Xuanzang and his two disciples also learned Pari and Sanskrit, the languages of the Buddhist scriptures. Wukong had been loyal to his master, though he could not engage in any intellectual activities due to his nature. As always, he preferred to fight and play with other animals in the wild. But he never forgot that he was wearing his master's magic headband all the time.

In the final year of their travels, they arrived at their destination: Vulture Peak in Rajagaha in the north-east of India. But Vulture Peak was surrounded by nine rings of high walls. The people who lived under the peak were destitute and the streets deserted. There were many soldiers guarding the walls. Xuanzang spent three days and three nights explaining to the gatekeepers that he had been sent by the emperor on a noble mission. But they were not moved by his entreaties. By the end of the third day Wukong had lost patience and began to attack the soldiers. Chaos was unleashed. The gatekeepers launched an offensive against the pilgrims. Though the master was protected by Wukong, Pigsy and Sandy were not and they were soon killed by the spears thrown by the gatekeepers. Xuanzang thrust himself before the menacing soldiers and addressed them with these words:

'I am a monk sent by His Majesty, the Great Tang Emperor of China, to worship the Lord Buddha and return with his scriptures. We left our home country twenty-three years ago and we have suffered diseases and have aged from this long journey. We are grateful to have finally reached the foot of this holy mountain, but what we have come to realise is that there is not a single happy person living here under the shadow of Vulture Peak. Blocking the way to the holy scriptures creates ignorance in human minds by not allowing people to understand the purest meaning of the Buddha's teaching. You must desist now. You must allow us free passage. I must see these ancient sutras and take them to China so that the deep wisdom of Buddha can be transmitted to the people of Chang-an. We will return the scriptures once we have finished translating them, and do so with profound gratitude to Buddha.'

The gatekeepers were moved by these words. The master and the monkey were finally given permission to enter the tower where the sutras were kept. And there, on the Vulture Peak, Xuanzang and Wukong saw and touched the holy scriptures for the first time.

On Westminster Bridge, just arrived in London, 2002

Arrival

'The girl is a peasant warrior, she will travel the Nine Continents.'

I was five and a half, clinging to my grandmother's skinny legs and listening with fear to the Taoist monk's prediction about my future. The wind was cold, blowing from the shadowy bamboo forest behind the temple, and little snakes were lurking all around us. I never visited that desolate temple again after my grandmother died. Sometimes I wondered if it still existed, or whether it had been renovated and was now home to a new set of young monks. But from that day on, my grandmother fixed the monk's words within her heart, and was steadfast in the idea that I would become the person he had dimly foreseen that day. Even now I don't really believe the old man foretold my future, my memory of a snake-infested temple and an old monk bent over a fire muttering is more powerful than his prophecy. But somehow his words became a kind of personal myth for me, a myth that manifested itself as my only possible destiny.

I spent a sleepless eleven hours sitting in the Air China Boeing 747 to London. I stared anxiously at the flight route map on the screen, ate whatever was put in front of me, and peered out of the window onto the great Mongolian plains and desert mountains below. Apparently my people, one strand of the Hui minority, had originated here. They had moved east, down into the lush rice paddies of the Chinese coast. And now I was leaving the coastline of my youth and moving west. After a few hours, mountains were replaced by flat, green farmland, and then clouds obscured the view. I was locked inside the confines of the plane. Unable to read or sleep, I entered a kind of purgatorial state, until eventually, exhausted and zombie-like, we landed at Heathrow Airport. At immigration, they checked my passport with its brand-new visa and my official Chevening Scholarship letter. The only question I remember them asking me was:

'Is this your first visit to the UK?'

I answered in my broken English, but with absolute earnestness, something like: 'My first time, sir. My amazing letter is bigger important. Prove first-time come here *arrrtest*.'

The immigration officer behind the counter raised his head, looked at me for a few seconds, and then asked: 'Arrrtest?'

I repeated the word a few times, then wrote it down on a piece of paper.

'Artist!' he exclaimed.

He shook his head, smiling and scowling at the same time, and stamped my passport with a very loud bang. He then fumbled with it, somehow ejecting it from the window so that it fell on the floor, next to my feet. I picked it up and blew the dust off from its surface, before entering Great Britain.

There was no one to pick me up, and all I had was a reservation letter for a student hostel near Marylebone Station in central London. Dragging my luggage, I jumped into a taxi.

Great Britain or – what was this country called exactly? The United Kingdom and Northern Ireland? As I looked out at the streets through the rain-drenched window of the taxi, it smelled damp and soggy. The air clung to my cheeks. The sky was dim, and the city drew a low and squat outline against the horizon: not very impressive. We travelled slowly, through unfamiliar, traffic-jammed streets. Everything felt threatening: the policemen moving about the street corner with their hands resting on their truncheons, long queues of grey-faced people at bus stops but no one talking, fire engines shooting through the traffic with howling sirens . . . I realised that I knew nothing about this country at all. I had planted myself in alien soil. And, most of all, my only tool of communication was a jumble of half-grammatically correct sentences in this tongue they called English. In China I had learned that the population of Britain was equal to that of my little province, Zhejiang. Perhaps it was true, since the streets didn't look that grand, especially the motorways, which were even uglier than the ones in China. Everything was one size smaller, or even two. Still, here I was. As the Chinese say: *ruxiang suisu* – once in the village, you must follow their customs.

For the first week in London, I spent my days walking underneath a sky leaden with wet clouds and in the few moments the sky was clear the streets were blasted by a fierce wind. The weather changed constantly, and rain threatened at every moment. My umbrella was my only companion, a royal escort. If the English light had felt dim upon my arrival, it was even gloomier from under an umbrella.

Before I left China, I was desperately looking for something. Freedom, the chance to live as an individual with dignity. This was impossible in my home country. But I was also blindly looking for something connected to the West, something non-ideological, something imaginative and romantic. But as I walked along the London streets, trying to save every penny for buses or food, I lost sight of my previous vision. London seemed no more spiritually fulfilling than home. Instead, I was faced with a world of practical problems and difficulties. Perhaps I was looking for great writers to meet or great books to read, but I could barely decipher a paragraph of English. Still, behind and beyond all the practicalities, in my naive mind, I was convinced I would find an artistic movement to be part of, something like the Beat Generation, or the Dadaists of the old Europe. Yet all I encountered were angry teenagers who screamed at me as they passed on their stolen bikes and grabbed my bag – they were the most frightening group I had ever met in my life. Before I came to England, I thought British teenagers attended elite boarding schools like Eton and all spoke posh and wore perfect black suits. It was a stupid assumption, no doubt. But all I had to go on were the English period dramas that showed rich people in plush mansions, as if that was how everyone lived in England. In the evenings, I hid my long hair in my coat and walked along the graffiti-smeared streets and piss-drenched alleyways, passing beggars with their dogs, and I asked myself: So is this what the rich West is really like? If that was the case, I wanted to cry. Cry for my own stupid illusions. What an idiot I was. Now I realised there had been some truth to my own country's Communist education: the West was not milk and honey.

Beaconsfield

After the temporary student hostel by Marylebone Station, I had to move to Beaconsfield, twenty miles from London, in Buckinghamshire. There were only two big buildings in the town:

a supermarket called Tesco and the National Film and Television School, where I was to spend a year studying documentary
film directing. I felt like a complete alien in Beaconsfield. I was
told that this was the richest village in all of Britain. For a Chinese person, *village* is synonymous with peasants, rice paddies
and buffaloes. Here, every home was surrounded by trimmed
rose bushes. Yellow roses in the front garden, red in the back.
And everyone seemed to own a pair of cars, parked alongside
their house. It was not quite *The Forsyte Saga*, but almost. If you
walked out of the village, there were neither rice fields nor farming land to be seen. Instead, a car factory lay on the outskirts,
alongside warehouses with trucks delivering goods to Waitrose
or Sainsbury's.

As I strolled along the monotonous village road (there was
only one narrow main road from the train station to the centre), I would occasionally see an old English lady passing with
her shopping. I was told that people were very polite here so I
smiled vaguely whenever I encountered a local. But I wasn't sure
if I was convincing. Often I stopped in front of one of the little
rose-bordered houses and tried to imagine the lives of the people
inside. Had they lived here all their lives? Or perhaps moved here
after wild adventures in places like India or Thailand or Ghana
when they were young? Most students commuted from London,
so I was a rarity in Beaconsfield. And on the weekends when
I went out looking for company I found the village absolutely
dead. No shops were open, no cafes served coffee, the only place
with an open door was a brightly lit pub called the Old Swan.
I had to admit that English pubs were something very special.
They always looked cosy, soft and warm, even though sometimes
the men were loud and unpleasant and never stopped talking

about football, beer mug in hand. I liked English pubs in general, because they had a particular smell that reminded me of my mother's silk factory in Wenling, with its heavy scent of steam, stale air, human sweat and scorched protein.

I used to spend my afternoons in the Old Swan. I'd go in just after it opened and read and write. 'A cup of hot water without a tea bag please,' I would say. The woman behind the counter began to take this as a sort of weird insult, knowing that I would be sitting in the corner for hours. I learned that I needed to be a good customer, so I began adding: 'I will order a plate of roast beef once your suppertime starts.' She winked at me, as if I was some alien monkey. After a few visits with my books and laptop, everyone started calling me Lucy. 'So how are your parents in Hong Kong?' they would ask. 'Do they want to visit England again?' I was so confused. I wasn't from Hong Kong nor were my parents, even though I secretly wished they were. Then I heard that there had been a girl from Hong Kong who lived here two or three years earlier, and also studied at the film school. Apparently she had the same long black hair as mine. They were so sure that I was Lucy from Hong Kong that I didn't want to correct them. And I began living the part to fit in, making up stories of my former life back in Hong Kong, absorbing bits of information they revealed to me.

'I haven't seen you in a long time, Lucy,' one of the barmaids said. 'I thought you went back to Hong Kong! How's your family, love?'

'Oh . . . they are very well, thanks,' I answered vaguely.

'I remember your dad visited you a while back, and he was very fond of our lager. Is he still working for HSBC? Or did he retire?'

'Yes, he just retired.' I guessed that was a plausible answer to her question. She smiled warmly and offered me another free cup of hot water.

My film-school experience wasn't as friendly as the English pub. My previous training in China was, I quickly discovered, the enemy of the style here. At the Beijing Film Academy, the teaching followed the Russian model, borrowing especially from the Moscow Film School, combined with La Fémis in Paris. Since our teachers had mainly been sent to Moscow and Paris, we had been taught to think of cinema as visual poetry, divorced from the traditions of theatre and literature. Furthermore, Chinese cinema had not yet been overwhelmed by Hollywood and we had formed our own way of making films. But at the National Film and Television School, the system was strongly influenced by the BBC and popular documentary journalism. I felt that 'Auteur Cinema' had little place here. Rather, there was mainly television documentary-making, often made with the standard BBC voice-over. It was only much later that I would come to appreciate British documentary film-making and to understand the tradition it had grown out of. At the time I had no context in which to place what the film school was trying to do, and I didn't understand the way in which British cultural life was dominated by 'consumer demand', which was something the Beijing Film Academy wasn't so interested in. The film-makers I had loved intensely when I was in Beijing such as Vertov, Pasolini, Fassbinder, Godard, Chantal Akerman, Chris Marker and Jean Rouch were old-fashioned artists here – they belonged only to European cinema. And if I ever pressed my point too much in class, the students would despise me, accusing me of being 'pretentious' and 'intellectual'. Of course, I felt their judgement was unfair.

For me, 'being pretentious' was the complete opposite of 'being intellectual'. A real intellectual hates empty pretension. But I didn't want to get into such an argument with the students and teachers here, because my English was too limited to say what I wanted. Instead, I spent most of my time alone in the Old Swan, studying English grammar and reading an English dictionary straight from the letter A.

During those desolate days I thought a lot about my childhood. I had been illiterate until the age of eight, and now, at the age of almost thirty, I was once again illiterate. I had to learn how to speak and write in another language otherwise I couldn't construct a life in the West. Identity seemed to be a pure construction – something I had only just realised. But this time the reconstruction felt much tougher than the first time. The pride I had brought with me from China didn't save me here; instead, it killed me. A feeling of being a 'second-class citizen' dominated my every day in Beaconsfield, and made me hang my head in despair.

London

Originally I thought I would live in Beaconsfield so that I could save time commuting between London and the film school. But after three months of wealth and deathly silence I felt like a weightless ghost, and I couldn't stand it any more. I felt youth had abandoned me and I had become one of the middle-aged people attached to their shopping trolleys who wandered up and down the leafy streets. So I moved out of my shared flat and headed to London. It was simpler than I thought – a

forty-minute train ride. And it was worth the cost. I felt life
return to me again.

Here I was, walking among all the other non-English speaking foreigners. Bengalis, Arabs, Brazilians, Spanish, Germans,
French, Italians, Vietnamese and even Icelanders! At least I wasn't
the only Asian face in the street.

All the years I've lived in London, I have ended up in the ugli-
est parts of the city. First there was a stingy, sad little house along a
railway line by Tottenham Hale Station, choked by a transient and
hopeless immigrant population. Later I moved to a flat on a council
estate on Hackney Road that felt like a prison. The whole area was
dominated by brown brick set against rusty shabbiness. The rows
of high fences were depressing. The Hackney of those days was
not the Hackney of now, which has gentrified considerably. In
2002 there were gangs, both adult and teenage, formed according
to the different blocks and postcodes. Often when I turned onto
my street gangs would burst out of nowhere, around a corner,
chasing some unfortunate soul who would be beaten violently in
a dark alley. It all made me shiver. In China, the peasants rioted
for equality, but you rarely saw open gang conflict on the streets.

During those long, rainy nights, with no friends and nowhere
to go, my loneliness crept up from my stomach and swallowed
me entirely. I couldn't read much and had difficulty sleeping. My
English wasn't good enough to go through a page of text before
I was so completely frustrated by constantly having to check the
dictionary. There was no one to talk to. I had no communication
with my Cantonese landlords either. Their lives seemed only to
revolve around their tiny takeaway restaurant. Their meat was
half rotten, they refroze the leftovers again and again, their vegetables were never washed before cooking, their sauces were long

overdue. They sold everything at minimum cost. As a result, the restaurant produced box after box of, for me, inedible food. They had no books in their house, and seemingly no thoughts in their heads. There was even less culture in this house than there had been in my grandmother's run-down dwelling in Shitang. Was the money they got worth the sacrifice of a meaningful life? I often got up in the night, stood by my window and looked out onto the empty, illuminated street. You might hear a police car rushing past, blasting its siren at a deafening volume; under some dim street light, an old bum would be slumped on a bench pulling a newspaper over himself for shelter; then a glass bottle would be smashed against a wall followed by a chorus of brutal swearing. What harsh, cold, rain-drenched and siren-whining nights they were! London seemed such a dark place, a place of deprivation. How did its people live here for years on end? I hadn't spent much time in the happier parts of this great capital, the 'posh' areas. I was sure the Queen, if ever she woke in the night, didn't look out onto such gloomy streets. Only the mindless ivy that grew along the rusty fences didn't notice the brutality of this side of London.

The only salvation from my overwhelming loneliness was to find a lover. The need didn't arise from any sexual desire, nor from any goal of building a home in the West. But from some basic things I wanted: warmth in the night, a male body, gentle and kindly, to love mine. Those cold nights would be soothed by an embrace, and I would be distracted from my feelings of loneliness as his body was pressed against mine.

Then I met Daniel. He was also studying at the film school in Beaconsfield and we often took the train back to London together. In some ways, Daniel typified the English traits I had encountered in my short time here: he was a vegetarian, an inveterate tea drinker, good at gardening and had strong connections to India. But he was also an artist and a political activist. Instead of taking me to see flowers in the park or art in galleries, he would show me around where he lived in Hackney. Often we ate in cheap greasy spoons, before walking under railway arches, passing smelly garages along the siren-song streets. I would spot a mentally ill man screaming and swearing on some desolate street corner. I had never witnessed so many desperate, angry, swearing men in my life. I felt rather disturbed by these scenes. But Daniel reassured me. 'You know they're not actually angry, just ill.' I instantly imagined myself penniless, mad and schizophrenic, roaming the treeless streets, swearing obscenities in Chinese. Perhaps I'd be driven to kill myself just as my grandfather had done.

As we walked along the rusty, scruffy east London roads, I began to get the sense that London must be a hard place to love. People from other countries moved here for jobs and opportunities, but this didn't necessarily make you love the place. If you felt affection for your home, you planted flowers on your windowsill, or a tree in your front garden. But all I saw were bare walls and CCTV cameras. Some lines from a poem called 'Slough' came to mind. It was by the English poet John Betjeman. I had read it when I was applying for the Chevening Scholarship back in Beijing. At the time I thought it would be something useful to learn. I didn't really understand it, as I had never been to Slough. But now the lines ran through my head:

> *Come friendly bombs and fall on Slough!*
> *It isn't fit for humans now,*
> *There isn't grass to graze a cow.*
> *Swarm over, Death!*

It isn't fit for humans now, there isn't grass to graze a cow. How precise.

'Why does the council have to put fences around those ugly houses?' I asked. 'Even the little patch where they grow grass is fenced. The rubbish disposal areas are fenced off. The bicycle chaining place is fenced . . . The city looks like a prison!'

'I know what you mean, I hate that too,' Daniel said. 'I hate London as much as you do.'

At the time Daniel was working as a deliveryman when we weren't studying, driving around in his dirty, misshapen hippy van, delivering goods to people's houses. He told me he suffered from migraines after spending all day in the city.

'I'm never happy in London. Every day is a struggle here, every day.'

'Every day? Really?' This sounded like what I was going through.

'Yes, every day. Fighting with the council, fighting with business people who want to steal money from you, fighting with those bastards in the street.'

'Then why don't you live somewhere else?'

'I did live somewhere else. I used to live in Wales. And I loved it there, people are much nicer. And I love the sea and the valleys.'

Wales! For me, the whole idea was exotic. The only thing I knew about Wales at that point was that it had a dragon on its flag just like imperial China. But it seemed strange to think of this Chinese dragon transplanted to such a faraway place, a tiny hilly corner of Britain.

'Can you take me there?'

'I would love to,' he smiled.

So when the summer holiday started, we left London for Wales.

South-West Wales

Even though the beauty of the British countryside has been extolled in song and verse by writers such as Wordsworth and Keats, I wasn't prepared for the empty, windy no-man's-land that I encountered in Wales. As it turned out, the trip was a deeply alienating experience for me, and led to me breaking up with Daniel.

Daniel used to live in Pembrokeshire, and he seemed impatient to introduce me to his old community. But the introduction apparently came with conditions. The first thing he said to me when we arrived at Fishguard train station, was:

'Change your shoes, or people here will think you're city folk – boring middle class.'

'What?'

I looked down at my shoes: a pair of modern leather boots. What was the problem? Although they looked a bit feminine, they didn't have high heels or fancy buckles. I didn't understand what was wrong with them. But he insisted. We rushed into a shop by the station and I bought a pair of plain wellies. Still, I chose a red colour rather than black. What was wrong with being middle class? I wondered. Weren't most people in the West middle class? In China, we were taught to strive for such a thing, to catch up with the West. A pair of modest-looking rain boots wasn't going to rid me of my middle-class vanity, I thought, and I kept the leather boots.

It soon became clear that Daniel's old home here was a hippy commune. All the people I met seemed proud of their own eccentricities, which was probably why Daniel worried about me looking middle class and boring. Ten families lived together in an old church and priory. Everyone seemed to be everyone else's ex-lover. They spent their time sitting around, or playing with each other's children. No one went to work. Planting beans seemed to be the main occupation, though this didn't take up much time. The food was simple – raw leaves, steamed beans and potatoes – a kind of culinary hell for a Chinese. And there was no proper loo. You just had to squat on the wet grass, depositing your waste alongside the cowpats.

'What's your problem?' Daniel said, sensing my disapproval. 'Did you have an indoor loo when you lived in your village in China?'

To top it all off, I soon discovered that half of the commune residents were drunk by midday. Nights started earlier in west Wales, around four or five in the afternoon. It always seemed to be dark, a land of eternal evening.

Pembrokeshire is occasionally referred to as little England beyond Wales. Maybe that's because of all the English hippies who came here from London in the sixties and seventies. On the third day, Daniel showed me an old church he had always wanted to purchase, lost in one of the valleys.

'Isn't it lovely?' he said, pointing to the old cemetery infested with tall grass and weeds that were slowly strangling the weathered gravestones.

Lovely was one of those enigmatic words that I discovered after arriving in England. The English used this word in ways that were baffling to me. Clearly, I was encountering some kind of aesthetic experience or concept that was alien to me. I contemplated the decaying churchyard with its scattering of defunct apple trees. Their leaves were coated in a white-greyish mildew that suggested a world in which time had stopped. I thought I would never grasp the idea of *loveliness*, there would always be something about Daniel I could never understand. Why would someone who was interested in becoming a film-maker want to end up in a decaying churchyard counting gravestones? For me, film-making involved a commitment to modern technology and certain social realities. It was progressive, whereas this vision to me was regressive: the sinking of all ambition into a quicksand that promised to suffocate us.

On one of the mountains – Carningli, in the Preseli Hills near the town of Newport – I encountered some people who had been living in isolation for years. One of them, a female poet, was deeply melancholic, and wrote about death and nature. She was a Sylvia Plath, brought back to life, but only halfway. I couldn't empathise with her. Instead, I felt like her bleakness was eating away at my optimism. I told her in my bad English: 'You should leave your husband, take your children and get out of this cold and dead farm, get out of here! It's this place that is killing you!' My bluntness shocked her immensely. But couldn't she see her problem? I left her house, infected with her depression. From that moment on, people thought I was the rudest and cruellest foreigner they had ever met. And I could feel that Daniel no longer wanted me there.

The weather in Wales was cold, wet, and windy. There never seemed to be anyone on the hills, nor farming their lands or working the soil. My feeling of dislocation was growing, like a stain darkening my body. That feeling of abandonment had always been there, in the background, but here it was being reawakened. The landscape was projecting it. Death was moving about on those wet hillsides, slithering like a lizard under a tangle of brush. It was waiting to reclaim me. How could I survive here, let alone find the intellectual and artistic milieu I wanted? No one here had any interest in my story. Cows and goats didn't give a damn about where I came from. I cursed the distant hills as I took my daily, solitary walks, my feet sucked down into the ravenous mud. I felt a mute dread come over me on those green valley paths, as if my body was being drowned in the monotony of greenness. I imagined losing my yellow-brown fighting spirit, being inked into the grey-green mist like an anonymous figure in a forgotten painting. I screamed and yelled in my heart. It was the loneliest moment of my life. At least during those years in Shitang I had the warm ocean, and the fishermen who generally said 'yes' to life. I followed Daniel along the edge of the Irish Sea at Newport Bay. In the freezing wind, I swore to myself that I would never return to this part of the world as long as I lived. I thought: this is the west of the West, and it's all I can take. I needed to be in a part of the West that had enough of the East in it for me to survive! Suddenly, I recalled a line from a Rudyard Kipling poem: '*East is East, and West is West, and never the twain shall meet.*' I had never agreed with this line. But right there, in my desolate heart, Kipling's words seemed to capture exactly how I felt. It was also in Wales that Daniel introduced me to some sad English poetry. One, by Philip Larkin, has stayed with me.

Never such innocence,
Never before or since,
As changed itself to past
Without a word – the men
Leaving the gardens tidy,
The thousands of marriages,
Lasting a little while longer:
Never such innocence again.

When Daniel read this poem, 'MCMXIV', to me in his draughty 200-year-old stone house, I kept wondering: what does it mean, 'never such innocence again'? Does it mean that men and women can never again fall in love with the absolute innocence and passion of the first time?

Certainly it felt like Daniel was unable to fall in love again, since he was much older than me and had a few failed relationships behind him. I found him almost too calm, and often detached. If any problem did arise, his first reaction would be to put the kettle on and make a cup of tea, as if everything could be solved with hot water from an old kettle. Well, never such innocence again. What about me? Yet again, I was facing the question of love and sex, both of which, in my case, had been conditioned by trauma from the past. After Hu Wenren's abuse and Jiang's violence, I felt that men always let me down, or hurt me, or sent me to a place which set off alarm bells inside me. Relationships. I didn't understand the concept. Coupling didn't make sense. Intimacy was invariably pierced by the bleakness of my heart, a shell-like thing with pins and hard edges that fiercely prevented any merging with another.

Then a letter arrived from my father, sent to my new address in Wales. Clearly he was confused about where I was exactly.

Where are you living these days? In school accommodation or a rented apartment in London? Which is the best address for me to send letters to? And how are your studies? Do you think you will be able to get any film work afterwards? I hope your education in England will be fruitful. Everyone in Wenling now knows about your prestigious scholarship and we are very proud of you . . .

I felt a deep shame upon reading this. I couldn't tell him the truth – that I was neither focusing on my studies nor looking for any film jobs. Instead, I was marooned on a wet Welsh mountaintop with a bunch of hippies. I was doing nothing productive. I could never share their ideals, nor could they understand why I had such an all-encompassing ambition to be an artist. It was clear that I could never put roots down in such bleak soil.

I missed the pulsating human energy of life in China: frenetic streets and crowded markets, kids laughing and fighting in the fields, delicious food smells from every kitchen window in the evening as I walked home. I even grew nostalgic for the sound of the loudspeakers and their propaganda broadcasts. I missed those ever-changing sights and sounds. It was on those barren hillsides that I realised that I couldn't, and wouldn't, cut myself off from China forever. I was born in the East and part of my heart had been left behind there. Indeed, it was only in west Wales that I understood how much I needed China as the driver of my imagination, a source of creativity, thought and understanding. From now on, never again would I turn my back on the China of my youth.

I didn't reply to my father's letter. I didn't want to lie to him. He would feel sad if he knew I was lost in these cold, rain-soaked mountains. To London I must return, that was clear. I had to go back to my film-making and writing as soon as possible, even if I had to break up with Daniel to do it. It occurred to me that relationships with men seldom made me happy. Perhaps I was expecting too much from them, despite not really believing such expectations could ever be realised. Being with Daniel made me feel more desolate than usual and isolated me from a world to which I had once belonged: literature, cinema and art. I felt a constant urge to write. So I packed my clothes and left. That experience in Wales and my days with Daniel, though difficult, gave me inspiration for themes I would later explore in my books and films: alienation, dislocation and the idea of home. I think these feelings had always been there, it was only a question of when and where I would finally write them down.

It was on that long train ride from rural Wales to the cityscape of London that I began to work on a feature-film script called *She, a Chinese*. It was a story about a Chinese peasant woman who leaves her village and comes to the West, before eventually realising she must now rely on herself, not on the men in her life. The film ends with her walking by the sea, heavily pregnant, looking across the water as if to the distant image of her childhood home.

Adopting a New Language

The year I came to England I was nearing thirty. I spent several months in panicked activity as the thought of my age came bearing down on me – to be a thirty-year-old woman in China was to be unbearably old! I still remember that celebration in London with some of my classmates from the film school. It was actually the first birthday party I had organised in my entire life. Like most Chinese families at the time, my family never celebrated birthdays. But there I was, cooking Chinese dumplings for my Western friends. Everyone declared that thirty was a good age, the age at which you started to know yourself a little, when you were no longer confused and started achieving goals. But I spent that year very confused. I had lost my main tool: language. Here, I was nothing but a witless, dumb, low-class foreigner.

At the end of the Chevening Scholarship I was supposed to go back to China. But I didn't want to. So I struggled to get all the required paperwork together and managed to extend my visa. Now the crucial question was: how do I make a living in the West? I had to survive somehow. But survival wasn't enough. I wanted dignity. I could only see myself making a living through writing, as I had done in China. But should I write in Chinese here, a foreign land, or enrol in a language class and study English grammar? If I continued to write in Chinese I would have no readers here. Besides, I would never create a community of fellow artists and thinkers in my Western life while speaking Chinese.

I didn't want to risk feeling even lonelier than I had done in China. It was not just the physical loneliness, but cultural and intellectual isolation. By the time my thirtieth-birthday party drew to a close, I was clear about my direction: I would have to start writing in another tongue. I would use my broken English, even though it would be extremely difficult. And yet, more positively, I would be free from state and self-censorship, which was an even more significant issue for me as a Chinese writer. State censorship was an obvious assault on our creativity, but few Chinese writers actually acknowledge the serious and endemic issue of self-censorship. For me it was as clear as the operation of the state's apparatus – without self-censorship an artist in China would get nowhere and had no voice. Self-censorship was like a shadow body embedded in every Chinese writer. It was necessary and useful. This self-protection enabled us to continue living safely in China doing what we loved. But now that I was living in the UK, I wouldn't need this foreign body that had lived inside me any more. I could flush it down the toilet, along with my consciousness of the propaganda machine.

When the birthday party was over, I mopped the floor and did the washing-up. An idea for a novel was already forming in my mind: I would make an advantage out of my disadvantage. I would write a book about a Chinese woman in England struggling with the culture and language. She would compose her own personal English dictionary. The novel would be a sort of phrasebook, recording the things she did and the people she met.

I had to overcome the huge obstacle of my poor English. I decided I didn't want to go to language classes because I knew my impatience would kill my will, my threshold for boredom being just too low. Instead, I decided to teach myself. Perhaps this was a huge mistake? As I studied day and night I grew more and more frustrated with English as a language, but also as a culture. The fundamental problem with English for me was that there is no direct connection between words and meanings; in Chinese most characters are drawn and composed from images. Calligraphy is one of the foundations of the written language. When you write the Chinese for *sun*, it is 太阳 or 日, which means 'an extreme manifestation of Yang energy'. *Yang* signifies things with strong, bright and hot energy. So 'extreme yang' can only mean the sun. But in English, *sun* is written with three letters, *s*, *u* and *n*, and none of them suggests any greater or deeper meaning. Nor does the word look anything like the sun! Visual imagination and philosophical understandings were useless when it came to European languages. Technically, the foremost difficulty for an Asian writer who wants to write in English is tense. Verb conjugations in English are, quite simply, a real drag. We Chinese never modify verbs for time or person, nor do we have anything like a subjunctive mood. All tenses are in the present. Because once you say something, you mean it in your current time and space. There is no past or future when making a statement. We only add specific time indicators to our verbs if we need them. Take the verb *to go*. In Chinese *to go* is 走, *zou*, and you can use *zou* in any context without needing to change it. But *zou* in English has all these forms: *goes, went, gone, going*. Mastering verb conjugations was a serious struggle for me, almost a dialectical critique of the metaphysics of grammar.

I particularly detested the *past perfect progressive tense*, which I called the Annoying PPP: a continuous action completed at some point in the past. I felt giddy every time I heard the Annoying PPP; I just couldn't understand how anyone was able to grasp something so complex. For example, my grammar book said: '*Peter had been painting his house for weeks, but he finally gave up*.' My immediate reaction even before I got to the grammatical explanation was: my God, how could someone paint his house for weeks and still give up? I just couldn't see how time itself could regulate people's actions as if they were little clocks! As for the grammar, the word order *had been* and the added flourishes like *ing* made my stomach churn. They were bizarre decorations that did nothing but obscure a simple, strong building. My instinct was to say something like: '*Peter tries to paint his house, but sadness overwhelms him, causing him to lay down his brushes and give up his dream.*'

But this was not the worst of it. I found something even more difficult: the dreaded *past progressive tense*. It was itself a philosophical enigma. For example: '*I was riding my bike all day yesterday.*' But if that was yesterday then the bike ride would be finished by today, therefore it couldn't be 'was riding', a continuing action. Also, a 'participle' is a weird thing for East Asians. The dictionary told me it is a word formed from a verb (e.g. *going, gone, being, been*) and used as an adjective (e.g. *working woman, burnt toast*). They are also used to make compound verb forms (e.g. *is going, has been*). I found the whole thing very abstract, even if I had to admit it might be more logical than Chinese grammar. But what's the point of logical? In China, it was almost akin to being impolite. 'Friend, you are too fat therefore you should not eat.'

In my state of despair, I asked myself, what kind of tenses did my hero Jack Kerouac write in? In the Chinese edition of *On the Road*, there were, of course, no tenses. The whole book is in the present, like a diary. So I went to a bookshop and bought the original version. To my astonishment, as I flipped through *On the Road*, I discovered that even my American hero turned out to be 'logical'; he had written the whole book in the past tense! I sat in the cafe next to the bookshop, and thought bitterly: where was Kerouac's mind as he feverishly typed his beloved Dean Moriarty's story? Surely a stream of consciousness, if it was anything, was a vivid form of present tense! Did that mean even youth culture in the West lived in the past? Where was their now? Did the present ever exist? I sighed. A sadness overwhelmed me. I laid down the Kerouac book and finally gave up on the idea of using only the present tense in my new, Western life.

Another curious realisation came when I discovered I used the first-person plural too much in my everyday speech. More than necessary, for sure. In the West, if I said 'We like to eat rice', it would confuse people. They couldn't understand who this 'we' was referring to. Instead, I should have said 'We Chinese like to eat rice'. After a few weeks, I swapped to the first-person singular, as in 'I like to eat rice'. But it made me uncomfortable. After all, how could someone who had grown up in a collective society get used to using the first-person singular all the time? The habitual use of 'I' requires thinking of yourself as a separate entity in a society of separate entities. But in China no one is a separate entity: either you were born to a non-political peasant household or to a Communist Party household. But here, in this foreign country, I had to build a world as a first-person singular – urgently.

Still, the desire and will to work on a first book in English propelled me through the difficulties. Every day, I wrote a detailed diary, filled with the new vocabulary I had learned. The diary became the raw material for my novel, the one I had imagined while mopping the floor after my thirtieth-birthday party: *A Concise Chinese–English Dictionary For Lovers*.

To Be Published and to Be Known

Christmas Day 2002. London. Cloudy. Gloomy. For most English people, this seemed to be the most important day of the year, certainly the day when the English hearth and home were busiest. Yet here I was, a young Chinese writer, a foreigner still growing accustomed to life in Britain, sitting alone in my dingy, rented flat, drinking cups and cups of tea. The heating was weak and the flat was draughty, and I started to understand why English people loved tea. I began early that morning, at eight thirty exactly. The ritual went as follows: Earl Grey (courtesy of Tesco), followed by camomile (honey-flavoured), mountain honeybush (product of India) and, for the finale, blackcurrant (low in tannins, high in antioxidants). I figured that I had managed at least half of an English-style Christmas, for although there had been no roast turkey or throng of shouting relatives, I had consumed my fair share of English tea. But by the time I downed my fourth cup, I had grown weary of this tea tasting. I decided to open a bottle of French 'Organic Red Wine', or so the label claimed. To be honest, I didn't much care whether it was French or English or South African, as long as it wasn't Great Wall or Dragon Seal Red.

And so I worked on my first novel in English. I had to use four different Chinese–English dictionaries – two Oxford, one Longman, one Xinhua. The novel was a diary recording my frustrations with learning another language and trying to make it mine. After Christmas and an even lonelier new year, I managed to finish the first draft. What should I call it? I stared at the tomes on my kitchen table. I should just call it *A Concise Chinese–English Dictionary For Lovers*, a homage to the source of my words.

After I finished the novel I didn't know what to do with it. I knew it would have little chance at ever being published, since I had written it using such broken English in a country awash with BBC voices and the perfect sentences of the Queen. And Britain was not like China, where writers could post their manuscripts directly to publishing houses. Here the system was different – as everyone told me. While pacing up and down in Waterstones one day and wondering how the hell all these books had been published, I happened upon the book *Wild Swans*. I leafed through it. In the acknowledgements, the author Jung Chang thanked her agent. At that point, my experience with agents was limited in the extreme, but common sense told me that an agent must be rather like a lawyer: a wheeler and dealer, someone capable of haggling shamelessly over prices, goods, terms and contracts . . . In other words, a good snakehead. This was exactly the sort of person who could help me get my book published. But I had to wonder: wasn't the merit of the writing alone enough to get it published? Was it really necessary to have a clever and expensive agent as well? In China, writers don't have agents because, in the world of Chinese socialism, agents have traditionally been viewed as parasites, members of the exploiting class. Although I had grown up with the same socialist propaganda and still held some of the same preconceptions about agents, I sent my book to Jung Chang's agent that very day. A man called Toby Eady, at an address I had gleaned from a random Internet search. Who was this man? I wondered. What were the chances that he would pay any attention to a manuscript by an unknown Chinese author? Might he be a terrible snob? Might he be the sort of Westerner interested solely in Chinese dissident literature and writings about bloodshed in Tiananmen Square?

A month later, one February morning, I received a call from
Mr Toby Eady's office requesting a meeting. On the appointed
day, I left my gritty lodgings in Hackney for his agency offices in
posh Hyde Park. I will never forget that day. London was awash
with a sea of bodies and police cars that afternoon. At first I didn't
understand why they were all there, and why helicopters were
seemingly hovering above every street corner. Unbeknownst
to me, it was the biggest protest in British history – a national
demonstration to stop the imminent US and British invasion of
Iraq. In fact, protests had been coordinated that day across six
hundred cities in the world. But an ignorant person like me, who
neither read the papers nor listened to the news, had little idea
about what was going on. All transport had been stopped for
the day, so I had to walk. I threaded my way through the chaos
and banners for three hours, only to find my way totally blocked
by manic crowds at Oxford Circus. Just then, I received a call
informing me that the famous agent had left the office and would
be unable to meet with me for the next few days. At that point,
I figured it was all over. I was just part of the collateral damage.

Three months later, I received an unexpected phone call
from my agent, who in the meantime I had finally managed to
meet, informing me that Random House wanted to meet me
to discuss the book. I was all nerves again. Leaving my flat at
least four hours ahead of the appointed time, I made my way to
Pimlico. This time I was too early. Sitting on a grey slab outside
a rain-stained brown mansion building called 'Random House',
I ate a prawn sandwich. I had no idea what the meeting would
be about since no one had told me anything in advance. In those
days I merely nodded my head, even before people began to
speak. Eventually, I walked into the reception area. Disorientated

by the number of floors and having to weave my way around
mazes of paper-piled desks, I finally met some editors. They were
very friendly and seemed to know a lot about me. One of them
made me a cup of Earl Grey. But I still didn't understand what
the meeting was about. And my English was not good enough
to understand the particular vocabulary of the Western publishing house. One of them mentioned a blurb and a jacket to me.
Blurb and jacket? I asked myself quietly. Did she mean the jacket
I was wearing was too blurry? Because I was wet from the rain?
I wiped myself with a napkin from the tea saucer, and smiled at
her again. By the time I left the office, I didn't even understand
that they had already made a good offer for my novel. At that
time, even this word 'offer' was alien to me. I didn't associate 'an
offer' with money or buying book rights, I thought it meant 'can I
offer you a cup of tea, or a piece of cake?' It took me a whole week
to understand that the offer was much bigger than a cup of tea.

Over the next few months I worked with the editors intensely
to improve the book. I felt much safer with their support. A year
later the novel was published and I was overwhelmed by the positive reviews. I hadn't expected such a warm reception. The book
went on to be translated into more than twenty languages – ironic
proof that even broken language can be translated if one has a
good ear for how to go wrong in language.

Since then, many English friends have asked me how I got
my book published in the West. How could a Chinese writer,
fresh off the boat, barely speaking much English, manage to get
her 'English' novel accepted? To be honest, I said to them, when
I arrived I had no idea of the difficulties involved in publishing a novel here. I didn't know that the process entailed waiting, having an agent and defining oneself in terms of a certain

literary genre. In China, many genres – such as 'self-help books' or 'culinary books' – had not existed until very recently. There were only two genres in Chinese literature: 'pure literature' (*chun wen xue*) and 'popular literature' (*liu xing wen xue*). Pure literature was of course the one to which most Chinese writers aspired. And I always thought 'genre' was a concept that belonged to the television world. Here, it seemed that writing was another form of industrial production, albeit one with many different assembly lines. The contrast with China and its massive illiterate population could not be more stark; most of my relatives back home could neither read nor write. Such a vast selection of books was of no use to them. As a writer, I wasn't sure which was better: being read by thousands in the West but still feeling misunderstood, or being read by very few in a country that understood me perfectly. At any rate, I had come to understand why the field of fiction in the West was so competitive, and what impact it had if you had the right editor and the right publisher behind you.

The Curse of Being a Writer

From the publication of my first English novel, I wrote intensely and all the time. I wrote three more books in English over the following three years. Apart from shopping, cooking and eating, I spent almost every waking hour in my flat, working and reading. I slept little. Although much of what I read has since been lost in the fog of inexactly understood words, reading was the only way to find my own voice in this new language. Once again, I went back to my old heroes, writers such as Marguerite

Duras and Italo Calvino. But now I read the English versions
rather than the Chinese translations.

I was in a vicious cycle: writing and reading seemed to be
the only way to beat back the loneliness, but they also reinforced
it. Financially, writing was also the only way for me to make
an income. Each line written, each paragraph composed, was
delivered in anxiety and desperation. My eyes were blurred,
strange flashes of light marred my vision. Floaters on my retinas
increased like heavy showers and moved around like a curtain
blocking my vision. I thought it was merely fatigue.

Then one day while out walking through London Fields, the
view before me suddenly became more wobbly and foggy than
usual. I wiped my eyes with a wet tissue and looked around me
again. I could barely make out the park. I blinked, and watched
as my vision became ever dimmer. At first I thought it was an
extreme reaction brought on by my hayfever – the maple trees
were releasing their pollen into the cloying summer air. But
within half an hour, I could no longer make out the faces of
passers-by, even though they were walking right in front of me.
I couldn't see the shopkeeper's face as I bought milk. I looked at
my phone; I couldn't read the text on the screen. I opened the
pages of my notebook – had I written on these pages? The lines
were undulating. The following day I was almost blind. But it
was the weekend. Not a good time to see a doctor. I waited for
Sunday to pass. Monday morning, my stress had only increased.
At dawn's first light I got up and made my way to the hospital.
After an examination, the doctor treated me with a Lucentis
injection in one of my eyes. I was told this might stop the blood
leaking into my retina, an apparent danger due to the macular
degeneration of my eyes.

Life was brutally interrupted. I couldn't read or write. I went out to buy a magnifying glass and cancelled my publication trips, as I couldn't even get myself to the airport. I walked outside in bright daylight, but my vision was dim like a faint candle burning down the last of its wick. I was in anguish at the thought of being disabled, being a useless presence for years to come. How would I function? I suddenly remembered an American book I had read some time ago, *Girl, Interrupted* by Susanna Kaysen, a memoir about the author's stay in a mental institution as a teenager. I remembered her acute feeling of hopelessness at the violence of the disruption to normal life caused by her mental illness and her confinement. Depression and frustration lurked in every corner, in the mundane tasks of an ordinary day.

For a while I could see nothing but a grey mass in the centre of my left eye. I couldn't even see the table right in front of me. My right eye too had high-degree myopia, registering minus twenty-four. I could see only the top letter A in the chart even while wearing my glasses. Since macular degeneration was now evident in both eyes, work became very difficult, and I began using the magnifying glass to read, as well as dictating my writing. But I knew: this was not a writer's life, a writer should be able to *see* and *read* her own words! Nothing is worse than a writer losing control of her own sentences. I don't believe in any God, but I silently implored the sky above: I cannot go blind, please! I cannot lose my eyesight. Being an artist defines who I am. Not my passport, my gender, my language, or my skin colour.

Bad eyesight was in the family, and I had long developed a particular sensitivity towards stories about blind writers like

Borges and Sartre: how it came on gradually and how they eventually lost the ability to read and write, and came to rely on secretaries. But these writers were twice my age when the blindness got them. I was not even forty! Borges took a philosophical attitude towards his fading vision. He refused to wallow in pity, either from within or from outside.

> *No one should read self-pity or reproach*
> *Into this statement of the majesty*
> *Of God; who with such splendid irony,*
> *Granted me books and night at one touch*

Despite my doubts, I decided to spend a considerable amount of money to attend Bates Method classes, a practice Aldous Huxley had used and described in *The Art of Seeing*. It was a five-hour course at University College London that spanned two weeks. I was told to shift my focus from a distant tree to a distant moving person, then swing my focus slowly between different objects at different distances. 'Pay attention to the warm sunlight,' my teacher said. 'You must close your eyes and bath them under the warmth of the sun. It is very important to take this sunbath every now and then, and you should try to visualise a blue sea in front of you with children playing on the beach . . .'

Beach and sun. But where could I find that in London? Sure, living in the mountains or by the sea would be a good way of fighting the depression brought on by the problems with my eyes. Perhaps big cities were not good for me. But where else could I go? I had made London my home.

Cutting up Nationality

Despite my declining vision, I managed to finish a new novel that I had been labouring on for years. *I Am China* is a parallel story about two Chinese lovers in exile – the external and internal exile I had felt since leaving China. Publication was due in a few months' time, but I began to worry if the upcoming publication would bring me trouble when I next tried to go back home since the novel concerned the student massacre on Tiananmen Square in 1989 and the nature of totalitarianism. What if I was denied entry because of this book? I decided to make preparations before the novel came out. So I applied for a British passport since I had been living in the UK for nearly ten years by then.

I spent some months gathering the necessary documents for my naturalisation. After a drawn-out struggle with immigration forms and lawyers, I managed to obtain a British passport. Now, I thought to myself, if there was any trouble with my books and films, I would feel a certain security in being a national of a Western country. Now I could go back to visit my sick father and see my family.

A week later, I applied for a Chinese visa with my British passport. After waiting at the Chinese Embassy in London for about half an hour, I found myself looking at the visa officer through a glass barrier. The woman wore horn-rimmed glasses and had her hair cut short, military-style. She looked like a resurrected Madame Mao. She took my British passport and scanned me up and down. Her face was stern, the muscles around her mouth stiff, just like all the other Communist officials, seemingly trained to keep their faces still this way.

'Do you have a Chinese passport?' She stared at me with a cold, calm intensity, clutching my British passport.

'Oh, yes.' I thought it was better to be honest since they would have all my details in their records anyway.

'Show me,' she demanded.

I had my Chinese passport in my bag, just in case. So I took it out and handed it to her through the narrow window.

She flipped through its pages. The way she handled it gave me a sudden stomach ache. I sensed something bad was coming.

'You know it's illegal to possess two passports as a Chinese citizen?' she remarked in her even-toned, slightly jarring voice.

'Illegal?' I repeated. My surprise was totally genuine. It had never occurred to me that having two passports was against Chinese law. I knew that in the West most countries allowed citizens to hold dual nationality.

The woman glanced at me from the corner of her eye. She was scrutinising me, her look designed to strip me of all exterior layers and bore right through me. I couldn't help but feel the judgement she had formed of me: a criminal! No, worse than that, I was a Chinese criminal who had muddied her own Chinese citizenship with that of a small, foreign state. And to top it all off, I was ignorant of the laws of my own country.

She then flipped through my visa application, which was attached to my British passport, and announced: 'Since this is the first time you are using your Western passport, we will only issue you a two-week visa for China.'

'What?' I was speechless. I had applied for a six-month family visit visa. Before I could even argue, I saw her take out a large pair of scissors and decisively cut the corner off my Chinese passport.

She then threw it back out at me, where it landed before me on the counter, disfigured and invalid.

I stared, without comprehension, at my once-trusted passport. The enormity of what had just happened slowly began registering itself in me. Although I was totally ignorant of most Chinese laws, I knew this for certain: when an embassy official cuts your passport, you are *no longer* a Chinese citizen. I stared back at Madame Mao with growing anger.

'How could you do that?' I stammered, like an idiot who knew nothing of how the world worked.

'This is the law. You have chosen the British passport. You can't keep the Chinese one.' Case closed. She folded my visa application into my British passport and handed them to another officer, who took it, and all the other waiting passports, to a back room for further processing. She returned her tense face towards me, but she was no longer looking at me. I was already invisible.

There I was, standing in front of the Chinese Embassy on Old Jewry, near Bank station. I was still struggling to believe what had just happened. Was that it? I had just lost my Chinese nationality? But I am Chinese, not British, I don't *feel* in any way British, despite my new passport. Little Madame Mao hadn't even asked me which passport I wanted to keep, the British or the Chinese. I suppose from her point of view I had already chosen by applying for another nationality, and in doing so, I had forfeited my birthright. For a few minutes I truly hated her, she became an emblem for everything I detested about my homeland, now no longer my country.

My tourist visa was ready a few days later. But for some reason, I never used it. Perhaps because I wasn't sure what I was

supposed to do with a two-week stay. From the day I lost my
Chinese passport, I came to the simple revelation that nationality didn't declare who I was. I was a woman raised in China and
in exile in Britain. I was a woman who wrote books and made
films. I could have applied for a German passport if I had lived
in Germany. But a passport and the nationality written on its
cover would never define me.

As the old Chinese saying goes, uproot a tree and it will die;
uproot a man and he will survive. I have always agreed with
this proverb, especially in the years before I left China. But after
the incident at the Chinese Embassy, I thought to myself: mere
survival is a life without imagination, but a drifter's life with
imagination is also a life without substance. As a new immigrant, everything felt intangible: I couldn't integrate fully with
the locals, nor penetrate the heart of the Western culture that
surrounded me. But the only way to overcome these problems
was to root myself here, to transplant myself into this land and
to grow steadily. So I began to plan a life exactly like every other
first-generation immigrant, starting with making myself a proper
home. One morning, as I was struggling to understand a mort-
gage plan on a website, I thought about my parents. My mind
formed an image of my mother, and I felt her accusing presence,
chiding me for not returning to China to visit them. Suddenly
the phone rang. With my mother's image still scalding, I picked
up the phone and was startled to hear her voice. 'Hello, Xiaolu,
is now a good time to talk?' I greeted her nervously. Why was
she ringing? Was my father dying? Or was my brother getting a
divorce? But my mother's tone was unusually positive. She told
me that my father had just undergone yet more surgery for his
cancer, but was recovering well after the procedure. I felt guilty

whenever I heard such news. But she hadn't phoned to tell me this.

'Your father and I are coming to stay.'

'What? Where?' I asked, still not comprehending.

'In Britain!' *Ying Guo*, the Chinese name for my new home, literally, English Land. Was she practising witchcraft? I thought for a moment. Had she somehow sensed that I had just lost my Chinese passport and was now a British citizen?

But they didn't even have passports, let alone visas. How could they come here? I heard my mother still talking, an upbeat tone in her voice.

'Remember your father had all those admirers of his paintings? He told one of them that he had always hoped, before he died, to go to Europe, visit his daughter, and to see those galleries and museums he had always read about.'

'What about passports?' I asked impatiently.

'This man, your father's admirer, is a big deal in international shipping. It was easy for him. He managed to arrange passports and visas for us. He even wanted to help us with the tickets. We're so grateful to him. We're flying next Tuesday.'

'What!' I couldn't think of anything else to say. There had been no warning, no discussion about this.

'Have you got a spare room for us?' my mother said, sensing my hestitation.

'Er . . . yes.' I muttered, lying.

'Should we bring anything for you from Wenling? Have you got a rice cooker yet?'

'Yes. Yes. I've got everything here.' I couldn't believe it, eight years had passed and my mother was still asking me about rice cookers.

The rest of the day I spent in a manic daze. I hadn't I told my parents much about my life in the West. They would find it utterly pathetic and insubstantial: renting a room in a shared house, no car, no fixed job, no family, not even a permanent boyfriend. The Hackney area I lived in was very dilapidated, with beggars shuffling along its dirty streets. I knew my mother would be disappointed. There would be no way for me to pretend that I was living in a rich area, the Queen's land where everybody lived in affluence. And, of course, I could never tell them that I had lost my Chinese citizenship. It would be inconceivable for them.

Yet, as I went out to buy a spare mattress for their stay, I thought: this will be their first ever trip abroad and probably their last. Maybe it was the only chance to improve our relationship. Or perhaps it was too late. We had always been like this, ever since they had abandoned me as a baby and then I had abandoned them as my adult life took over far away. There had always been a separation. It was the pattern in our family.

An Old Couple in a Land of Wonders

The day came. After a long, miserable flight, my parents walked through the arrival gate at Heathrow with two large suitcases, the very picture of two Chinese peasants lost among the urban Westerners. Their clothes were shabby and wrinkled, their bodies stiff and disorientated. I noticed that my mother had dyed her grey hair black, and my father looked much skinnier than I remembered. After what felt like an endless taxi ride across

London from the west to the east, we eventually arrived. Staring at the mountains of rubbish bags and graffitied walls in the courtyard, they silently entered the flat. Instantly they realised that there was nothing much for them to see in my Western home: a small kitchen and a tiny bedroom, no chaise longue, no super-wide leather sofa, only a leaky bathroom without the marble basin or glass walls that were obligatory in the house of a Chinese entrepreneur. The rest of the flat comprised a narrow corridor and my flatmate's bedroom. I had put a brand-new single mattress in the corridor, where I would sleep.

'I feel so unreal coming to England,' my mother reflected, sitting down on a chair. 'On the plane, after flying five or six hours, I kept thinking, what if we actually took the wrong flight? So I got up from my seat and found the air stewardess. I asked her: "Where is this plane going?" She stared at me like I had two heads. She opened her eyes wide and asked: "Where are you going?" I thought, I won't tell her that I wanted to go to London, in case she says something different. So I didn't answer her. Then she got really serious and asked me again. I had to tell her London. She said that was where the plane was going and I shouldn't keep asking.'

I was about to laugh, but stopped myself when I saw my mother's troubled expression.

Opening their suitcases, the first thing my mother showed me was their travel insurance papers. 'Keep this! In case anything happens to us.'

I glanced down. The title read 'Certificate for Overseas Emergency and Medical Insurance'. I started scanning what was covered.

Mortal remains handling benefit:
1. repatriation of mortal remains (approximately 100,000 yuan)
2. repatriation of ashes (approximately 2,000 yuan)
3. local burial (20,000 yuan according to current British service costs)

I stopped and gasped. I didn't want to read through the rest. They were bringing death with them from China to England. I told my mother to keep the documents safe in her suitcase, hinting that way I would know where to find them in case of emergency. For them to die here, in a foreign land, would be the saddest thing that could happen to them.

As I was making some tea for my parents, they began pulling their belongings one by one from the suitcases: hot-water bottle, tea, raincoat, hat . . . I brought my father a cup of tea. He was standing by the bedroom window, looking outside. The view was of a large, rusty Victorian gasometer tank on the banks of the industrial canal. Now it was abandoned, one of the 'landmarks' of east London according to local estate agents. Many English people seemed attached to this sort of industrial clutter, but I had never been a fan of the rust-belt urban aesthetic. Urban people in London sometimes seemed to take bleakness as a charming feature; it felt strange for us Chinese. My father was visibly disappointed by the view. He must have been wondering: where are the famous English rose gardens and rivers? I wanted to tell him that they were in the rich parts of the city, but I didn't say anything. Instead, I drew the curtains across the view outside and handed my father the cup.

'You must be one of the people they would call *poor* here,' my mother's voice announced behind me.

'No, I'm not poor. Didn't you see the beggars on Hackney Road? They are poor. I'm doing fine here.' I tried to educate my mother about the reality of living in a big city like London, but I knew she had already made up her mind. She judged everything on first appearances. Like most Chinese, she assumed that a decently well-off person would own a Gucci bag or a pair of Prada shoes, at the very least. She couldn't understand that I found these empty labels disgusting; they reminded me that the world was flooded – no, being swallowed up – by expensive but superfluous products. I didn't want to argue with my mother, however, so I returned to the kitchen to keep an eye on dinner. My father began to splutter and struggle for breath, that sort of very particular cough developed after a laryngeal cancer operation. My mother immediately fetched his medicine.

'It's a miracle that your father has survived this long. I can't stop thanking Heaven,' my mother mumbled as she handed my father some pills: 'But his operation cost us a fortune. We got the bill from the hospital a week later and the total was 640,000 yuan! I didn't dare show your father. Can you imagine that? Can anyone's life be worth 640,000 yuan? Maybe only Chairman Mao deserved such a sum! Even so, he only made it to eighty-three!'

'So what did you do with the bill in the end?' I asked.

'We couldn't pay it of course! I took it straight to the town hall and asked to meet the mayor. They received me and listened to my plea. Given your father's reputation, the local government couldn't ignore his situation so they paid 80 per cent of it. Without that, we would have had no choice but to wait for our very last breath.'

Since the day my father had lost the ability to speak, my mother had done all the talking for him. 'Still aching from that enormous bill, we went back to the hospital and asked them how long your father would last after this operation. They said maybe three to four years. *Maybe*? They like to use words like that, don't they? That's why we're walking around without our heads these days.'

As we sat down to eat, my mother brought out a present for me: a large glass jar of roasted red chilli peppers in oil. 'You must be missing this,' she said. She knew I had been fond of spicy food in my younger years, even though I had lived without it for so long now.

Our first family dinner together in London was simple: chicken noodle soup with vegetables. They ate in full concentration. As they drained the last bit of soup from their bowls, my mother began telling me about my brother. 'We had such high hopes for your brother, but you turned out better,' she sighed, clearly disheartened. 'He's still an alcoholic, still bad-tempered. Not much has changed. But since he moved away from us and got married we haven't had to face his problems every day. All I can say is that without his wife, he couldn't function. She is a good woman, so I can't really complain.'

What could I say? I knew my brother had disappointed my parents because he had never managed to 'become someone', which was all any ordinary Chinese family hoped for a son. I barely knew him anyway. He was someone from my past, not someone I desired to have intimate contact with. I knew my brother had just had a baby girl, and his wife had given up her job as a hotel receptionist in order to take care of the family. There was only one person in our family still drifting along, who had contributed no money or grandchildren for the elderly, and that person was me. I was struck by the guilt of my unfilial behaviour every time I spoke to them. But I kept telling myself: they knew too well that I was never going to be the one to sit beside them as they lay on their deathbed.

An Arranged Marriage

There was an unwelcome strangeness in sleeping in a flat with my aged parents lying on the other side of the wall. I couldn't remember the last time our bodies had been so close in the darkness. It felt like premature burial, as if my body had been covered in a thick blanket of earth and I now lay breathless and imprisoned. We were here in my flat in London, but the presence of my parents had transported me back to the family home in Wenling, to the stifling summer nights with their droning mosquitoes and ghostly shadows cast by naked light bulbs. I was an unhappy daughter there, but I had escaped all that – I had made a new life as far as I could from my old life. I didn't like feeling that it was coming back to me, even though now my mother was old and weak and could never again raise her hand to beat me. But I don't think she ever regretted how she treated me, I was sure about that. Yes, I forgave her. Or rather I accepted the past, just as she now accepted the daughter I had become. Yet I could hear her snoring, fast asleep, as I lay awake and restless. I could hear my father's lungs rattling with phlegm, and him getting up in the night. All I could think about was whether he would survive long enough to make it back to China, or die here an exile, his body returned lifeless in a box on the plane. I pictured my mother's accusing eyes, the crease on her forehead knotted in judgement. I had killed my father by seducing him over the ocean to this senseless continent.

I survived the night, and took my parents to a nearby cafe the next morning for a full English breakfast. Food would bring us closer, I thought. But my parents looked bemused by the contents of their plates: cooked tomatoes with fried sausage, tinned beans and mashed potatoes.

'The cook must have made this meal based on a nutrition wheel,' my mother said, her eyes moving from the plate to the knife and fork that lay beside it.

I went to the counter and asked for two big spoons.

'Don't they eat buns and wonton soup in the morning here?' My mother took the spoon from me, turning to see if there were other options. Around us, an old pensioner was eating alone, his plate indistinguishable from ours. My mother resigned herself to the food in front of her. But they seemed to like it, and before long everything was gone apart from the mashed potatoes. As my father chewed on his last oily sausage, my mother began to look restless and impatient – something was nagging at her. I could see that she was about to say something serious. She wiped her hands on a napkin, fished out some photographs from her pocket and laid them in front of me.

At first I didn't pay any attention to the photographs, but as my mother sat there wordlessly I was forced to ask: 'Who are they?'

She separated the photos and looked at me meaningfully. 'Take a good look. Which of these men do you like?'

I couldn't believe my ears. So that was why she had come! I was still sure that my father wanted to visit me and see Europe, but now I knew she had her own reason too. She was here to marry me off!

Partly to satisfy her with a perfunctory response and partly to amuse myself, I looked down at the photographs. There were five portraits altogether, printed on glossy paper. They all wore nice clothes, aged somewhere between thirty-five and fifty. One or two looked like well-to-do businessmen. The others looked like privileged white-collar workers. Four of them stood in front of grand examples of European architecture.

'Do these men live in China, or do they have green cards in the West?' I joked.

'What do you think?' My mother was almost offended. 'Do you really think your mother would choose some peasants for you? Or that I would force you to return to China? They all live in Europe, and are very successful businessmen. It took me a very long time to get their contacts and photos for you!' My mother gulped down her tea with some indignation.

My father was shaking his head slightly. I knew he was innocent of any of this. He never got involved in my mother's plans for my 'future'.

'I'm quite sure you've spent lots of time and energy on this!' I said. sarcastically. 'But where do they come from? I mean, how did you find them? Online?' I asked, shuffling the photos in disbelief.

'Online? Internet? No! You know we don't even know what a computer is. But your parents have lived in Wenling for more than sixty years and we know all the wealthy families in town. We've got two million people living in Wenling, so it's not that difficult to dig out five decent families with unmarried sons living abroad!'

By now, my mother had emptied her cup and wanted a refill.

'I know you think your home town is just some tiny shitty place. But it's not like that any more. We've got lots of millionaires, even billionaires! The city government has collected statistics and they say around six thousand people from Wenling have emigrated to the West. Most of them are very well-established entrepreneurs in the USA and Europe.'

I was forced to go through each photo as my mother gave the commentary. Her greasy fingers smeared across the cheeks of one of the smiling Chinese men.

'This is the cousin of my friend from the silk factory,' she went on enthusiastically. 'He now lives in Spain, somewhere near the sea, I was told. He runs two restaurants and he also owns a vintage furniture shop. Apparently he has very high standards when it comes to girlfriends, and has never been married. Isn't that rare these days? Although he is five years younger than you, I thought you might give him a try. His mother will make an introduction, or I will. Look here, that's his name, contact number and email address,' my mother said as she turned over the photo.

Then she moved on to the next one.

'And this one, isn't he handsome? His name is Jiang Qinglin and he's seven years older than you. Good age for a man. He lives somewhere in Italy and runs a clothing factory. There is only one con with this one: his mother's sister told me he's divorced and has a child with his ex-wife. Maybe that's not so important. He's single now and his aunt told me he's looking for a girlfriend who also lives abroad. Britain and Italy are not so far apart, are they? I haven't had time to look at a map yet . . . '

I stood up, went to the counter and ordered another cup of tea for my mother. When I came back she was ready to show me the third photo. By the time she got to the fourth, I couldn't take it any more.

'But, Mother, I have a boyfriend here already!' I was going to have to invent him quickly. 'Besides, I refuse to date Chinese men, not after my experiences. I've told you that before.'

Her face abruptly changed colour. Just seconds before, she had been excited by my rosy-coloured future. She turned away and her face saddened.

'Then why didn't you tell me you had a boyfriend already? Where is he?'

'I didn't have time to tell you, Mother! You just arrived yesterday, and my boyfriend left two days ago for a holiday with his family!'

Mother shot me a suspicious look as she gathered up the photos. Just then, my father rose from his chair and made a sign for the bill. He wasn't happy. As always, he was on my side. He had never really agreed with his wife's plans for life and the future in general. He was often frustrated and could hide in his painting studio for days. Once again, I wondered how my mother and my father had managed to live together day in and day out for the last forty years. In the old tale *The Weaver Girl and the Cowherd*, Mother Heaven created the Milky Way to prevent her daughter from seeing the cowherd. But perhaps the Milky Way was part of a marriage settlement: the reality to be endured in any marriage between a woman and a man. My grandparents had lived with their version of the Milky Way. And my parents had continued the tradition, each living on their own side of a tidal wave of stars, yet somehow joined nevertheless. For me, love could not take any such interstellar form. We had to be on one planet. There would be differences, to be sure, but I was

determined never to live in such profound disagreement with
a future partner.

A Colonial Education

On the third day of my parents' stay in London, I found myself
filming them with a video camera. Once I had started, I couldn't
put the camera down. Why was I doing that? I asked myself. Not
because I was a film-maker by training, but because I thought
that images would be less prejudiced, a more objective way to
make contact with my parents, especially my mother. I had hated
her when I was a young girl, and I still couldn't forgive her for
abandoning me, and later neglecting me when I was taken back.
Filming her would be therapeutic, but also anthropological. It
would perhaps bring some sort of truth to the surface about her
and about our relationship after all these years of separation. Yet
my parents were absolutely oblivious to my camera and the whole
filming process, which I found quite amusing in the context of
our humourless coexistence as a family. A year later, when the
film was premiered at the Museum of Modern Art in New York
with a full house and then toured hundreds of international
film festivals, I was surprised by the enthusiastic response this
humbly-made home video received. Perhaps these audiences
would have done the same thing had they been in my position?
But at the time I had no intention of making a work of art. I was
acting almost instinctively.

I also wanted to record their interactions with the alien
Western environment. I had suffered cultural isolation ever
since I left China, and this was a way of understanding that

isolation, through the lens of my parents. So I took them, and my camera, around. My neighbourhood in east London was very mixed with large communities from India, Bengal, Africa and the Caribbean. This was the very phenomenon that confused my parents: they didn't recognise this as the 'England of the English'. It was nothing like our monoculture of 'China for the Chinese'. I told them that a mixed culture demonstrated the level of tolerance and freedom of a society. China didn't embrace this mix of cultures and wouldn't have it for a long time. My father thought about my comment for some seconds and nodded. My mother didn't dispute it, but nor did she agree with me. In the manner of a wise peasant, all she said was: 'If you mix things up, how can you sort them out again later?' For her, the movement of people around the world was a mistake and she never saw the point of it. She hadn't enjoyed the trip so far. Although I might have described myself as a 'global peasant', she would never be one.

Despite all our exchanges about the meaning of a 'free' society, I wanted to show them something concrete. So I took them to the local shops where they could buy vegetables and fish. We walked to the fishmonger's at the end of Broadway Market, run by an old Jamaican man. Everyone called him 'Spirit'. When we got there, he was unloading sugar cane and yams. With a big white beard and a bulging, multicoloured Rastafarian hat, he resembled an aged Bob Marley who had spent years as the guru of some mysterious tribe. Spirit was always very friendly to me. Perhaps it was because I was one of his best customers. As I introduced my parents to him, he cheerfully took my father's hand and shook it rigorously. It looked like a summit at the UN, the delegates from China and Africa formally greeting one another.

My mother held herself back, her demeanour reserved, her body tight, as if a show of friendship would be akin to physical assault.

I switched on my video camera. Spirit seemed not to be bothered by my filming. Instead, he was making funny gestures at my lens. I knew why this man was so happy to meet people from China. He had once told me with deep nostalgia that his first love back in Jamaica had been a Chinese girl. That was about fifty years ago. 'She was very special, the quietest in our class,' Spirit had said. They had studied together for years but he never managed to tell her how he felt. By the time they graduated, she was engaged to another boy. He had been heartbroken and soon left Jamaica for Britain. Since that confession, Spirit and I had formed a kind of secret bond.

'London is not as good as I imagined,' my mother proclaimed as we walked home. I couldn't help but feel this judgement included me in its scope. I sensed her jaundiced and weary eyes casting a glance over my life, just as they had done upon entering my flat, and finding it deficient. But what perhaps surprised me a little in the whole situation was my cold, stone-hard awareness of this. I couldn't have cared less about her judgements and expressions of disgruntlement. They meant nothing to me. I had stopped caring a long time ago. Indeed, my camera, the dispassionate lens directed at her, expressed all of this. I was indifferent, a scientist observing two insects scrabbling at the bottom of a glass jar. I found my parents' behaviour in this foreign land interesting, sometimes surprising, but it had nothing to do with me.

In order to show them a better side of London, I took my parents from Bethnal Green to Buckingham Palace. As we approached, the sun came out and it suddenly made England seem momentarily glorious and friendly. My parents were thrilled just to stand in front of the palace, imagining the Queen in her immaculate mansion enjoying a rest or having tea and cakes with some elderly lords or foreign presidents. But after ten minutes, heavy clouds covered the sky again and the wind started to howl. It immediately affected their mood. I knew what they were feeling, as for years my moods had been subjected to the whims of the British sky. We began to shiver in our thin coats. A helicopter appeared from nowhere, circling above the palace as if it had detected possible terrorist activity inside. For a second the hostility of the atmosphere and the piercing sound of the rotors seemed about to annihilate us.

All my mother could say was: 'So the Queen lives alone in such a big house?'

I made something up, as I didn't really know. 'Well, not alone. With her five hundred servants. They also have their state banquets here.'

'State banquets, hmm.' My mother was suspicious. 'It doesn't look very alive. Maybe to keep good hygiene.'

Just as we were about to flee, the sun pierced through the dark clouds again and illuminated everything. The helicopter lost interest in us and hovered off.

My father looked relieved and then went back to admiring the palace. He wrote on his damp notepad: 'It's not as grand as our Summer Palace, or the Forbidden City.'

We walked into St James's Park and rested on a bench. As if under a spell, my parents began to stare at the glorious red tulips in front of them, each seemingly absorbed in thought. I wondered how they felt about this part of London. It felt to me that the royal landscape isolated us from our surroundings. The 'royal parks' were always overly manicured: the neatly cut lawns, the mismatched flower beds that were somehow also lifeless, and even the lemon trees were shaved into confinement. Apparently the red geranium beds are planted to match the tunics of the Queen's Guard at Buckingham Palace, but I would never have made such an association if I hadn't read it on the park noticeboard.

My mother sighed. 'It's so clean and beautiful here, my heavens. But . . .' Her voice was almost melancholic.

She had always been a practical, materialistic person. There was some hint of discontent in her praise – a knowledge that she would never be able to live in this foreign landscape. She couldn't really enjoy something full-heartedly when she saw there was no connection to her own reality. Her gaze across the park landscape felt almost bleak and desolate to me, and I shared the same feeling. But in my mother's case perhaps her bleakness came from the contrast to the hardship of her past, and the blandness of her present. She had no feeling or sentiment towards this grand foreign place, it only made her feel more alienated than she already was. She had come to Britain because her husband wanted to see the West, but she had had an ulterior motive: a marriage quest for her daughter. One last hope. She had come armed with photos and CVs: one of whom I would choose to be her son-in-law. But she knew now there was little hope I would give in to her designs. In her wordless sighing, I could sense that she was deeply disappointed that she had absolutely no influence over me in my adult life. And it made me happy, with a certain degree of mercilessness, that she was now small and wrinkled, a woman who had lost her power to cast further shadows over my life. I knew she knew it, but she should have realised it long ago. It should have been obvious even when I was still a young girl in the town of Wenling.

A French Pilgrim

After multiple visits to famous gardens, my father had had enough of hectic London. He wanted to see France and Italy. He was told by some Chinese tourists that he could do a tour of five European cities in three days, 'because Europe is so small'. Reluctantly, I nodded. It was his first and last trip abroad, and I would have to put up with it.

First, my father wanted to visit the Louvre in Paris. 'We can skip the rusty iron tower. What is it called? Right, the Eiffel Tower. It looks like one of our tarnished telegraph poles. But I must see the Mona Lisa in the Louvre,' he wrote in his clear hand on his notepad. My mother was also enthusiastic about the idea of Paris. She had seen the old Hollywood film *An American in Paris* and had absolutely loved it without understanding a word of the singing or the dialogue. Perhaps it had reminded her of her days in the revolutionary opera in Wenling – her most glorious of her youth, when she had still been a young, vibrant woman. They would enjoy Paris and Rome, I thought.

In Paris we headed straight for the Louvre. The queue under the glass pyramid extended like a snake across the courtyard, and it took forever for us to get in. We joined the mob there to absorb the aura of Leonardo's masterpiece. Having struggled for nearly two hours, we finally found her. But the painting was blocked by hundreds of visitors, chatting in a multitude of languages. Even on my toes, I could hardly catch a glimpse of the not-quite-smiling enigma. My father squeezed in front of the crowd in desperation. He stood there for quite a while, perhaps about two minutes (certainly longer than the average twelve seconds according to the Louvre). When I finally broke through to stand beside him, I noticed that he was not looking at the Mona Lisa herself. He was studying the landscape in the background behind her. His eyesight was poor, but he was trying hard to make out the mountains and mists. I knew that, for him, they were far more beautiful than Mona Lisa's elusive smile. As a Chinese ink painter, apart from his propaganda phase during the Cultural Revolution, my father didn't like painting faces or figures. Humans were not objects for the imagination, and certainly not spiritual. The Chinese do not associate the sacred with the human form. Western church paintings of Christ and the Apostles have little emotional effect on us. Here, standing before one of the great works of Western art, I wondered if my father had changed his mind. Then I heard my mother comment: 'She must have been very rich to afford an artist to paint her.'

She wasn't wrong. I thought of my grandmother, who had never even had a photo taken of her. She had been the poorest person in our family and, surely, the most ignored. She hadn't even been graced with a name. The Mona Lisa, whoever she was, had enjoyed both portrait and title. She had lived on in the regard of others as an individual.

Once we extricated ourselves from the crowd, my father lost interest in seeing anything else and my mother began to complain about her aching feet. As we were exiting the Louvre, I thought to myself that perhaps I preferred Marcel Duchamp's Mona Lisa parody, a reproduction of the lady with a moustache and goatee. The Louvre was a great mausoleum of culture: a tomb for art. Grave-robbing tourists filled its halls. Duchamp's Mona Lisa was a punk gesture towards the establishment and the meaning of art. In China, we had taken the same logic to its political extreme in the Cultural Revolution. But in the West, instead of launching revolutions, they built museums.

After wandering around in Paris for two days, we came to the Gare du Nord and I bought some more tickets.

'Where are we going?' my mother protested. I knew she just wanted to stay put in a hotel, put her feet up and guzzle a bowl of noodle soup.

'We're going to visit a little village called Auvers-sur-Oise, because Father wants to see where Van Gogh lived out his last days.'

I didn't want to mention that it was the place where Van Gogh had shot himself. My mother didn't know anything about Van Gogh. My father and I had both read *Lust For Life*. Twenty years had passed, but our mutual fascination with Van Gogh was just as fervent. We arrived on a rainy Sunday to deserted streets. We walked to the famous Maison de Van Gogh, now a restaurant with a sophisticated menu and a long wine list. The artist's bedroom had been preserved upstairs, and was accessed by a very narrow wooden staircase. It was tiny, cramped and felt strangely miniature. The idea that the troubled painter had eked out his last nights here filled us with a strange sense of intimacy with a dead past. My father reached out and touched the bed frame, stooping silently as if in some sort of benediction, then turned to leave. My mother was gazing out through the tiny bedroom window, looking impatient and ill at ease, her breath laboured from the exertion of climbing the stairs.

We walked back downstairs again and entered the restaurant. My mother was hungry, but my father was inspired and roamed around, restlessly soaking in everything around him. Maybe I should buy a meal at Van Gogh's house for them, even though it would be expensive? Timidly, we sat down. I was given a menu with herring and salmon entrées for twelve euros and beef bourguignon for twenty-eight. I decided to order everything on the page, just to impress my parents. Of course, as Chinese, we refrained from the cheese and dessert. 'What's the point?' as my mother would say about Western dessert culture. 'Eat more rice if you're still hungry!' We even ordered a glass of red wine for my father. Everyone was happy, although my mother kept asking for more rice. I had to keep begging the grumpy waiter, 'Plus de riz, s'il vous plait!'

We wandered around the village one more time before our train back to Paris, taking in the famous wheat fields nearby – the subject of Van Gogh's last painting. They were tall and nearly ready for harvest. The houses in the distance looked peaceful but melancholic, and the sky was pale and still. There were no crows, none of the agitated, doom-laden, black shapes of Van Gogh's brushwork. I felt slightly disappointed by the scenery. It felt flat, almost banal. Ordinariness obliterated any higher meaning. While my father was instantly taken by the landscape, like visiting a shrine – he had been, touched the relics, and could now return home – I wished I had never come. I wanted to keep it all in my imagination only.

At the end of the day I started filming again. I shot my mother wiping mud from her newly bought leather shoes with a dozen sunflower-design napkins stolen from the Van Gogh restaurant. I caught my father soaking in the late-afternoon light as it fell upon his aged features and the yellow heads of wheat. The fields were melting into a golden, shimmering form, until finally, through the growing gloom, we made out a few black crows fluttering in the distance. It was too dark to film the descendants of Van Gogh's black blobs of paint, so I put away my camera. The church bells rang, marking the end of the day. It was time to go.

When in Rome

It was evening by the time we arrived in Rome. We rushed to the Colosseum before it could be swallowed by the dark. The massive ruin was illuminated in gold, which left a strong impression on my parents. Rome was their last stop before heading back to China. Back at my London flat, my father had pointed quite specifically to Rome on a map. 'If I get the chance to see Rome,' he wrote, 'I will understand, even just a little, where Western civilisation comes from.' I had nodded, not wanting to mention ancient Greece and Athens. It would have been a lot of extra work for me to take them to Greece. I was also keen to go to Rome. I was attracted to the city because of all the old Italian films, especially Fellini's *Roma* and Passolini's *Mamma Roma*. Their Rome was rough, cruel, and without morals. I had always wondered if it had retained that atmosphere.

But the city laid out before us was vibrant, romantic even. We chose to stay next to the Colosseum. Everything inside was made from marble, which satisfied my mother's idea of a posh Western hotel. But the toilet was broken and wouldn't flush. We were told by a hotel maid to defecate elsewhere. Once we were settled, my parents wanted to eat some Chinese food. So we went out into the dark, and roamed around trying to find somewhere suitable, but the Romans didn't think it necessary to build a Chinese restaurant close to their glorious Colosseum. We couldn't find anything even remotely Chinese in the area, apart from a sad-looking takeaway with a Cantonese-style buffet. But they had rice and tofu. That was enough to fulfil my parents' longing for home. We bought takeaway and sat outside on some steps, chewing on rice and stale tofu. The Colosseum at night looked almost ridiculous to us, like a heavily wounded monster drained of its power. Or perhaps it was us who were ridiculous to the Colosseum.

I watched my father tear a piece from the side of his cardboard container and try to write something on it.

'So was this where they held gladiatorial contests? They really watched people killing each other for fun?'

'Yes,' I answered, 'but that was two thousand years ago!' Then, after a brief pause, 'Didn't we do that in China too?'

I reminded my parents that only seventy years ago, the death penalty was carried out in public in China, especially in local markets. People would rush to watch the decapitations. Perhaps my father had seen a few heads roll when he was a child. But maybe he hadn't found it amusing. I didn't want to ask. After all, the Colosseum had also served as the venue for sophisticated theatre performances and other glorious events.

We stayed in Rome for three days, wandering from one medieval fountain to another. I liked the energy of Rome – it was messy, alive, spectacular and radiant. It reminded me of the China I used to know. And yet Beijing had gone down the opposite path: every morsel of history apart from the Forbidden City had been gobbled up by rapid modernisation. My father was fond of Rome too, he had always loved old architecture and traditional ways of life. The European cities satisfied his notion of cultural inheritance. I could sense regret in my father's gaze – we had nothing like this in China. Yet my mother was totally oblivious. She had never heard of the Roman Empire, and she missed her rice and noodles. All she wanted was to go home as soon as possible.

As we rode out to the airport, I felt a tension from my mother. She wanted to talk about something with me, but she couldn't find a way.

'Xiaolu,' she said eventually, 'you're not young any more. You have to think about children, before it's too late.'

'But I've told you, Mother, I don't want children.'

My mother fell silent and stared at her hands. Then, all of sudden, she started talking about my brother, or rather, his dead child. I had never been told about this. I didn't even know my brother's wife had been pregnant before their current daughter.

'It aged your brother overnight. Really. His hair turned white from the shock and distress.'

My father looked away, casting his eyes upon the passing landscape outside the train window. Perhaps he didn't want to hear this story again. Perhaps he wasn't even listening.

'What happened?' I asked, a bit fearfully.

'Well, no one wants to be reminded about it. I never mention it in front of your brother and his wife. But I guess the story won't bother you that much.'

I nodded my head bitterly. Yes, sure, I was the selfish daughter who cared nothing for her family. Why should she be affected by another unpleasant story that had ripped at their hearts?

'Sixteen months ago, your brother's wife was due to give birth. The ultrasound machine said it would be a boy. Imagine how happy your father and I felt! Our only grandson, we thought, since we couldn't expect you to give us any. On the day she went into labour, the child was delivered but he didn't look well. He was deformed. The hospital told us that the baby would die within hours and we should know that there was no hope. Your brother and his wife were in tears. They couldn't cope. I looked at the poor, dying little animal and told them I would take care of the rest. They shouldn't worry about the baby any more. So I took the little one home, thinking that would be a good way of preventing them seeing the deformed thing again. When I got home, the little baby was still breathing. I wrapped him in a little blanket and put him on the sofa. I thought I should go to the shop to buy some milk for him. I went out very quickly and as soon as I got back with the bottle, I saw the baby was dead in the blanket. There was no breath coming out from his little nose. Nothing. I thought to myself, that's it. The poor thing has died. Now what do I do?'

My mother paused, as if seeing the dead baby before her eyes. I was utterly gripped, and unable to say anything in response.

'Then I thought, I better borrow a spade and bury him. I didn't want your brother and his wife to witness it once they returned from the hospital. So I went to the neighbours to ask if anyone had a spade. One of them lent me a small one. I went back home, wrapped the baby in a plastic bag and went straight to the hill behind our house. I found a quiet spot where there were some bamboo. It took me at least half an hour to dig a hole for the poor thing. Then I buried him there. When I returned home, your brother and his wife were still at the hospital. I phoned them and they told me that the mother was too weak to walk. I said, don't worry, I've already dealt with the baby. They could forget about the whole thing now.'

'They never asked what happened to the baby's body?' I was astonished.

'Never! Do you think they really wanted to know? It would have haunted them day and night. They thought the hospital and I had made some arrangement. Your brother was destroyed. He never mentioned the child again, but you could see what it had done to him, his hair had gone white. I told him: don't brood on this! Once your wife recovers you should try to conceive again. Time will heal it. And now, you see, they have a healthy girl. So far, they are coping well. Heaven bless the little one.'

Rome International Departures was crowded with families. As my parents waved goodbye at the gate, my mind couldn't erase the image of the spade. My mother carrying the dead baby in a plastic bag and digging a hole for her newborn grandson. A spade. What a tool! Perhaps only my mother could have managed such a tragedy with such practical efficiency. She didn't mention praying or weeping after putting him in the hole, or if she ever secretly visited the grave again.

I wandered around Fiumicino Airport alone, I didn't know where to go now. The camera in my backpack was heavy and my shoulders hurt. My flight to London was the following day and I would have to find a way to kill time until then. I thought about the moment my mother gave me away. Thirty-eight years ago now. She would have done that with practical efficiency too, whether or not she had done so cold-heartedly or wept I would never know. Perhaps she walked with me in her arms, up into the mountains, until she found the Wong family house? Or perhaps she took a long-distance bus to get there? Or perhaps the couple were waiting in the labour ward while my mother was giving birth? This too I would never know. She would never tell me. Silence was the way we communicated, a family tradition carried down to my brother and me from my parents and their parents. My father's silence after his throat cancer operation was just another version. Silence was common in Chinese culture, it served a purpose. Never mention the tragedies, and never question them. Move on, get on with life, since you couldn't change the fact of your birth.

Father's Final Departure

While my parents had been with me, I had keenly felt their presence as an imposition – as if they were an uncomfortable shirt I had to wear pricking my skin, or hair constantly in my eyes blocking my vision. It was like the smell of my mother always in my nostrils, that I have to clear. But as the days passed after their departure, a sense of nakedness returned to me, and their absence became another unwanted presence. Some part of me wanted to reach out to my father, and inside I felt I was having a conversation with him, even though he was now mute. It struck me that my father didn't know me at all. He knew fragments of a girl, of a child, of a young woman. Perhaps he recognised parts of himself in me. I would never know what my father really saw in me. He would die. He would take his images of me into himself and expire with them, and they would be burnt up with his body on the day of cremation.

Three months after my parents' European tour, I received a phone call from a hospital in Shanghai where my father was hospitalised. My mother told me to fly back immediately. I dropped everything in London and flew to Shanghai and went straight to my father's cancer ward. His deterioration was shocking – he had become skeletal and was depressed and in despair about the end. The cancer had viciously spread to his bones, and he was on daily doses of morphine. But it had now lost its effect and the pain was all-consuming. He could still recognise me, but his eyes were no longer the eyes I knew. Now he was a man far away from the things he loved: art, painting and nature. Expressionless and motionless, he was preparing himself for death.

The father I remembered, the father I had kept with me all these years, was a man who never felt depressed and never gave up hope. He hated the very idea. He told me once that he couldn't understand how people could commit suicide since life was so precious. He rarely discussed my grandfather's suicide. For the last decade, cancer had reared its head many times. But each time he had fought back. Every day for the last twenty years, apart from his days in hospital, he had got up at five in the morning, walked through the fresh dawn wind to the mountain near our house and practised qigong, before going to his studio to paint. We always believed that as long as he painted and created, he would not surrender to death. 'Art is bigger than life', that's what he told us when we were young, and that was how he had always conducted himself. But now, he could no longer even lift his pen. Had the art died already in his body and in his mind? Or had he come to the conclusion that his will could no longer rule over his body?

He slept most of that final week. His face blank and dull. Occasionally he opened his eyes and made manifest the miserable pain his body was suffering. I tried to make him recall the happy moments in his life, such as his recent trip to Europe. 'Father, do you remember Van Gogh's house in France? Van

Gogh?' No response. 'His bedroom was so small that it could only take a little bed!' My father looked at me with his sunken eyes and I stopped asking him stupid questions. Tears fell down my cheeks. I went out and stood in the corridor, waiting for the tears to stop. As each minute passed, I knew his body was shutting down. He died the next morning, with our family around his deathbed.

On the English south coast, filming *She, A Chinese*, 2008

PART V | In the Face of Birth and Death

Decades before, when Xuanzang and his disciples left for India, China was the most prosperous country in the whole world. By the time they returned, the country was in turmoil: warlords in different regions were fighting against each other and the population had shrunk by half. Greed was the main force now dominating the once glorious land. Rumour reported that the emperor was on his deathbed. Xuanzang and Wukong the monkey were shocked by the cries and lamentations from the people in the streets of the capital city Chang-an. There were beggars everywhere. They saw children naked in the cold air and adults starving to death. In the Imperial Palace they found the emperor lying in his bed, ancient and diseased, coughing up the last of his blood.

The emperor's spirits lifted as his eyes came to rest upon Xuanzang. Yet he felt his death might come at any moment. He said to Xuanzang: 'The country has lost its prosperity and faith because the people have had no strong spiritual force to guide them for all these years. It will be your mission to bring the people of the Tang Dynasty together again.' The emperor summoned all his officials to win their support for Xuanzang's appointed task. They would build monasteries and libraries to assist the master monk. The court felt the return of optimism about the future, and vowed to the emperor that they would do everything to encourage the right spirit in the country.

After the emperor died Xuanzang left the court and was ready to dedicate his life to the translation of the scriptures. Before his departure, he asked Wukong to join him. Knowing the monkey's favourite fruit was peach, he suggested that they plant ten thousand peach trees around his Buddhist temple. But Wukong, the Emptiness Knower, having witnessed too many human tragedies, shook his head and said:

'Neither eternal peaches nor countless nuts would promise happiness for me, because my mind has been so infected by human unhappiness.'

He begged his master to let him return to being a free creature, so he could go back to the wild without seeing another human being. Xuanzang accepted the monkey's plea, but he also pointed out that now the monkey had become the Emptiness Knower, he would no longer be a savage creature.

The monkey bowed to his master, then bowed to the four directions of the world. Off he leapt, fast as lightning, light as a spring wind, riding on a pink cloud howling joyfully. In the blink of an eye, he disappeared into the ethereal mist above the East China Sea, dissolving with a cracking pop. For a long while, only a mauve glow remained on the horizon, like a luminous face spread across the sky with its ever alive spirit, playful but profound.

With Moon, two months old, 2013

A Mother

Even though I still continue to travel and live in different places across Europe and America, I have really spent the last decade in London. This is where I have made myself a home. It seems to me that people decide to settle somewhere not because they love the place, but because they value and cherish what they have invested in it. I often imagine myself as a fern, growing in a cool climate under the filtered sunlight. Most of the time there is deep shade and plenty of heavy raindrops falling from the sky onto my leaves. These are conditions for flourishing – perfect conditions for ferns, and how they have lived for millions of years. Perhaps I could learn something from them.

I met Steve, a philosopher from Australia, in east London. Perhaps our coming together was inevitable. We both lived around our local park, London Fields: he in a flat by the west gate, me by the east gate. We both wrote our books in local cafes. We first noticed each other in a Greek cafe and instantly felt a mutual attraction. Perhaps it was because we found ourselves discussing Sartre and Buddhism during our very first conversation. He stirred something in me. I felt like I was back at the Beijing Film Academy hanging out with those hard-headed artists again. A silly exchange on our first meeting was a sign of what was to come:

'So do you, an Australian, think your country is in Asia or in some other continent?' I asked, half joking.

'You mean, is Australia part of the East or the West?' Steve adjusted my question.

I laughed, and nodded.

'Well, it's part of Oceania. But what is Oceania? A bunch of colonised islands whose identities have been taken over by European influence. Islanders on the wrong side of history,' he said, almost serious.

'But you still haven't answered my question,' I insisted.

He thought for a few seconds, then said, 'I prefer the idea that Australia belongs to Asia. Aboriginal culture is really alien to us Westerners, ours is more like "white fella culture". We took their land, and pretend that we are still living in the West.'

The cafe was not really the place for such a discussion, and if truth be told, we were not really taking the discussion too seriously anyway. Clearly, something else was going on. I cut the debate short. 'I really miss eating seaweed.' We agreed to meet two hours later at a Japanese restaurant.

The next few weeks passed in a crazed longing. Nights spent alone in our respective flats were unbearable. 'What is this incompleteness?' we asked ourselves, under our own, separate duvets. Love was in the air, and we realised we had to give it a space to grow. We found a flat, still right next to our favourite park. Despite being so far away from the places we had grown up, we often looked at the weather reports in Beijing and Melbourne. I cooked Chinese food for almost every meal. Steve would describe the beauty of the forest and the water in Tasmania. 'You can stand in the shallows and pick wild oysters straight from the seabed and eat them right there,' he murmured in a dreamy state. Clearly, nostalgia makes itself felt in the stomach. Salty samphire took me back to the beach in Shitang and its green-brown bed of kelp. In the evenings we ate rice and fried tofu with chopsticks while watching BBC4. 'Why don't they ever talk about China?' I complained. Television was repetitive, seemingly always about royalty or fashions from the dim recesses of British history. Perhaps the Hairy Bikers were discovering Cantonese stir-fries in Hong Kong, but that was the extent of content about my homeland. The programmes made me feel unfulfilled, and stupid.

I had spent the last decade with one foot in each world: West and East. I couldn't say I was fully here, and I certainly wasn't fully there. Of course I found myself longing for the sounds of my childhood and its familiar flavours. But I swallowed that longing. I told myself: I have lost my country and I am in exile, even if it is self-imposed. My work is all I have and my work is my only meaningful identity. But is that enough? Am I really living fully? I questioned myself repeatedly. Perhaps I will build something else with Steve, in this foreign land. Build something together – a physical home. But what did that mean exactly for someone like me?

I had decided at a young age that I didn't want to have children. I didn't want to become another one of those mothers, trapped in domesticity, and disrespected by her husband. It wasn't a decision borne out of a militant feminism; it was totally personal. Those years living in my grandparents' house by the sea had been a hard lesson. The domestic violence that surrounded me then felt so inescapable that I couldn't imagine there could be a positive version of domesticity ahead of me, especially if I became a mother. Witnessing how my grandfather abused my grandmother and her silence after the beatings had left a painful conviction in my head: family life was awful and being a woman was awful. And my time in the West hadn't convinced me yet that there could be another type of womanhood, one in which women were respected inside and outside the home, where women were not merely child producers, and where they could fall in love again even after having become mothers. My growing environmental awareness only added more fuel to the argument for not having children. And the logic of never-ending consumption didn't just harm the environment, but actually killed people too. In 2008, a scandal came to light about 54,000 Chinese babies hospitalised after drinking formula milk adulterated with melamine. It was just another terrible incident of which we heard more and more every day. To bring more humans into the world would only add to an already threatened planet.

But far back in my 'positive' Chinese mind I still felt I had a right to reproduce, to bring hope through the creation of a new generation. The China of my youth is far away now; the past is another country. Our children are our future. They will create something new in a way my generation and my father's generation failed to do. The new generation will have to be more ecologically aware.

Of all the negative and positive voices in my mind, the positive prevailed. So that just after my father's death, on the verge of turning forty, I found myself asking the same question again: should I spend the rest of my life brooding hopelessly on the failings of humanity, or should I bring hope into the world by having a child and creating a person to whom I could give the best knowledge I had? I chose my future child.

Nine months of being pregnant felt unbearably drawn out at the time, but when I look back now, it feels short and quite magical. I have always been a very impatient person. I have struggled to write long books or carry through on year-long film productions because of my low threshold for distraction. But with this, there was no way to speed up the process. All I could do was wait. The only nine months of my life I have ever truly waited, with full participation, apprehension, excitement and fear.

I have never been a sentimental person – I don't weep easily while watching films or attending funerals. But while pregnant, I would burst into tears at cheesy Hollywood movies. Even the cry of a child in a television soap would affect me and make my eyes wet. Just before midnight on New Year's Eve 2013, one day before my due date, Steve and I decided to take a gentle walk through Hackney. We went from crowded Mare Street to the quiet back roads of Victoria Park. The sensations in my belly were intensified by strong kicking from the baby. I couldn't distinguish between her feet pushing from inside me and the onset of labour. I was nervous, and very emotional. As the fireworks burst above us, I watched and wept.

On the second day of 2013, our child was born. Weighing nearly nine pounds, she was robust and didn't look particularly like either her mother or her father. She was a mix, a Eurasian, with brownish hair, fair skin and dark eyes. We named her Moon. As her small round face lay against my breast, I thought about my parents. My father never had the chance to see his rebellious daughter become a mother, or meet the granddaughter that had been named after one of his favourite things to paint. She would have made him so happy.

Two months later, on the eve of the Qingming Festival for the dead, my new family was on a plane to China. Moon was oblivious to time; screaming, crying, sucking and then falling asleep on me in a twelve-hour cycle, she was living in the moment. 'Don't cry,' I said. 'I'm taking you to see the place where I was born.'

The Final Visit

The experience of childbirth made it seem like half a lifetime since I had seen my mother. Everything was blurry because of a lack of sleep, including the face and figure of my mother. There she was, a middle-aged peasant woman, waving through the glass of the arrival-hall doors. I could have walked past her without realising that this short, humble woman was my mother. I held Moon tight to my chest and dragged our luggage towards her. Steve followed with the pram and another bag. My heart felt heavy.

'Ah, what a lovely little one . . . ' Then my mother hugged me with a weary look. She was much thinner than the last time I had seen her. Her skin was yellow and her steps were weak, as if she had just left hospital. She turned to the squirming baby wrapped in my arms. There was surprise and a little joy in her eyes, but her mood seemed to be clouded by something else. She didn't take the baby into her arms as a typical grandmother would. She wasn't fully prepared, perhaps. When Steve tried to greet her and shake her hand, she paid him no attention. We followed her to a taxi.

'It's not easy raising a child abroad alone,' she said suddenly, when we reached the car.

'But I'm not alone, Mother!' I pointed to the Western man standing behind me, towering above all the Chinese men around

him. How could she have not noticed him? My mother turned
and gave Steve a glance, my chance to make a short introduction. It was hard to know how my mother really felt about him.
She knew I was still not married and I probably never would
get married. In her eyes, a foreign boyfriend without a wedding
ceremony and an official certificate meant nothing. I was fine
with her attitude. She didn't have to agree with my choices.

Once home, she reached for her hair and removed it, revealing her bald head underneath. I was in a state of shock. Then,
before I could say anything, she told me in a matter-of-fact voice:

'Have you ever heard of widow's cancer? That's what your
mother's got.'

'Widow's cancer?'

'Yes. Stomach cancer, late stage. The doctor said I might have
three months.'

I was thunderstruck. It explained her strange appearance at
the airport, her reluctance to hold Moon, her distance. Now I
also understood why she had urged me to return to China when
I had called. She hadn't wanted to tell me about the cancer over
the phone. She didn't want me to worry about her while breastfeeding the baby.

Like a lot of women, she believed a new mother's milk would
stop under emotional stress. As I was making a bed on the sofa
for the baby, she told me the doctor said she was too far gone for
surgery, but she was undergoing chemotherapy. It was a miserable experience, she said, she was vomiting all the time and felt
very sick.

That evening my brother and his family drove a few hours
to meet us. He was only two years older than me, but he looked
puffy, weary and far more middle-aged than a man of forty-two

years should. His little daughter was healthy and energetic, as if she had sucked his spirit into her body. My brother's wife was happy to meet us. 'I've heard so much about you, Xiaolu! I can't believe you're finally here!' She was the most excited to meet our baby Moon. We went to a seafood restaurant to celebrate the reunion. It was our first family meal with all three generations around the same dining table – only Father was missing. We ordered mountains of food, and my brother kept adding dishes from the menu. But my mother ate only a small bowl of porridge. She could hardly swallow. At one point the waitress brought a large bowl of crab soup. Vivid red legs and pincers swimming in a gingered broth. I didn't expect my brother to order sea crabs. No one in the family had good teeth, and my Australian didn't have much experience eating hard-shelled crabs. We drank the soup but left the monstrous creature in the bowl. Staring at those red pincers and two beady eyes, I suddenly remembered the opera from my childhood, *Madame White Snake*, in which an evil tortoise turned monk, resentful of the earthly happiness of others, seeks revenge on loving couples but ends up hiding himself in the stomach of a crab. Any human who ate the yellow part of the crab suffered stomach aches. The fear had stuck with me as a child. I still remember screaming at my grandmother not to swallow. Had my mother bitten from the cursed sea creature? Terminal stomach cancer. The monk had taken his revenge yet again on another woman.

During our two-week stay in Wenling, we walked around with my mother, usually between the hospital and our home. The town had now grown into a city of two million inhabitants, and shiny skyscrapers had grown out of the mud and old socialist factory compounds. It was disorientating for me. Where were all the peasant workers in blue uniforms? Our house used to be fringed by rapeseed fields and untouched bamboo mountains, but now these were crowded with new buildings and traffic. We passed a row of grey concrete buildings – Wenling Silk Factory where my mother used to work. It was now a dead space, awaiting the wrecking ball. A certain nostalgia washed over me, and I tried to remember the taste of the roasted silkworms on skewers that I had eaten so often as a child on those desolate afternoons after school. But I couldn't recall the taste on my tongue. Everywhere was the scourge of pollution: black discharge pouring into the river from pipes, the very same water in which I used to catch shrimps and small crabs; mountains stripped of vegetation and now littered with shredded plastic rubbish bags. Still, I heard children laughing and playing – not in my imagination, but right in front of me – on the riverbank next to the oily black water.

The Return

But the sea was calling me. Swaddled in a warm blanket, we took Moon to visit my grandparents' fishing village. The bus trip to Shitang was easy and quick compared with when I was a child. As we arrived, I discovered that even the station had been relocated. Standing on the asphalted promontory, I breathed in the familiar air. It had the same fishy salty taste, and the same perfume of kelp and ribbonfish hung in the air, but now this was mixed with a strong odour of petrol. As we walked down the hill towards the open sea, I spotted large industrial fishing boats parked in the harbour and my heart leapt. They were different to the ones of my youth, but I loved the sight of them, creating elaborate ripple patterns in the water. As we got closer, I could hear the workers speaking Mandarin Chinese to each other. 'How are the fish today?' I asked one of them in Shitang dialect. He didn't react, so I tried another question. 'Did you catch any big snapper?' But everyone stared back at me with blank expressions. They were migrants, I realised, they didn't know the local tongue. Of course Shitang had always been home to migrant fishermen. My grandfather had been one. I had forgotten, somewhere in the thirty years since his death.

As we stood by the churning waves, Moon woke up in the sling and opened her eyes. Her small head stretched out a little from my jacket, and seemed to peer out at the vast body of water in front of her. What did she see? I wondered. Was it the grey waves of my childhood? Would this picture survive into her later life to form a dim memory of the past? Or, was the sea nothing more than another part of her mother's body and being?

Carrying Moon in the sling, we tried to find our way back to my grandparents' house, but we were soon lost in a maze of new buildings and streets. Whenever I passed some old people sitting out on the street, I wondered if they recognised me. Yet I couldn't recall any of these wrinkled faces. And neither could I find my childhood home. We stopped and I asked a white-haired man if he knew a street named Front Barrier Slope. The old man stared at me for almost half a minute, not responding but only sucking on his cigarette. I then tried again in the local dialect: 'Front Barrier Slope, it used to be called Anti-Pirate Passage.' An obscure smile squeezed itself out across his face and he pointed with his nicotine-stained finger.

Finally, I spotted the old stone house, squashed in between two new premises. It was *our* house. My feet slowed as we approached. The outside hadn't changed at all, although now it was a hair salon filled with fashionable teenagers. Standing outside for a while, I wasn't sure if I should go in and introduce myself to the owner.

After some hesitation, I entered with Moon in my arms. A middle-aged man was cutting the hair of a young girl. Two teen-aged boys sat on a bench playing with their phones. I introduced myself to the man: my name, and my family name, Guo.

'Guo?' The man's eyes sparkled, as if he might just recognise me.

'Yes. We owned this house twenty-five years ago, or more actually, twenty-seven years ago, when my grandmother was still alive.'

The man holding the scissors immediately understood who I was. 'I know! I know! Your father sold this house to us! How is he? All well?'

I nodded. I didn't want to explain. He dropped what he was doing, leaving his customer on the chair, and called to his wife to say hello to me. It was an awkward situation. We were invited inside for tea. The sofa we sat on was where my grandmother used to have her old bamboo bed, and where we had slept every night. This was also where, on the very night my grandmother died, I sat with my parents and watched over her coffin under candlelight. As I sat on the edge of the sofa, holding the teacup, I wondered about the upstairs room. My grandfather's room. There was no sound coming from the top floor.

'Oh, the ceiling upstairs has been leaking for a while. We don't use that room,' the wife said, as if she could read my thoughts.

Sunset cast a golden light across the wavy sea and the grey sand. We took the bus back to Wenling before nightfall. Despite my mother's illness, I was longing to return to Britain. There was no use in us staying here with her. We had nothing more to say to each other. Physical closeness hadn't brought us together in any way emotionally. Our minds had occupied different universes for too long, and we couldn't bridge the chasm that had been created. Our relationship had always gone unacknowledged. It was just a fact, like breathing air, or rain in typhoon season. It was unconscious. As if we were performing a script which neither of us had written. We never wanted or liked it, but it had been handed to us by fate. Perhaps I had never looked into my mother's eyes with the hope of understanding her situation, and she had never done the same for me. I had no memory of a motherly look. There was only the culturally programmed habits of duty, hers of a mother and mine of a filial child. That programme had replaced any true understanding between us. It had conditioned me, indeed, had made me guilty from the very beginning, as the unworthy, wayward daughter. It had killed any natural love I might have had for my birth family. It had never been there in the first place. Of course, I was aware of how my own child would feel about all this when she grew up, since her childhood would take place in the West – a totally different reality from mine. I will have to wait and see how our relationship turns out.

A few days later we said goodbye to my mother. We stood by the taxi, which was about to take us to the airport, and I looked at my mother. She looked back at me, but somehow our eyes didn't meet. I took in her broad face, aged and wrinkled, but still childlike in some way. I could tell she felt miserable. My heart was pained by a coldness, a feeling that there was no love in me. There was just a kind of weight, unbearable weight, and a lethargy of the spirit. In the next life, I would be a good daughter, I thought. She wore her wig, like an actor performing one of the opera roles of her youth, and kept up a stream of simple comments about catching the flight and breastfeeding Moon. I nodded but said nothing. Both of us knew, I guessed, that there would be no next time.

The Circle of Life

We returned to London. Two months passed in a swirl of activity, mostly breastfeeding and struggling to cope with sleep deprivation. We were also in the midst of buying a flat in east London and trying to plan a better family life. Then one day I received a phone call from China. It was my brother. His voice was jagged. Our mother had lost consciousness three days previously. She could die at any moment, she survived only by being fed oxygen through a tube in her nose. I listened, watching the removal men loading our furniture into the back of their van as the traffic police yelled at them to get out of the way.

Two days later, I was unpacking boxes in our new flat and I received another call from China. 'Yes, she just died,' my brother reported in a flat, spiritless voice. 'I assume you won't come back for her funeral. We'll cremate her in the next few days.' He hung up the phone. We had no words to exchange, and no shared pain to express.

I sat alone on the floor, surrounded by more unopened boxes. A dull depression was sinking into my body, forming a dark, inert mass that absorbed all light. I was being dragged downwards, like a body tied to a stone sinking to the bottom of a stagnant lake. But then, I felt a rush of relief and liberation, buoying me up. The stone fell away and I emerged through the surface of the water. The feeling wasn't levity or joy. It was a sense of clarity. Now my father and my mother were gone, I had been orphaned for a second time.

The protagonists of my favourite books were all orphans. They were parentless, self-made heroes. They had had to create themselves, since they had come from nothing and no inheritance. In my own way I too was self-made. I was born and then flung aside, to survive in a rocky village by the ocean. If I had to pinpoint a moment when this thought crystallised in my mind, it was that day on the beach in Shitang when I met the art students drawing in their sketch pads facing a sunless, wavy-grey sea. I was six years old and consumed by an ineffable loneliness. I watched the young girl in particular as she contemplated the monotonous scene before us, and then started to apply paint to her paper. Her brush made a shimmering blue and a burning sunset appear across the page. I was suddenly captivated by the girl's imaginative act: that one could reshape a drab and colourless reality into a luminous world.

Now, surrounded by boxes in a London flat, the narrative of my past had been brought to a close. The beginning and end echoed each other. My childhood was gone. Finally I felt free from the burden of my family. I no longer needed to find them. I was my own home now. And at last, I could breathe fully, taking fresh new air into my own lungs.

Ode to the Light, Xiuling Guo, a typical seascape by my father

ACKNOWLEDGMENTS

I am deeply indebted to Sasha Mudd and Stephen Barker for their comments on early drafts. I feel extremely grateful to Anna Holmwood for her elegant and thoughtful edit. As always, I thank wholeheartedly Juliet Brooke for her intense editorial work and Rebecca Carter and Cullen Stanley from Janklow & Nesbit who have supported each stage of my writing.

I am so very fortunate to have found a home with my publishers – the Chatto & Windus team in the UK, Amy Hundley and Morgan Entrekin from Grove Atlantic in the US, Claudia Vidoni from Knaus Verlag, Andrea Berrini and Gaia Amaducci at Metropoli d'Asia, Dag Hernried from Alfabeta Bokförlag, Gesa Schneider, Thomas Geiger from Zurich and the following great individuals who have supported me over the years: Clara Farmer, Claire Paterson, Rebecca Folland, Kirsty Gordon, Sam Coates, Monique Corless, Anne Rademacher, Shalene Moodie, Vanni Bianconi, Philippe Ciompi, Suzanne Dean, Mari Yamazaki and John Freeman.

And my last expression of gratitude is to Wu Cheng'en, the ancient writer who wrote *Xi Yon Ji* (*The Journey to the West*), a legend that has inspired me since I was a child.

Xiaolu Guo, Berlin and London, 2016

Read on for an essay by Xiaolu Guo.

"I'll See You In Berlin" first appeared on the *Freeman's* channel at *Literary Hub* on October 12, 2017. A version of this essay can be found online at lithub.com/ill-see-you-in-berlin-xiaolu-guo-on-a-fresh-start-in-a-new-city.

I'll See You In Berlin

He said: "See you in Berlin."

I said: "See you . . . Bye."

I was leaving Britain. A large part of me felt is was "for good." Though that strange phrase in English, "for good," struck me in one way as optimistic, since it was for something better. But it was also pessimistic; "for good" seemed to suggest a sacrifice.

For better or for worse, I had just said goodbye to S. This happened just as we reached the entrance of King's Cross tube station. We said we would see if this time the separation would indeed make sense or be for "the good." We would live in different countries, and know something of solitude for a while, and maybe the dense fog that seemed to have settled about us would lift. But actually my will had formed itself into an arrow, and I wanted to shoot myself out of London and everything else forever. My arrow would come to ground in Berlin.

It was the beginning of 2012. I was traveling light. The only book I had with me was Christopher Isherwood's *Goodbye to Berlin*. I was going to Berlin but traveling with a book about saying farewell to the place I was going to inhabit. Isherwood's

Berlin was pre-war. My yet-to-be Berlin was post-wall. So perhaps there was no conflict after all. War and time had separated
his city from mine almost entirely. But actually, I wasn't keen to
reflect on history. It was the opening sentences of the book, that
had persuaded me to take it:

'I am a camera. Not feeling, only recording.'
    When feeling was just a fog, then seeing was what I wanted.
Recording everything, being a camera, felt like an act of
cleansing myself. So, I would go to Berlin as a camera, and
surrender to seeing. The events of life would just imprint
themselves on my mind like images on a digital tape.
    I flew an hour and a half and arrived at Schonefeld, a sad,
slightly shabby airport, and got through immigration without incident. I then made my way, through the cold and
across what was once some meadow for cows, to the train
station nearby. I got the S-Bahn to Ostkreuz, then got off,
waited for the S9 that took me to right across the city. I had
memorized the Berlin U&S Bahn map during my previous
visits to Berlin, and I recorded everything as I went. Already
the sense of lifting fog was there. How simple it was. One
decision, then the first few steps. Not completely without
fear, but feeling the possibility of new fearless life.

    "Your apartment is in Storkwinkel, at the end of the
Ku'damm—Kurfustendamm," said the DAAD artist residency
secretary who was managing my stay. I was beginning a year-long
fellowship in Berlin. She gave me a string of keys, including a tiny
one for my mailbox. She then opened a detailed city map, and
showed me the small street at the end of Ku'Damm. I nodded,

but said nothing. It had not been my ideal. The residency was on the edge of the city, in the further west of West Berlin. I had wanted to be in Kreuzberg or anywhere central. But there it was. I folded the map and put it in my pocket.

Later that afternoon I made my way to the residence, after walking up the length of Kurfurstendamm, the great showcase Boulevard of former West Berlin, the supposed envy of the East. As I went on foot, the glitz of the shops slowly diminished and was completely gone by the time I reached a bridge overlooking Halensee S-bahn with a curry wurst stand on it. Inside was a blue-bloodshot eyed man waiting to dish out trays of red-sauced wurst with plastic forks, along with large bottles of dark beer. His thin but long hair added strands to the mix on the plastic plates. Perhaps, I thought, I was witnessing my daily meal.

I finally arrived at Storkwinkel, the street with my flat. It was, as I expected, a non-descript lane, lined by five-story Berlin facades. As everywhere in Berlin, a sense of history made itself felt with an electric tingling at the back of my neck. But I did not pursue the feeling. I was a new woman here, a new person in a new country. And I was recording everything around me. My eyes were a camera.

There were no elevators. I climbed five flights of steps to the top floor, where my name had already been placed in neat print- ing on the wooden, over-painted door. Inside was a rambling former attic, now a flat, overlooking Berlin's grey ring road and the S-Bahn stop of Halensee. I saw no sign of the "sea" in the distance—the supposed lake. But the apartment had a generous layout. It was furnished in modest modern style: white tables, wooden chairs, a basic kitchen set. It was nothing like Isher- wood's lodging in 1920s. I remembered his description of his first time seeing the rented room: *unnecessarily solid, abnormally heavy, dangerously sharp.*

The light and white furniture suited my new mood. It was strangely pleasant. I thought I could live in this flat. No, not "flat"; in Germany they called it *wohnung.* And I would live here alone, without S. Even though he said "See you in Berlin." Perhaps he just said those words without thinking, the way people say "goodbye." No promise or intention lay behind them. I opened the window to let the fresh air in. I was feeling deflated, a little blown by the wind, sensitive to the foreign smells, but I felt I had a foot in something like a home.

I had been to Berlin before and knew people; I met a few film-makers here in the past and had kept loosely in touch. Before I left Britain, I contacted my friend Martin and informed him I was coming. I thought Martin would show me around, especially with his cinematic eyes. He was the cinematographer of the film *Good Bye Lenin!,* and I had seen the film way before I had met him. But as I reflect now, I had seen another film shot by him, decades ago in China, before I came to Europe. It was one of my favorite films of all time: Wim Wenders' *Wings of Desire,* and Martin was one of the camera operators on that film. It was made in 1987.

I was only a 14-year-old school girl in my Chinese province when Martin was filming in a helicopter above the Brandenburg Gate and the Tower of Victory. I had no idea what was Germany then—apart from two names mentioned in our textbooks: Karl Marx and Adolf Hitler. When Martin made that film, the Berlin Wall still existed. It was still the zone of death in Berlin, a place for corpses to lie in dirty snow. Martin had witnessed the fall of the Wall, with his camera eyes, and with his own blue eyes. Now those war time photo archives were placed everywhere in Berlin streets. They were even lining the capitalistic Kufersterdamm, even in front of MacDonald and Gucci shops. What would Martin say about this? Bringing out my mobile, I rang him. Instantly, it came out in his slightly accented English: "Wellkommen! But sorry Xiaolu, I am shooting a film in Frankfurt at the moment!" What a pity. I would have to wait to see him for a few weeks, or even months. I sent him regards and hung up the phone. Putting on my shoes, I picked up my unfamiliar keys.

I descended slowly, touching the old wooden railing. I made my way to the nearest supermarket *Kaiser's*. I felt a hunger, and I wanted to fill my stomach with meat. Now that I was alone, not living with S—a vegetarian—I could eat anything he would not eat.

Over the next few days I made contact with some of Martin's friends. They were filmmakers who lived in Kreuzberg. We met near the canal by the Ankerklause. Oberg was tall and lanky, with no hair and a constant flow of fidgeting and witticisms— like an elongated Woody Allen without glasses. He had made a semi-erotic sci fi film in Japan, and was working on a new script. He told me of his plans in a slightly nasal voice, but with great animation. "Germany is boring! I want to move to Spain, to become an irresponsible foreigner!" Then he kissed the current girlfriend beside him passionately.

"I am going to introduce you to some great people." Oberg continued: "Tonight there is a barbecue in Kreuzberg 66. Clemenz is the chef. He loves to cook sardines on hot plates, with Brazilian music. You can meet Barbara there too, one of Germany's great actresses. She is a policewoman in that hot TV series—*Tatort.* You probably don't know this program. People love crime in this country." Then he looked at me with pity: "Poor you, live all the way over there in that dead West, what is it called, Storkwinkel? A strange name for a street. Is it where you enter *the other world*?"

More people arrived astride heavy, German bikes, built like tanks. They wore the post-punk uniforms one sees around Berlin—dark green rain-proof jackets. They were smiling broadly. I was affected by their generous mood and easygoingness—there was good *chi* in the atmosphere. As always, I wanted to conquer people with my "outgoing" personality—draw them in so that my foreign friendships might spark and bring me some warmth. So I began to talk, randomly, about London, about Beijing, about films and books I saw and read in the last few months.

That night, after I returned to the edge of West Berlin, I had a bowl of rice with two white sausages on the side (a choice I deliberately made to educate myself about German culture), and a black beer. The sausage was interesting, if not as *interesting* as the locals claimed. But the beer was genuinely flavorful. Leaving the dirty dishes in the sink, I lay in the bed in my train-rustling wohnung and continued reading *Good Bye to Berlin.* Isherwood seemed to be drifting aimlessly in Berlin, and the city felt alien but exotic to an Englishman like him. And that woman, the divinely decadent Sally Bowles! She was a real person too, but she and Isherwood and all the other characters are dead now. Strangely, Berlin in between two World Wars felt like the London I had lived in during the last several years. I somehow knew well of those disillusioned artists, those cheap lodging places, amateur language teachers, and dodgy night clubs. All this brought me back to the Britain I had lived. I thought about S, but only briefly.

I finished reading the book the next morning. Then I walked around my blocks, enveloped by a sense of dislocation. No one was out. All the windows shut. The wind was blowing, and it felt cold and dull. I thought, perhaps these feelings were transmitted from Isherwood's world to mine—a foreign life without orientation, a gloomy daily atmosphere leading towards a forthcoming war. Under the rainy clouds, I walked up to the bridge by Halensee and felt I could see our own war like a distant storm already beginning to thunder on the horizon.

One afternoon I took the train to Wannsee, and wandered around the shore. I thought about *Wings of Desire* again. I missed Martin. When I first came to Berlin some years ago, Martin was the person who introduced me to the lakes around Berlin. We had stood by the quietly lapping Wannsee, contemplating the famous wartime spy bridge in the distance—the Glienicke Bridge. It used to be the border separating East Germany and West Berlin. A strange border, I thought. It looked so innocent above the quiet waterway. We then took a long walk through the dark forested area along equally dark water. The lake's surface seemed troubled, I remember, and the path appeared broken and awkwardly placed. Some logs lay drowned at the lake's edge, pail and inert. He then took me up to an abandoned radio tower that stood above the forest like an alien presence. During the DDR period this tower was used for surveillance. Now it looked bleak and desolate. Martin looked at the tower, and said something like: "I prefer the South, the heat and sunlight, like in Portugal or Spain. I always feel cold in this country." Martin's eyes were clear blue, beneath the scant, straw-colored hair. I found the eyes unsettling. As if their blue depth knew something that even he was unaware of.

That was two years ago. I wondered if Martin still had this desolation in him, as I stared into the blue green water. When the sky turned dark and the air felt cold, I left the lake and took the train back home.

The next morning, as I woke up, I received two emails from S. He asked me how I was doing in the new city, and when should he come over? "The weather is very bad in London, it will be good to get out," he added. Outside my window, the sky was blue, but I didn't tell him that. I missed his company, but this separation was a trial for us. And he should know that I wanted to be alone here, even though my body didn't want to be alone. So I answered his email with a few vague lines.

A week later, to my surprise, S arrived in Berlin. He was pleasant, energetic, and interested in everything around him. He even liked the shabby and unattractive little Storkwinkel in front of my building block. We went out for dinners, walking all the way to Kantstrasse where the Chinese restaurants are located. We would eat dumplings and walk all the way back to the end of Kurfurstendamm. Sometimes the walk would take an hour, if we got lost on the side streets. I always thought that on one of these long walks I would suggest a real separation. A hard and final one. A separation without us ever seeing each other again. But I never managed to fully express my desire.

The truth was that I couldn't make up my mind. Why? Because I felt lonely again in this foreign city with a language even foreigner than my second language, English? Or, because I was not ready to fall in love with other men? I wondered. With many doubts and thoughts in my head and in my heart, we continued to stroll along Ku'damm under those wartime maple trees.

Finally Martin appeared. He returned from his film production in south Germany. We met in a café in Kantstrasse, on the street where he lived. He looked very tired. He said he would have to go soon, because his wife was waiting for him to see a play. We talked briefly about our future projects, and his fondness of the time he spent when he was making *Good Bye Lenin!*. When we finished coffee, I mentioned that I was separating from S. Or rather—I tried to explain—I had to make a decision if I should remain in the relationship or come out. I thought Berlin might be a good place for me to make this decision.

Martin didn't react. Instead, he seemed to be troubled by a problem. His stomach ached. He said he could not eat much at all. He complained that his stomach would torture him as soon as he returned to the film set, even though he was taking painkillers everyday. "I probably need to quit my film career; I am finished." He smiled sadly. "The film world is for young people anyway," he sighed, but remained dignified, like a proper German. I looked at Martin across the table. He had clearly lost some weight, but I didn't think something lethal was going on in his body. Nor did he. When we hugged for goodbye in the street, I didn't realize this would be the last time I would ever see him again.

When the residency finished, I didn't stay in Berlin. S took me back to London, or rather I decided to return to London with him. I had made the spontaneous decision that I would make a home with S. Or perhaps the decision just made itself, and I followed in the dark. A phone call was made to Martin before we flew back to the UK. Immediately, he announced the bad news: he had been diagnosed with Stage II stomach cancer. "But don't worry, I just told my wife that I am going to get an operation—taking out my stomach." My mind was silent. A cold wave of incomprehension dulled my senses. Nevertheless, S and I made our way to Schonefeld Airport. We took our plane. In the sky, I looked down at the Berlin I was once entangled with. The wings of desire fly us to places we somehow can never fully inhabit.

Three months later, when S and I went to see our local General Practitioner in London, we found that I was pregnant. A sudden feeling of terror snatched me, mixed with excitement. In front of the clinic, we talked about making a real home together. "But it will be in London, not in Berlin, right?" S said, humorously. I nodded. But since he mentioned Berlin, I thought I should ring Martin to find out his situation. I called straightway, but no one answered. I called again. No answer. I felt uneasy. I searched numbers in my contact list, and dialed our mutual Berlin friend Oberg.

"Oh, you don't know then. Martin died a week ago," Oberg answered flatly in his nasal voice.

"Died?" I repeated the term a few times like an automaton, breathing stiffly into the phone.

"Yes, they took his stomach out. But still . . . too late."

My eyes fixed on a heavily pregnant woman entering the clinic. She was staggering, hands supporting her belly. I was amazed by her life—unfolding, clumsy, but alive. Unlike Martin. Then I noticed someone take my left arm. It was S. He dragged me away.

Upon returning home, I called Germany again. I called Martin's wife. While I was waiting for the phone to be picked up, I pictured Martin's 19th century building right in the middle of Kantstrasse, a street not as pretty as other streets in Charlottenberg. I remember Martin once telling me that his fantasy was to live in a seaside southern town, somewhere like Marseille or Barcelona. Too sad that he didn't make it, just like many of us. Martin's wife, a sometime actress and school teacher, finally answered.

After brief condolences, I could not bring myself to say anything sensible. Instead, I said to her: "So sorry . . . do you want to visit us in London? It might be good to say goodbye to Berlin just for a little while, for a change."

"Goodbye to Berlin?" She repeated on the phone, with a weary voice. She paused for a second, then answered: "No. I don't think so. I will stay here." Then her last words: "I hope to see you in Berlin."

"Yes, I hope so. Please take care of yourself." I hung up the phone, looking back at S who was putting chopped orange and apple into a blender. He pressed the button. A deafening noise immediately filled the flat. I waited until the noise ceased.

"You know what? I regret that in all those months in Berlin, we didn't visit even once Nollendorfstrasse."

"Nollendorfstrasse?" S turned, passing me a glass of juice.

"Yes, the street where Isherwood lived in *Goodbye to Berlin*."

A month later, S and I came out from a clinic in a street right next to Nollendorfstrasse in Berlin. The German gynecologist had printed out a picture of the fetus from the scan result, and he told us the baby's sex. As we passed Nollendorfplatz U-bahn station, I stopped, leaning on the railing and took a careful look at the small photo of my future child. It was black and white, indistinct, with the shadow of a tiny heart like a chestnut incased in its pod. I stared at it for a long time, wondering about the forms of life and the forms of the death.